# MY FAMILY AND
# 50 OTHER
# ANIMALS

*To Carolyn, Emily and Samuel, with grateful thanks for your love and sense of fun.*

Published in 2009 by André Deutsch
An imprint of the Carlton Publishing Group
20 Mortimer Street
London W1T 3JW

10 9 8 7 6 5 4 3 2 1

A CIP catalogue record for this book is available from the British Library.

ISBN  978 0 233 00278 1

Printed in the UK

The publishers would like to thank the following sources for their kind permission to reproduce the pictures in this book: p.i: (top and bottom) © Carolyn Couzens; p.ii: (top and bottom) © Carolyn Couzens; p.iii: (top and bottom) © Carolyn Couzens; p.iva: (top) © Carolyn Couzens; (bottom) © Charles Gibson / iStockphoto.com; p.v: (top and bottom) © Carolyn Couzens; p.vi: (top) © Peter Wey / iStockphoto.com; (bottom) © Heiko Grossmann / iStockphoto.com; p.vii: (top) Philippe Clement / Nature Picture Library; (bottom left) Layton Thompson / © National Trust Photo Library; (bottom right) © Eric Isselee / iStockphoto.com; p.viii (top) © Carolyn Couzens; (bottom) © Klaas Lingbeek van Kranen / iStockphoto.com. Drawings (throughout) very kindly supplied by Emily Couzens and Sam Couzens. Every effort has been made to acknowledge correctly and contact the source and/or copyright holder of each picture and Carlton Books Limited apologises for any unintentional errors or omissions, which will be corrected in future editions of this book.

# MY FAMILY AND
# 50 OTHER ANIMALS

**A year-long quest to see Britain's mammals**

## Dominic Couzens

ANDRE
DEUTSCH

BAT

wood mose

# CONTENTS

fox

# Foreword

Carry out a straw-poll of most wildlife enthusiasts' favourite fauna and I'd bet my bottom dollar that you'll come to the conclusion in no time that "feather" invariably beats "fur" in the popularity stakes. In fact so far are birds ahead of the competition, that the term "bird-watching" has entered such common parlance I even heard it mentioned twice on BBC Radio 4's "Today" programme this morning. Bird-watching has become such a widely practised pursuit that it can now even be subdivided into "birding" and "twitching" – both encompassing the actual art of watching of birds, with the former being considered a healthy pastime (and what I generally do), whilst the latter, which involves chasing rarities, is largely thought of as an expensive macho addiction (I might have done this a few times before too). By contrast, not only is the term "mammal-watching" a wholly unfamiliar phrase, but it is also an unwieldy mouthful.

This seeming lack of interest in mammals, as opposed to birds, is reflected in the amount of popular support the two respective animal groups' main charities receive. Whilst the Royal Society for the Protection of Birds (or RSPB) is the proud possessor of over a million members, the Mammal Society can only call on the support of a paltry 1,620 patrons.

So why on earth should mammals – of which let's not forget, we are one too – whilst of course cherished, be so far down the pecking order amongst many nature-spotters? Surely we should hold a particularly special place for the beasts with which we have so many shared attributes, including a common ancestor?

Well for starters the vast majority of mammals are not easily seen, either being crepuscular (busiest at dawn and dusk), or downright nocturnal. This means that many mammals are active and therefore most noticeable at times when most sane people are either settling in for a night in front of the telly or tucked up in bed.

Even when stumbled upon accidentally by either a late-night reveller staggering back from the pub or an early commuter dashing for a train, most mammals' persecution-complex means that they are often very timid, giving us little time to appreciate their finer points before they duck out of view. For those sticking around for more than just a glimpse (and with the very obvious exceptions of squirrels, foxes and badgers), many mammals can also be devilishly difficult to identify correctly. The only way, for example, to definitively differentiate between a Wood Mouse and the very similar Yellow-Necked Mouse, is to pop the rodent in a clear polythene bag in order to see if it has washed its neck… and to even get to that stage you first have to find and then catch the little critter!

If you think that mice are both physically and figuratively tough to get to grips with, then their identification is "a walk in the park" when compared to Whiskered and Brandt's Bats. These two batty cousins are so similar that naturalists only realised that Brandt's Bat was actually a British species in 1972. I'm reliably informed that the males of these two virtually identical species have slightly different shaped penises, which can only be used as an identification feature if first, the bat is in your hand and secondly, you are of course looking at a boy bat. In fact the only guaranteed way to separate this daring insectivorous duo is by checking out the arrangement of their teeth, which believe me, on a small, gnashing and wriggling animal that you are desperately trying not to injure whilst holding it, is hellishly difficult.

Compared to the biologically diverse group that is birds, we are not hugely blessed with an enormous variety of British mammals. With a small group of hardcore twitchers having logged over 500 different bird species in and around the shores of the UK, I doubt very much whether any UK naturalist has seen more than 80 mammals in their country of residence. This is because at least half of the mammals recorded on the British list are either incredibly rare immigrants that turn up (if we're lucky) once a decade, or, whilst being bearers of a British passport, are just so incredibly rare that they are nigh-on-impossible to see anyway.

Being unashamedly (like Mr Couzens) a birder first and foremost, I can recall British bird-watching trips on which every time I lifted my binoculars I seemingly spotted a different species. For example at the RSPB Minsmere reserve in Suffolk in late spring, it would not be misplaced to guarantee at least 100 different bird species that can be either seen or heard before breakfast. When it comes to mammals, the most I've recorded in a whole 24-hour period has to be no more than seven or eight.

Additionally, birds also tend to be much more predictable than mammals. You would, for example, have to be pretty unfortunate and/ or inexperienced not to either see (or at least hear) a Sedge Warbler in a reed-bed in spring, a Tufted Duck on your local reservoir in winter or a Blue Tit on your peanuts at any time. However, despite an estimated population of 75 million field voles during an average British spring, it is difficult to name with certainty any one location where a sighting can be virtually guaranteed at any time, and don't get me talking about Otters – or "notters" as I call them!

My final offering on the "birds versus mammals" popularity debate is that for those with an ornithological bent, the only equipment really needed to spot and identify our feathered friends is a pair of binoculars and a field guide. For those with a penchant for ticking a fair proportion of Britain's "get-able" mammals, essentials to add to your kit-list include a bat detector, some live mammal traps, a good night-torch, some gloves, various experts, a sprinkling of permits, a pair of sea-legs and lots of luck.

In summary, it is fairly obvious why mammal-watchers are a much rarer breed. But just because mammals require more effort, planning and patience to track them down, it doesn't mean they should be any less appreciated than, say, butterflies or dragonflies – other eminently twitch-able groups, making them popular amongst list-making naturalists. Mammals are wholly deserving of our admiration, support and protection too.

Reading this book, I feel I have seen mammals in a new light. It also struck me, in addition to the fact that two children under the age of seven have seen several mammals which I haven't (and I won't reveal which ones they are for risk of spoiling the book), the mammals most to be admired are the four members of the Couzens family themselves. And I'll go further by saying that Sam and Emily's parents are indeed a particularly rare breed themselves, who believe that their children's education should not end at the classroom and whose spare time should stretch beyond the TV, their toys and video games to include the great outdoors and all the natural wonders it holds.

…and more power to their elbow.

*Mike Dilger – Naturalist and Presenter*
March 2009

# Introduction

There are many great endeavours that mankind has attempted. There are those who have braved sub-zero temperatures and great hardship to reach the Poles. There are those that have defied both terror and gravity to conquer mountains. There are those who have abandoned civilization and their everyday lives to cross the world in small boats. There are those who have, in various ways, overcome deprivation and extreme difficulty to surmount almost impossible physical and logistical challenges, and somehow come out on top.

This book isn't about any of these.

It is about a challenge, though. And quite an unusual one, at that.

A challenge, you say? What do you need to overcome a challenge? You need excellent forward planning, total dedication, considerable flexibility, money, sponsorship, well-trained staff and top of the range equipment. And that's just for starters.

We didn't have any of those. Just a family of four and a second-hand Vauxhall Zafira.

But honestly, it was a challenge. It was a difficult challenge, too, and one that had never been done before. Our family may not be ready to tackle headline-grabbing assaults on mountains, but then why should we? Lots of people climb mountains, swim across lakes and hang-glide across glaciers. That's a bit old-hat. And perhaps more relevantly, I'm a 40-something father in less than peak condition, my wife is a busy housewife, my daughter is five and my son three. We don't do extreme anything.

But a few days before the start of 2008 I was reading a book and I had an idea. The book was *Where to Watch Mammals in Britain and Ireland*, by Richard Moores, and I idly wondered how many of these furry creatures I had already seen. I counted and I was shocked. It was embarrassing.

If that seems a little on the oversensitive side – after all, if you're going to be shocked, at least you should be shocked by proper things such as the extent of world poverty, global warming or the speed of Madonna and Guy Richie's divorce – then a word of explanation is required. I am, by trade, a writer on wildlife, mainly birds. It's my job to know what colour the nose of a Nathusius' Pipistrelle is, and to know how badly the population of Polar Bears is doing. That's my field. When I write about it, I am supposed to know what I'm going on about. I should have my own experiences to call on. I should have a strong track record of meeting a large range of British wildlife face to face.

And so I should really have seen more than 30 species of mammals. There and then, I resolved to do better. Much better.

But of course, for every such determined resolution there's a depressing snag. For every confident step forward, there's a faltering slip backwards – science and nature's equal and opposite reaction. And, to add to the proverb, there's a time for every purpose, and this wasn't it. How could I improve on my paltry score at any time soon? I had a book to write. I had a mortgage to pay. And – oh, yes – I was the joint shareholder in a family that needed me at home. I could hardly trot off to all parts of Britain to have encounters with Minke Whales and Wildcats while the kids had to content themselves with "64 Zoo Lane" on the telly.

No, it was not even a possibility.

Unless, perhaps, the family came too. Maybe we could all go and see some wild mammals? Yet another snag. My wife isn't that keen on wildlife-watching. The kids don't know a Weasel from an easel. If you took Samuel to the Himalayas and sat him down in front of a Yeti, he would still think that the toy fire engine he was playing with in his lap was considerably more exciting. He's three, and not versed in the art of the outdoors, except to get very, very muddy. And then there's Emily. Emily is the most wonderful enthusiast, and very keen on all kinds of animals. But could we ever get her to wear a warm, snug all-weather outfit that wasn't exactly the right colour, and didn't have the remotest thing to do with princesses? It seemed unlikely.

Overall, the whole idea was pretty unpromising. And that is why it was also irresistible. It is good to have challenges, and to mould the improbable into the inevitable, using the joyous unpredictability and perversity of life, something that tends to loom large in the presence of children. So here was the germ of an idea: why didn't we all commit to a mad year of running around and seeing mammals?

And actually, when Carolyn and I sat down and thought a bit harder about it, the idea did seem to have more than a little merit. For one thing, if we resolved to do one thing all year as a family, then that meant we would have plenty of time spent as a unit, rather than splitting into factions along the lines of birds, friends, princesses and fire engines. Furthermore, if we did all this together, we would have shared adventures. We would have travelled together and discovered things all at once, and we would be able to appreciate our responses collectively. Even if we failed miserably to see some mammals, then it wouldn't really matter, as long as we had plenty of fun along the way.

And there was another benefit, too. As an environmental writer, I have a bit of a thing about the outdoors for its own sake. I have been a natural history junkie from the start, and I find it generally incomprehensible that anyone should not get excited about our natural heritage; you know – about Hedgehogs, Blue Tits, autumn leaves and Bluebell woodland – that sort of thing. I find it genuinely alarming that, as the National Trust have found, most children can't even recognise an Oak leaf. I mean, we're not talking about a leaf from some hideously obscure specimen, we're talking about that of an Oak. One of the commonest trees in Britain. How on earth can a child not be taught how to recognise the tree that gives the British countryside its unique character? Furthermore, another recent survey lamented that, these days, the average A&E Department at a local hospital receives more children injured from falling off beds than falling out of trees. And, while I have no intention of adding to A&E figures for anything, I would find it a bit worrying if my children were forever locked in their rooms looking at computer screens or the TV. Call me old-fashioned, but I want my children to know the feel of leaf-litter on their feet and wind in their hair. I want them to camp out in the fresh air as well as having sleep-overs with their friends. I want them to have real-life adventures and some real-life risk, not just adventures in cyberspace.

And one way to ensure this, for a year at least, was to take them out to observe mammals.

Mammals were also ideal subjects. While there are lots of birds in Britain, and they are very obvious, I have found, much to my chagrin, that they don't tend to turn very young children on much. This is probably because children don't hear stories about Velveteen Gulls, but Velveteen Rabbits. They don't go on Heron Hunts, they go on Bear Hunts. And Jemima Puddle-Duck is hardly a role model, is she? So it's the furry stuff the children naturally love, at least early on. They get excited about Grey Ssquirrels and Badgers and Foxes, and maybe even Otters and Hares, and less so about Crows and Blue Tits and Blackbirds.

Another advantage about mammals is that they are, perversely, much more difficult to see than birds. Why is this an advantage? Well, by right of their elusiveness, mammal-watching requires, if not more effort, then certainly a different kind of effort than bird-watching. From the start, as Carolyn and I discussed our putative project, we knew that we would be doing much more than spending our time waiting around in draughty hides. We would need to be more hands-on. We would need to see some animals, such as rodents, caught in humane traps, and we would need to go to some unusual places to see bats. We would also have to spend quite a few night hours to watch and find nocturnal creatures, which we knew would appeal greatly to the kids. In all these ways, mammal-watching seemed to fit the bill.

It was all very well having a challenge, but what form exactly was the challenge going to take? If we were climbing a mountain, the aim is obvious – to plonk a flag on the summit. If we were walking across the world, we would have to make every possible footstep towards that obvious goal ourselves. But having fun and seeing some wild animals, while an admirable intention, wasn't enough. Our overall aims would have to be defined.

As far as we were concerned, there was no escaping the need for a number of species as our target, a target to reach in the 12 months of 2008. Although this would probably steer the project towards simply ticking off things, and rendering fleeting sightings as good as more fulsome ones, it seemed unavoidable. We couldn't just aim to see an Otter and a Badger. We needed to see a very high proportion of Britain's animals at least once. It was regrettable that an instantaneous fly-past from an obscure bat would therefore be as important towards the goal as two hours in the company of frolicking Foxes, but it was also a driving force towards something concrete. And how many? Well, I made a list of all possible species and soon found that about 100 animals had been seen in Britain. Of these, quite a few were just sea mammals that had been washed up dead or had swum past occasionally, so I crossed these off, together with a swathe of rare stray bats and seals. That left about 70 possibilities. OK, that was way beyond reach, so how about something difficult but at least feasible? The idea of seeing 50 began to form in our heads.

Later on in the year, the figure was put to the experts. All agreed it was difficult but do-able for a single-minded enthusiast with time and money. With children it would be, to put it mildly, a challenge.

Finally, we decided that – just to make sure we would be running our yearly marathon with all the possible shackles attached to our legs – we would combine our mammal-watching year with all the machinery of normal life. We wouldn't drop anything, just for some madcap project. We would still take the children to school and preschool. We would keep up our attendance at church as best we could. We would visit grandparents and meet up with our friends. We would still go to parents' evenings. We would still watch some TV, and the kids would still go to parties and clubs. We had also promised Emily long ago that we would go to EuroDisney when she was five years old, and since this was the most significant promise we had ever made to our fledgling, we weren't about to break it either. In short, life would tick over and, while normality might be stretched or disrupted, it would not be sacrificed.

Thus, with a few conversations and frank exchanges (gas and air, if you like), our project was given birth. We would show the children 50 species of wild mammal in Britain in a year…. And maintain normal life…. Of course we would.

# January

## January 1st – Coming, Ready or Not

The great thing about New Year resolutions is that, on the whole, they live up to their name, being confined to the New Year. Quite naturally, nobody takes their resolutions seriously further on into the future than a few days, and certainly no longer than the banks accept cheques with last year's date. New Year's resolutions are supposed to be transitory, and are all the better for it. Not everybody can be fit, or reliable, or free of bad habits.

It is probably fair to say that, on this New Year's Day, we took our mammal project along with us in the same vein. The challenge, we knew, was an idea that we could cast off as quickly as those oddly patterned socks that aunts send for Christmas, if we found that it didn't suit us. If the early days of mammal-watching proved intolerable or impractical, we could abandon any commitment towards later days. We would wear the idea lightly, and toy with it and test it out. If we didn't like it, then Carolyn and I could always visit the gym three times a week instead.

On this particular day, therefore, we felt like customers who were enjoying the benefits of a trial period. For this day, at least, the stakes were about as low as they could possibly be.

And this was just as well. After all, for a family who were embarking on what was a potentially challenging and effort-hungry project, we were woefully underprepared. We had, after all, only had the idea in the first place a few days earlier. Most undertakings of this kind spend the requisite time in germination, and then a number of months in the planning. There were people to contact and, ideally, sponsors to woo. I should have proposed the idea to a book publisher and written up a synopsis. We should already have got our outdoor clothes sorted, our mammal-watching equipment provided, our hotel rooms booked in advance, our car serviced and had the furry creatures lined up one by one. We had done none of these things – in fact, we had made no preparation at all. And just to complicate matters further, Samuel was in the middle of being potty-trained.

Despite this chaos, however, we did at least have a plan for the first of January. A bird-watcher friend of mine had been out a couple of days before in the west of our county, Dorset, and amidst describing the various feathered delights he had encountered, he happened to mention that there were two Common Porpoises off Burton Bradstock.

To him it was a footnote; to us it was a foothold. Common Porpoises are, despite their name, by no means easy to see off the South Coast anywhere. If, therefore, we could replicate his sighting, it would make a truly terrific start to a year's mammal-watching. Perhaps it was a sign.

We didn't quite jump in the car and travel with high hopes, singing Cliff Richard songs of joy and cheer along the way, because Carolyn and I did know a bit about watching for sea mammals, and knew what a hit-and-miss business it could be. Or at least, a miss business. We had once spent a week's whale-watching in the Azores, which consisted of five minutes of whales and the rest watching the blank sea – literally. And neither of us had ever even seen a Common Porpoise. And, if the truth be told, we would be hard-pressed to know if we were looking at one, either. The preparation for our great year of mammal-watching had not yet reached the stage of learning how to identify anything.

But anyway, Burton Bradstock was awash with people revelling in the mild start to the year – or trying to walk off their wild, start-of-year revelling. The atmosphere was cheery – even carnival – and we heard more

"Good afternoons" in a couple of hours than we probably heard for the rest of the year, although some were, admittedly, a little slurred.

Everybody in West Dorset, it seemed, was outdoors. There were families with children, loads of dogs (perhaps still worrying about their futures – would they just be for Christmas?), contented-looking pensioners, people in wheelchairs and, as you might expect, a higher number of large parties than usual – in other words, normal families dragging along the aunts and uncles and in-laws and sundry relations they feel obliged to associate with over the festive period, and awkward step-families just praying for it all to end. Yet not a single one of them appeared to have slightest knowledge about, or interest in, Common Porpoises. There were no binoculars, telescopes, nor even longing glances towards the flat, calm sea.

It was almost embarrassing to set up my trusty, seriously professional-looking Zeiss telescope along the cliff walk and point it importantly towards the waves. If we had done the same in Piccadilly Circus we might conceivably have attracted fewer sideways glances and bewildered expressions from the streams of people passing than we did here. Clearly, nobody expected anybody to be studying the open sea so carefully, especially since, to every brief glance, there was nothing there. To make matters worse, the children were complete novices in the art of using wildlife-spotting optics of any kind, so we found ourselves indulging in a sort of comedic farce in full public view.

"Put one eye to the telescope."

"That's right. Now shut the other eye."

"No, not the eye you are using to look through the telescope. Keep that open."

"No, don't shut both eyes!"

And so on. The instructions weren't helped by the fact that, inevitably, each child found it enormously amusing to loom up in front of the telescope while somebody was trying to look through it, and to peer through the wrong end intentionally. At the same time Samuel, in particular, liked to grab the telescope and point it in any direction other than the sea. To my knowledge, Common Porpoises cannot fly, so this method didn't contribute much to the collective scan.

The kids managed much better with binoculars and, to be truthful, using a telescope is actually quite tricky if you have never done it before. I'm not sure the kids had ever tried opening one eye and keeping the other shut before, whether behind an eyepiece or not – at least not formally. It was also tricky to set the tripod at the correct height for them.

All in all, our search for the Porpoises wasn't going very well. Even if a fully-grown adult Blue Whale had taken a running jump, leapt high into the air and managed a wave of its fins before crashing with thunderous force back into the sea, we would probably have missed it. In the well-tested Bridget Jones fashion, Carolyn and I made a "note to self": teach the children how to watch.

And much as we adults watched, we didn't see so much as a fin appearing above the surface, not for a microsecond, and not across a single cubic metre of the water that we checked, not for the couple of hours that we must have been watching. The sea was blank. We had no luck, let alone a fluke.

Now you might get the idea that our own, personal January 1$^{st}$ was therefore not a success, but about this you would be entirely wrong. The day was a complete triumph, and all because of a small incident on a hilltop on a West Dorset road.

It was Samuel who precipitated the moment. He spoke magic words, we parked, there was an anxious wait and then it happened.

The potty filled.

He has never looked back. Within a month or two he was standing up beside me all over the country, in driving rain, harsh winds and snow, peeing at will. If you're a parent, I'm sure you will understand the sheer sense of wondrous triumph that we felt at that moment, knowing that, with this small step, we had a key to an easier future.

But our main objective had still eluded us. On the way home we even made a short diversion to Portland Bill, a well-known spot for Bottlenose Dolphins, which would also have made a good start to the year. But our search was a little half-hearted, and the wind was now howling, battering anyone who foolishly braved the fresh air to clear their heads. It was a no-show. All we saw was a belligerent sea.

So the day that began with qualified hopes became an unqualified letter-down of those hopes, and if the previous presence of Porpoises was a sign, it was pointing in the wrong direction. Yet the reality of watching out for sea mammals, and the togetherness that it engendered, and the fact that nobody in the family came to any harm, did not allow us to feel let down. We weren't inspired, but we weren't gutted, either.

And besides, we saw a Rabbit on the way home.

# January 2nd - Notes from HQ, Part I

I suppose you could call us mammal-spotters now. In the same way, the sages say that to be a writer all you have to do is write, and whether or not your work is published is immaterial. So, by the same token, the Rabbit in the field in the fading light of the first of January had made us into bona fide mammalian adventurers. And it felt strangely satisfying.

Today I mused on the task confronting us, and especially I wondered why, to our knowledge, nobody had ever undertaken such a challenge before. For those who don't follow wildlife matters avidly, setting a target for seeing a certain number of species of something in a year is not at all unusual. Bird-watchers do it all the time, all over the world. In Britain, every year, there is a quite wondrously silly contest over who can see the most species in that year, and it is often marked by fast cars and egos and dirty tricks and sullied reputations and nursery-style traumas. Not surprisingly, the same happens in the United States, where the angst is the same but the population has 192 million firearms. I don't think there has been a murder yet...

Elsewhere the contests have spread to such inoffensive creatures as butterflies, and even moths. But you just don't seem to hear about people setting mammal targets, especially not in Britain. Why should this be?

As I sat down to research our task (yes, I know, I should have done it months ago), I came up with what seemed like some reasonable solutions to this puzzle. It seems that, especially compared to other forms of wildlife-watching, mammal-spotting is exceedingly difficult. A high proportion of Britain's furry creatures are highly elusive, shy, nocturnal, or any combination of these. Indeed, you quite often hear people making such statements as "I've never seen a live Mole in my life" (assuming, that is, that you have raised the subject first. If they said that without prompting, then you may have cause to worry about them), and you realise how true this is. And the Mole isn't even nocturnal. Similarly, an animal such as a Common Shrew, with a British population in tens of millions, is an extraordinarily difficult creature to see in the wild, because it is shy and spends its time running around in dense vegetation.

That's assuming, of course, that you can identify it as a Common Shrew in the first place. That's the second serious problem. Mammal identification is difficult. Shrews are hard, rodents are awkward, and bats – well bats are sometimes impossible, even for experts. And let's face it, it's a bit of a damp squib not actually being able to identify what you are seeing.

And this point about bats also touches on another problem. In Britain, at least, rather a lot of the mammals are bats and rodents (and there are also many obscure sea mammals on the British list – Sowerby's Beaked Whale, anyone?) Together the two groups account for nearly a third of all our furry creatures. So unless you are going to get to grips with bats and rodents, you are never going to appreciate a high proportion of British mammals. For my part, I had a sneaking suspicion that, while the members of these groups might appear to look pretty much the same, we were likely to come across some hidden and unexpected delights. But unless you have a nose for unearthing the obscure, you are not going to appreciate the less glamorous groups at all.

And reputation affects mammals more than birds, because a Snow Leopard is exponentially more exciting than a Pipistrelle Bat, whereas an eagle doesn't put a sparrow in the shade in quite the same way. In my kids' books there are lions and tigers and monkeys and elephants (even a patchwork version of the latter), and these are all so exciting and wonderful that a Hazel Dormouse simply cannot compete, despite being a good deal cuter than the lot of them. The TV programmes don't help, either. Even when covering British creatures, it's usually Otters and Foxes, Badgers or deer that fill our screens, leaving the rest behind. The other mammals' stories, which might be just as interesting, remain untold.

And that, in a way, felt like yet another reason for our family to follow through with our task and become serious mammal-watchers for a year. If many of the British animals were underappreciated and poorly watched, then we would be treading in some fairly novel furrows as we went along. As we saw more and more species, we would learn about their lives at the same time, simply as part of our quest. And we would uncover for ourselves new things about the familiar, and delve deep into the unfamiliar, both on our doorstep and beyond.

It's amazing how your life can change when you see a Rabbit.

Bring it on!

# January 3rd – In Search of Snow

My children would tell you they've never seen snow. Actually, they did once in the far-off days of their toddler-hood, but living on the south coast of England, when a harsh winter these days is defined by a few frosty mornings, snow is a rare experience. And this is inconvenient, because children's literature and culture is knee-deep in the stuff. Father Christmas always seems to be battling his way through snow, whether on Christmas cards or in stories, and Angelina Ballerina was clearly born somewhere north of the Arctic Circle. You can't even go on a bear-hunt without encountering a blizzard. It's not surprising, therefore, that many British children ask awkward questions about the lack of sledges, snowmen and chilly-looking robins when the nights start drawing in.

When the opportunity arises, therefore, the responsible modern-day parent is honour-bound to take it, and show their children the magical white stuff falling from the heavens. And today, with the weather forecast promising snowfalls moving ever southward, we decided to devote a day to finding at least a dusting. We took the car and headed north to the Downs, to some moderately high ground where the chances of some settling would be greatly enhanced.

It had already been a satisfactory day, blessed by watching Grey Squirrels feeding and frolicking in the garden. Of course, in the context of seeing 50 species in a year, this animal hardly registers quite as high on the achievement scale as a Minke Whale, but it's easy to peer down your nose and overlook what a splendid entertainer the tree-rat is, particularly for children. And, as it turns out, especially in winter. The human beings of Southern England might at that moment have been bracing themselves for an Arctic-style plunge in temperature, but the Grey Squirrels weren't fussed at all. After an autumn of plenty they had all the provisions they needed to survive with ease, having stashed a horde of acorns and other nuts in various small caches in the ground. Add to this a warm winter coat, and well-built dens (tree holes) and dreys in which to shelter, and the Squirrels were well prepared for a weedy Dorset winter. They were, indeed, in the peak of condition.

There was another reason for their *joie de vivre*, too. Now that they had spread their seeds around during their autumnal hoarding, it was time to do exactly the same again among themselves, this time up in the trees. In January, courtship chases are a common sight and sound, and if you have Squirrels you can hardly miss them.

The animals living in the wood behind our house were in, shall we say, a vigorous mood this morning. There were at least two animals chasing a third, certainly the female, and they simply couldn't leave her alone on her visits to the bird feeder. Once disturbed she would run off vertically and the three would helter-skelter round the trees at full pelt, stopping occasionally for a breather and a loud chatter. Then they would be off again, dashing up as high as they could into the narrowest branches and leaping to the next tree, showing off their exceptional acrobatic abilities to whomever was watching.

Apparently, this high-octane chase is precipitated by the female and, to be quite honest, she must rank as one of the worst leaders-on in the entire animal kingdom (and boy, has she got competition). First she wafts her scent through the treetops to tell of her availability, the sort of Squirrel equivalent of putting your profile on a dating website. Then she sits back and waits for results. It's that simple and the males invariably come running (sorry, girls, if this isn't your experience), but actually, this is partly because male Squirrels are completely immune to the concept of choice. Anything with a suitably bushy tail is irresistible to them. The females, however, are a little bit more choosy; what they want more than anything is a male with stamina. The idea of the constant game of high-speed catch-me-if-you-can is that, after a few hours or even days of unrelenting and exhausting pursuit, all but the very best (or desperate) males fall by the wayside, knackered. The last one standing, even if he is a little jelly-legged, is allowed to copulate. Happily, when this stage is reached, the Greys are blessed with a degree of decorum, and the consummation of the chase usually takes place out of sight, so one can trust them to entertain the children without opening their young eyes to adult shenanigans.

Anyway, with two mammals to our name we felt free to pursue the snowfall instead, not entirely caring where it took us. But if this sounds like some serendipitous jaunt of romantic freedom, with our trusty jalopy tracing complex patterns through the cobwebbed back-roads of rural England, the fact is we took the eastbound M27. And there, in a field beside the carriageway, I spotted some deer.

"Deer," I called, logically enough.

"Oh yes," replied Carolyn, peering in the right direction.

There was silence from the back.

"Deer." I repeated. "Roes."

Still nothing.

"Did you see them?" I asked the children.

They shook their heads. "Look, I've put Cinderella in her new outfit," Emily said, reassuringly, showing us the fruits of her back-seat preoccupation.

Clearly, the children had missed the Roe Deer, and that set me thinking. There was no problem about them missing these, but what would happen if they missed something really important? Say we took them on a special trip to see an Otter, and they missed it despite the animal showing in front of them? Should we then count it on the basis that we gave them the chance to see it, which, by reasons of misfortune, they didn't? And what if only one of them saw it? Should we add it to our tally of mammals then? It was clear that we needed some ground rules.

It wasn't very difficult to decide on the ideal plan. Since this was very much a family project, we decided that no animals would count unless at least one child saw one of them. The reason for this latitude was Sam. Being a mere three years old, Sam was in no position to be an especially reliable witness (for example: "It wasn't me," next to opened packet, chocolate on face), and furthermore, we weren't sure that he was, as yet, fully in touch with what we were doing. So, should Emily alone bear positive witness to the animal, we would count it. And as for us parents, we decided on the same rule – that just one of us needed to see it. Why? Well, although for most of the time both of us would make the effort to see everything, it seemed sensible that, on occasion, Carolyn at least should the spared the full force of endless mammal quests.

Anyway, our quest took us at length through the murky, somewhat depressing English countryside. No wonder everyone fantasises about winter snow, I thought, observing the limp, almost colourless landscape. Everything was tired and ragged. The fields' green was a fatigued, end-of-the-line green. Even the berries that had shone blood red or blue-black a few months back had lost their lustre and were tired, now resigned merely to being unsold goods left behind by the birds – in fact, the countryside was exactly like the washed-out décor of a store that was closing down. The trees were as still and stark as turned-over tables and chairs, and the woolly old-man's-beard that draped over them seemed to sag like dustsheets over condemned furniture. We passed by hedgerows, where just about the most vivid thing to see was the occasional etiolated leaf that had somehow defied autumn and remained defiantly and pointlessly upon its uninterested, closed-down branch.

And we couldn't find the snow. It had stopped at Birmingham.

We stopped in the pretty town of Alresford for a special lunch – my birthday. The place was a tonic. With Christmas a fresh memory all the decorations were still up and the main street was spruce and cheerful, with multi-coloured lights in the line of trees that strode along it. The children weren't used to that unmistakable pattern of antiquity, whereby every house on the street was slightly different from its neighbour, having evolved along different lines and different moods, and they revelled in its unexpectedness. They delighted in the different doors and entrances by the pavement, some grand and some modest, and the different angles of houses to each other, their odd shapes and sizes, their chimneys. One of the delights of walking along with small children is that their curiosity pricks yours, and you can use your brood's lack of decorum as an excuse for peering into places where you wouldn't normally do so. Thus, we looked down alleyways and through curtains, spotting the odd log fire or, conversely, a widescreen TV. We would read the signs on the bells, full of stranger's names, and spot those small giveaways to the inhabitants within, such as posters for dog charities, notices of talks and the local Neighbourhood Watch. Everything pointed to an ease with affluence, and unabashed, commuter-belt comfort. Alresford was confident of itself, its past and its present.

We let the siren call of the bridgeside pub lure us in, and took a table overlooking Alresford pond. Nothing really beats family meals, especially when you sit in comfort and your view affords wildness. The pond was in lackadaisical mood: the ducks swam over the water and skirmished as if trying to stir some life into it. But it just lapped at the reedbeds and seemed to sulk.

"We sometimes see Otters here," ventured the waitress, noticing our regular stares out of the window.

It seemed perfect. An Otter served up with a latte. But, despite the fact that we stayed there much longer than we probably should have, no Otter showed, even as the short winter's day began to call time on the light.

# January 12<sup>th</sup> – A Meeting with the Underclass

If ever we needed a jolt to our respective systems to remind us that this year was not going to be entirely conventional, it was the knowledge that, on this apparently ordinary Saturday, when all our friends were going shopping, or killing time at soft play centres, or blobbing in front of the telly and reading the papers (heaven!), we were going to look for Bank Voles. I mean, who in their right mind looks for Bank Voles? Nobody, surely? When was the last time you ever heard anyone remarking: "I'll just pop out to check the voles", or "Saw a couple of lovely, furry voles only yesterday"? It just doesn't happen.

But that's what we were doing. And with a high degree of earnestness, too. To be honest, we needed to see these rodents. They were significant to us.

The animals had been seen by some friends of mine underneath a bird table at the nearby nature reserve of Blashford Lakes. The incidental manner of the sighting is instructive. The friends, and everybody else, goes to this nature reserve to see birds. But while looking at the finches and tits, and a few woodpeckers, the friends happened to notice these small, furry, mouse-like creatures running around, and identified them as Bank Voles. You get the point. My friends didn't go there for Bank Voles, nor would they have done, ever in their lives. Nobody I know would have done so. The voles were subtexts to their plot. Voles are always subtexts, they are never the main event. Voles are absolutely, gut-wrenchingly insignificant.

But they were the reason for our visit, and that, in a way, was mildly unsettling. Were we mad?

Carolyn wasn't. She had gone shopping, under our newly decided one-parent rule.

The more I pondered upon the vole's colourless reputation – as we drove the short distance to Blashford, Emily merrily singing and Samuel playing with his beloved toy cars, the more I realised that all this could hardly be fair. Voles are valid animals – just like cute Grey Squirrels or cunning Foxes – and they are, in population terms at least, way more abundant than either. It is estimated that there are some 23 million Bank Voles in Britain, which equals 10 voles to every Grey Squirrel and 100 to every Fox. Yet nobody seems to take much notice of them.

Indeed, you might never even have heard of a vole. Perhaps you had, but weren't aware of how it differs from a mouse. Well, I must admit, until recently, neither had I. For your information, voles are the same size as mice, but they have proportionally smaller eyes, smaller ears and shorter tails. While mice usually come out at night, voles come out by day and night. And the other main difference is in their diet: mice eats all sorts of food, including vegetable matter, some insects and other meat; voles are strictly vegetarian, eating mainly seeds, berries and grass.

If you delve even a little into the natural history of these mini-animals, one thing is particularly striking. Almost everything carnivorous seems to feed on them. It is almost amusingly predictable. Find details of anything in Britain with a decent set of teeth or claws and, with unwavering regularity, there among the list of dietary items it will say "voles". Among the many enemies of voles are Common Buzzards, Kestrels, Tawny Owls, Foxes, Stoats, Wildcats and Domestic Cats, Minks and even the Adder. Several animals eat voles as niche items, almost to the exclusion of other meat, including some owl species and, in certain areas, the Weasel. Chillingly, it is estimated that the latter may, in a given year, eat 20 to 40 per cent of a given vole population. Imagine that! If you were a vole and had nine friends, the chances dictate that four of you would go down the gullet of a Weasel or an owl within the next 12 months.

Intriguingly, one of the vole's many weaknesses (along with being small, abundant and active night and day) is that it suffers, to put it bluntly, from incontinence. In common with other rodents, voles live in a world where the olfactory sense is as important as sight or sound, and voles use smell to make sense of a lot of life. They can recognise each other by scent, and they declare their own presence by peeing everywhere and spreading their smell abroad, as with many other mammals. Actually, they pee every few minutes, for one reason or another. Unfortunately for them, the smell lingers around enough for a Weasel to detect where a vole is, even when the latter is tucked away in a burrow underground. And Kestrels, those small predatory birds that customarily hover over motorway verges and other rough ground, can actually see where a vole has been peeing, because vole urine has a chemical component that is visible in the ultraviolet spectrum. All in all, their need to wee plays an important part in their downfall.

Anyway, as we were preparing to see these oppressed Bank Voles, I was beginning to form a picture of an animal that, in its own way, and contrary to every impression I had ever gathered, is very special indeed. It is nothing if not stoic, surviving against the toughest of odds, a creature living under the permanent cloud of almost universal predation. It's a wonder a vole ever bothers to venture out at all for fear of imminent death, yet it still heroically does so, like a Gazelle on the African plains, which instinctively knows that it is merely an extra in a film about Lions or Cheetahs or Leopards. But who will appreciate the vole – in anything other than the culinary sense? I resolved that, for a few moments today, we would give the animals the attention they were due.

It was only a short walk from the car park at Blashford to the Woodland Hide, where the voles had been showing. The children weren't yet primed much to mammal-watching this early in our quest, and they showed far greater interest in a pile of firewood beside the path than in any need to keep going. Promptly they began to dismantle the pile. They then began to beat sticks against the trees, giggling wildly. By the time we reached the hide, our arrival was hardly news to those watching the animals and birds from inside. We entered to a tense, stony silence, broken only by my embarrassed apologies.

But, while the birds had largely vacated the viewing area by the time my herd of little elephants arrived, it turned out that the voles were made of a little more fibre than their feathered counterparts (maybe that's why they are so good to eat?) Almost as soon as we had sat down to scan the woodland floor beneath the bird feeders, a vole duly appeared, creeping out from underneath a fallen log. Soon it began to scoff a piece of birdseed, holding its paws to its mouth in hamster fashion, apparently nibbling without a care in the world. I had expected it to be a complete bag of nerves, dashing one way or another, watching all around it, up and down, the picture of fear and foreboding. But, in a way, it was perfectly peaceful. It stood still enough for me to point each child in the right direction so that both could actually make it out, and it even scurried away slowly enough, when disturbed, for them to follow its movement.

It was also a handsome creature. I never thought I would ever say such a thing about a rodent, but it was. Bank Voles are rather well-proportioned animals and, while they lack the large ears and eyes that can make mice look delightful enough to have spawned cartoon characters, they don't have that snake-like tail which makes rats so unappealing. This individual was also covered in richly coloured, warm-brown fur, a far cry from the blandness of your average mouse.

We didn't stay watching for long. People were coming regularly into the hide for a dose of quiet, and close-up birding action, whilst the kids' concentration had more or less evaporated within a few minutes of entering. And so, we left the hide and went for a three-quarter family walk, the kids venturing alarmingly near the visitor-centre pond, fiddling with the stuffed animals inside the centre, playing with a large, admittedly irresistible wooden broom that had been neatly placed on standby outside the door, and generally leaving no object of curiosity untouched. By the time we had reached the car, I was parentally frazzled.

We drove off in semi-disgrace, leaving a small trail of destruction behind us. But as we left, I calmed down and thought about what we had achieved. Yes, we might have annoyed a few people looking for quiet in the hide; we might have slightly upset the wardens of the reserve by disturbing their woodpiles and brooms; but we had also seen a shy and hard-to-see British mammal, completely in the wild – our third species of the year. I was sure that we had not caused our quarry the slightest disturbance. The whole trip had been very worthwhile.

Except that, if we were to sit down together and chat about our stress levels, the Bank Vole would have to admit that it had a more relaxing afternoon than me.

# February

## February 1ˢᵗ – Notes from HQ, Part II

To see the wild Bank Voles had been satisfying, and had proven that it was possible to see poorly known animals in the wild, even with family members that were high on noise and short on concentration span.

However, the Bank Vole quickly proved to be an isolated incident. In a way, the voles had been delivered on a plate (sorry about the metaphor, rodents), with accurate information that we managed to follow up easily. But I soon discovered that leads to sightings are in short supply in the world of mammal-watching. You sometimes hear about very rare animals, such as stranded whales or seals, but the ordinary, run-of-the-mill British natives are an information blackspot. Take the Weasel, for instance. It is Britain's most abundant carnivore, but there seems to be nowhere in the entire country where sightings of this mammal can be guaranteed. The House Mouse is just as bad. You hear about the fact that it is everywhere (the most widespread non-human mammal in the world), but I tried to find where to locate one, and no one in cyberspace was willing to tell. I spent a lot of time searching the internet for tips to try to plan our year, but it became a frustrating, almost fruitless exercise.

We were thwarted in other ways, too. I enquired about several commercially-operated Badger-watching spots, because I was keen to see this mammal next month, when it was at its friskiest, but got no replies. Eager to see a Mole, I made enquiries with a couple of professional Mole-catchers, to see whether they might want to live-trap one of their arch-enemies so that a couple of kids could admire them – and I would have been happy to pay for the service, too. But strangely, they didn't want to know, and were entirely dismissive. Maybe they thought that I was having them on.

There were also certain sensibilities to maintain. It so happens that in our area there are a goodly number of farms and potentially friendly farmers. It seemed absolutely sensible to me to enquire about the mammals that might be inhabiting their properties, but Carolyn was strongly resistant to this idea.

"You can't ask to see the rats and mice in their barns," she said incredulously, rolling her eyes. "We don't know them."

My protestations that we certainly would get to know them if we went ahead and asked were firmly rejected.

Thus, the first month of our mammal challenge went by without a great deal of progress. We scored pitifully few mammals and didn't get many useful leads, either. The lack of organisation and resolve that had hampered us from the very start was beginning to tell. So was the fact that we were, essentially, trailblazing. Except that, if this was a blaze, we had hardly even lit the match yet.

## February 2ⁿᵈ – The Past and the Future in the Forest

A challenge like seeing 50 wild mammals in Britain in a year requires all manner of fair winds. We knew we would have to get ourselves better organised, meet helpful people, enjoy friendly logistics (i.e. no car breakdowns, accurate maps) and, undoubtedly, benefit from a good dose of luck at times. We would need exceedingly elusive animals to become somehow viewable, if only once, and animals with scattered populations would need to scatter across our path. We would require alternatives to those species we missed, and contingencies for being persistent with animals we couldn't afford to miss. Thus, in reality, our single challenge was really a series of challenges.

Above all in our challenge, we also needed a few of the least variable variables: the "home-bankers". These were animals that we could completely rely on finding, so that, in theory, we could leave them until we had plenty of difficult species on board. They are the sort of species that you might not see in your back garden, perhaps, but require just a short journey and not much real effort to locate. We had seen a couple of them already – the Grey Squirrel and the Rabbit – but there were plenty more around.

Well, the idea of holding off on such reliable creatures was fine in theory, but by the end of January our list of bagged species was so small that we felt it necessary to flout our own rule, and go in search of one or two "unmissables". We had begun to tell people about our challenge and, when the inevitable question of "How many have you seen so far?" came up, it became embarrassing to admit that it was only three. It undermined the whole project, not just for our friends, who might bashfully have seen more mammals than us by now, but also for ourselves. It was a matter of identity. No matter how advanced our plans for mammal-spotting domination, until we had a respectable number of sightings on board, we weren't real spotters at all. We needed to withdraw a few home-bankers from our guaranteed account.

Among the easiest of all wild creatures to see in Britain are deer. This is partly because, on the whole, they are bigger than most mammals – the Red Deer being the largest native land animal still found at large in Britain – and partly because several species are restricted to patchy, relatively confined areas that you can visit with high hopes of seeing them. Deer also have the pleasing habit of running around during the day, and are therefore easily visible before even a three-year-old's bedtime. They are also active throughout the year, and many of them live in groups dotted across woodland rides like antelopes spread over the African savannah. Thus, the six British deer should, by rights, find themselves on any serious mammal-spotter's list.

Moreover, we also hold the considerable advantage of living close to one of the best sites for deer in the whole of Britain, the New Forest. Within its admittedly large area (580 square kilometres/220 square miles), there are about 2,500 individual deer of five different sorts, all roaming free. You can hardly get from one side of the National Park to the other without tripping over a Fallow Deer (1,600 individuals), while there are healthy numbers of the more solitary Roe Deer (400) and Red Deer (350), together with a few elusive Sika Deer and Muntjacs. Many of the deer get run over every year by drivers exceeding the modest speed limit of 40 miles per hour. Of those that don't meet this end, quite a number are culled every year by the rangers, so that their populations, and the damage they do to the forest vegetation, doesn't get out of hand. In short, you'd be hard-pressed to miss a deer in the forest, especially if you were looking for one (or driving fast).

So we set off on this sunny afternoon in a search of the inevitable. We only had to cross the border of the National Park to see signs of these animals' presence. In all the woodlands we passed, the branches never drooped down to the ground, but all their growth seemed to start around 1.5 metres (5 feet) from the forest floor, something that applied even to the boughs of the prickly shrubs such as holly. This was the "browse line", the level reached by the forest's larger herbivores when grazing. Below this line was nothing but the tired, warm-brown tangle of bracken to break the monotony of last autumn's rotting leaf-fall.

At Bolderwood, in roughly the middle of the National Park, the deer lead an idyllic existence because, in a glade surrounded by deep woodland, they are given handouts of food every afternoon, a nice dose of corn and grass to make the leaves and acorns (that they might deign to find in the forest) go down well. They are a tourist attraction, so all they have to do is to show up and look pretty, which isn't very difficult, since, to our eyes at least, their gentle black eyes, pert tails, shapely legs and – in the males – sharp-pointed antlers make them inherently pleasing on the eye. They don't really seem to do much for most of the year (which gives them plenty in common with human models) except graze on vegetable matter (same again) and presumably get enough exercise to keep them in shape. The latter function isn't to keep them safe any more: deer predators have long gone from this country, but there is always the chance of an audition for a trim deer in Autumnwatch and – the ultimate for any aspiring cervine model – to be whispered at by Simon King.

So we couldn't really miss the deer at Bolderwood, and we didn't. It almost felt like cheating. About 10 of them were sitting around in the hallowed clearing, waiting for the day's handout (or perhaps for their mobile phones to ring), and they were simply doing nothing at all. We peered at them, trying to be enthusiastic. It was clear that they were Fallow Deer – the antlers were wide-rimmed at the tip, a bit like cauliflower ears – but their lives looked a little fallow, too. They occasionally looked at us, chewing the cud in that same vacant, clueless way that a gum-masticating football manager always seems to adopt when his team is losing a match. But really, they were almost expressionless.

This was a shame, because, in the New Forest, Fallow Deer have a long and lively history. In a way, each of their footsteps dances over the ancient and bloody past of the forest itself, its disasters and its turbulences. Fallow Deer were present in Britain up to about 100,000 years ago, but the last glaciation did it for them and they would never have made it back here had it not been for the hand of man. From their refuge in southern Europe, Fallow Deer were slowly reintroduced to the northern continent after the climate warmed up again, arriving here in Britain with the Normans in the eleventh century. So they were part of the famous spoof history book's "…and all that" rider to the events of 1066. The slain British king Harold should never have worried: invaders often bring good things as well as bad.

And it was William the Conqueror himself that created the New Forest, ring-fencing it as a royal "Nova Foresta" in 1079. What so excited him was, above all, the deer populations, which now, of course, included the Fallows brought in by his own armies. Living out the trend of the powerful at the time, and indulging in royal tendencies that continue to this day, the conquering king adored hunting which, let's face it, wasn't too different from his day-job of wiping out human enemies. However, the Royal Family's association with this area and its larger grazers was not always a happy one, for two of William's sons died in the forest at the hands of deer, or as a result of deer-hunting: Prince Richard was mauled to death by a stag in 1081 and William Rufus was found mysteriously shot by an arrow while out hunting in 1100, probably as a result of poor aim by his colleagues.

Back in the present, we gazed at these Fallows, these present-day descendents of the original Norman herds. We imagined them soon after their introduction, when, at large in the vast wilderness of this huge area (the New Forest is still one of the largest patches of undeveloped lowland in Western Europe), they must have had the chance of leading lives without ever seeing a human being – at least in the early days. We imagined them leaping away from kings on the hunt and poachers who would have been sentenced to death if caught. We imagined them in their prime, frisky and alert, fleet-footed and quick of antler. And then we sighed at the current lot, deer that seemed to spend half their lives lying down, and didn't look as though they could maul a fly.

One of the great delights about the New Forest is that there is always something unusual, or even strange, happening there. For example, I have come across the British Bonsai Club stripping young pine trees from the acidic soil in the middle of nowhere, and I have run into army units practising their orienteering skills, groups of full-time mushroom-pickers on the loose for a pre-breakfast profit, and dozens of youngsters on their Duke of Edinburgh's Award schemes, usually lost and on the point of eating acorns to survive. The forest is a spectacular place, an unusual landscape and a backdrop for the out-of-the-ordinary. This time we happened to come across a wedding.

It was no ordinary wedding, of course, but a major bash at a stately home called Rhinefield House, and for her big day, the bride had chosen to arrive on an antique pony and trap. The horsebox and cart took up much of the car park and, close to the appointed time, the whole area seemed to beat to the usual pre-wedding drum of fussing and waiting, with smart-frocked women wearing concerned faces, and men in suits trying to make jokes. Only the horses, of which there were two, both tall-limbed chestnuts with white-streaked noses and thick black manes, seemed unaffected by the occasion, hiding behind their blinkers and happily munching the contents of bags placed in front of them. We watched as the bride, dressed in blazing red, risked her dignity and heels by clambering into the wooden carriage, which shook alarmingly as her father joined her above the high wheels. At this the horseman, looking a little self-conscious in a costume that could have been loaned from the BBC Drama Department, made a gentle "mush" call, and the carriage swept the bride unsteadily around the corner, towards her new life.

But as diverting as the whole scene was, there weren't many more deer to see here in the enchanted forest. That isn't to say we didn't try looking for them; it's just that, in an area as big as this, everything wild is inevitably often elsewhere. Nevertheless we went for short walks in search of Reds, Roes and Sikas, and the children stamped on the ice coating of the puddles. Emily sang songs, her breath streaming through the air and Samuel – at this point in life obsessed with fire engines – put out imaginary conflagrations every few metres.

We had given up on the day's quest, to the point of driving to Lyndhurst for fish and chips, when Carolyn, still admirably alert, shouted "Deer!"

I backed up the car and parked up next to a small patch of very young woodland of densely packed, narrow oak trunks, its floor thickly covered by leaf-litter as brittle and powdery as snowfall. A few metres within it was the unmistakable shape of a deer, on its own, and peering at us with almost courteous concentration. It was a Roe Deer, small, dark and wild-looking, a female, and she was ready to run. In whispers we directed the kids' gaze to the right place, trying to keep them quiet and make slow movements. But they couldn't miss it when the Roe finally spooked, dashing off with that extraordinarily elegant and agile four-footed skip that they use, a gait known as a "stott". As it went the Roe's most distinctive feature became obvious: its bottom. It had a creamy round patch around the most feeble-looking, all-white tail. When deer are running, their bottoms are so conspicuous that it helps them to keep together.

So the fish and chips became a celebration. We had bagged two deer, just as the deer hereabouts had once bagged two royals. Yet I also felt a tinge of consternation. If it had taken half a day to see two cast-iron certainties, what would it be like when we were searching for mammals that were genuinely elusive?

# February 9th – Up and Running

Although a month old, our project was barely up on its feet. Seeing the deer had at least mathematically made finding 50 mammals viable, with five down and 11 months to go, but we were sorely lacking in any respectable encounters. The only faintly unusual mammal we had notched up was a Bank Vole, but, with due respect to this inoffensive rodent, it is hardly the stuff of legend. We weren't likely to be saying to ourselves, "With a Bank Vole behind us, we can take on the world." We needed some inspiration and, generally speaking, we were struggling. We weren't sure how much effort to put in – whether to wait until the summer and then go all-out for mammal sightings, or to drip-feed ourselves slowly, so that the target number gradually reduced. We had barely started to plan how we were going to find the majority of our mammals, or whom to contact to help us. In truth, deep down, we still weren't really convinced about our quest at all, let alone feeling sufficiently competent to pursue it.

For example, it seemed sensible to see Badgers by attracting them to our garden, but this turned out to be more difficult than we had first thought. We knew that Badgers occupied the rough ground behind us because, a few years ago, some neighbours had invited us round for Badger-spotting drinks, but that was pre-kids, and we hadn't encountered the animals since. Assuming the occupants of the sett were still around, how would we bring them in, and how long would it take? And what should we feed them? Feeding garden animals is a minefield. If you feed Foxes, some neighbours will complain about encouraging pests round to defecate at will and leave scraps. If you feed Hedgehogs with bread and milk, the problem, apparently, is that you will give them constipation, which can be harmful in extreme cases. If you feed squirrels, you might get black looks from the owners of the bird table next door, since you're causing their favourite Robins and Blue Tits trouble. Magazines and blogs are full of poison-pen warnings about giving food to various sorts of wildlife. You've got to tread carefully. You can feed your own kids on fast food and biscuits, but woe betide you if you give Badgers anything other than pre-approved gourmet food that has passed through 10 layers of health-and-safety checks and is years in advance of its sell-by date.

Thus it was, on this particular Saturday, that I sent Carolyn to Sainsbury's with strict instructions to buy exactly the right sort of food for our Badgers. My book had recommended a certain brand of cat food called "Gilpa Valu", so we decided that nothing else would do. Carolyn and the kids scoured the appropriate aisles for long enough to attract the interest of the in-store security, but they couldn't find the right stuff. Perhaps this was not surprising: none of the family had ever scanned the pet section in a supermarket before. Instead, the whole trip became a skirmish between the children. Emily was going through a cat-mad phase and insisted on looking at every brand of moggie food, while Samuel, determined to assert himself, lobbied for everything doggy on the opposite aisle. Carolyn was pulled in both directions, caught between a catfight and dogfight.

In the end, we gave up on cat food and decided to put out peanuts instead, night after night, just outside the garden gate – it was a recommendation from a friend. But it still didn't work. The Badgers stayed away and fed elsewhere, no doubt outside a more reliable dwelling, perhaps in a higher council-tax band. The Grey Squirrels ate the peanuts and got fat and healthy. Our neighbours' population of Blue Tits looked on, and scolded.

For the moment, however, in the fledgling weeks of our project, we had nothing but a certain stubbornness to keep us going. Seeing any mammals was difficult; we knew that, and the last few weeks had proved what we had been led to expect. But we were equally unconvinced that, despite our shaky start, we should give up. After all, nobody had tried our project before, and, since we had no measure of how we should be doing, there was nothing to suggest that we were on a course for failure.

It did, however, take a morning of parental hell to propel us out into the mammal-watching world again. The children's spat at the supermarket was, it turned out, merely the first exchange in what became a full-blown campaign of internecine fives-and-under conflict. It became so utterly intolerable by lunchtime that, to avoid the temptation of henceforth signing off our children's care to social workers, we set out in the car just to get out of the house, Carolyn in the back seat between the rival factions. By the time the Zafira had steered us into the calming, curvaceous landscape of South Wiltshire's chalk belt, Emily and Samuel were no longer spitting blood. Now all we needed was a serious distraction.

It soon occurred to me that this type of countryside held considerable promise for seeing Brown Hares. I had noticed them not far from here in the past, crouching in the open on these anonymous close-cropped swards and ploughed fields stretching away into the distance on both sides of the road. Hares are completely open-country animals, eschewing the homely underground warrens dug by Rabbits for a chilly bivouac amongst thick grass above ground – the Hare's "form". So, while Rabbits tread lightly and cautiously any distance from their holes and cover, Hares are the ones you tend to see right out in the middle of fields, obvious but alert, their brash confidence underscored by the ability to run and run fast. They are often easy to see from cars, even at some distance. Furthermore, with the sun touching the tinder of pre-spring green and lighting up the Hares' grassland stage, I wondered whether the atmosphere might induce a tinge of "madness", and we might see the animals dashing about in a lust-induced state of wild abandon.

You might immediately think, reading this, that February is a bit early to expect the Hares to be getting frisky. After all, you can be "mad as a March Hare", but not, in the lexicon at least, be a February Hare. The alliteration, though, hides a more complicated picture. Hares do indeed get hot under the collar in March, but they can equally lose their heads any time between January and August. They have a long breeding season, lasting throughout the summer, and the young Hares, the leverets, can be seen as late as October. However, the extended season masks the fact that a Hare's sexual possibilities are severely constrained, because females only enter into receptive oestrus for a few hours every six weeks. That's a very narrow window and, let's face it, enough to make any bloke a little desperate. To make matters worse, Hares live in a hierarchy that keeps none but the dominant males satisfied, even when the female is receptive. If a subordinate male attempts to copulate, he might suffer the indignity, not just of being boxed and given a clip round his ample ear by a rival, but equally by the female he is attempting to woo. All in all, the Hare's reproductive world is a little explosive, to say the least. And like most explosions, it might be spectacular, but it is also short-lived. If you wish to see excited Hares, you have to be there at exactly the right time on the right day.

Of course, if we had had Sir David Attenborough with us, the Hares would have covered every hillside, chasing, boxing and copulating as if their very lives depended on it. The man is amazing in what he can induce wildlife to do, isn't he? Until David arrives the lions in Africa are in a seemingly perpetual state of slumber, enough to make even the most excited tourist slump down in their safari bus and wonder what the fuss is about. But as soon as he and his film crews arrive, off the big cats go on a spectacular hunt and bring down a wildebeest faster than the youngster at our local drag can summon up a Big Mac. But we didn't have Sir David with us, and the Hares weren't playing ball.

But all our project truly compelled us to do was to find one Hare, not a field full of them. As we drove along we had several false alarms, especially emanating from the kids, but even the least outlandish claims turned out to be Rabbits. Carolyn, for her part, had never knowingly seen a Hare before, so she found herself expecting to see nothing more than big versions of Rabbits; so, every time one of the ubiquitous bunnies looked a little better fed than usual, she had the urge to stop the car. But, as an experienced Hare-watcher might tell you, Hares are very different creatures indeed. They just don't really look like Rabbits very much, not even at a distance. They are big and athletic, nothing like their couch-potato relatives.

When we finally did come across a Hare, it looked initially like a clod of earth more than anything else. But it was a "suspicious" clod of earth, somehow indefinably animate. The sight of it was enough for us to park the car by the side of the road, risking even the indignant (and inevitable) wrath of the vehicles behind us in order to check the clod out. Through my binoculars I could tell what it was straight away, even though its body was flat to the ground and its signature ears were lowered. It was entirely still, body not twitching but eyes watchful, probably relishing its anonymity in the dirt. But, like a commuter on a train whose immediate neighbour breaks ranks by starting a conversation, the Hare's peace and quiet had been shattered by our unwelcome arrival. Neverthless, we left the car so that I could set up the telescope, and the kids could appreciate this wild and rangy animal in its normal environment.

It's true to say that the Hare looked almost scary when magnified by the telescope. Hares are like sensory machines, with huge ears, wide eyes and a substantial nose, and they certainly don't look friendly. The eyes, in particular, stare at you with a sort of mad expression that might belong to the relative no one in the family ever talks about. The ears have an almost robotic twitchiness; their black tips can be used as the most reliable way to tell for sure that it is a Hare, not a Rabbit, that you are looking at.

"Gosh," said Carolyn. "It's really big. I had no idea."

Emily, too, was impressed. She worked the telescope well, shutting one eye, and feasted on the novelty of the view. Ever the enthusiast, she squeaked in delight: "It's the same colour as my coat."

And it was true. The Hare was a warmer brown than any Rabbit you will see, especially in the late afternoon sunshine.

Much as we were delighting in it, the Hare was beginning to get more and more nervous. Very soon it sprinted off as only a Hare can, its legs a-blur, its speed miraculous. When stretched, Hares can get to a peak of 55 kilometres (35 miles) per hour, but that dry number is nothing compared to the reality of seeing this animal go. Who needs to see a Hare box when it can thrill you with a mere sprint? But just to give us an extra show, as the Hare reached what appeared to be a safe haven, it slowed and shadow-boxed in the direction of a couple of nearby Rooks, which cawed in irritation.

On the way back the car was filled with excited conversation. Carolyn was impressed at how different Hares were to familiar Rabbits, while the kids, all differences forgotten, recalled the bedtime story that we had read to them many times over the last few years, featuring the very nut-brown Hares that we had just seen.

To celebrate the great event we treated ourselves to ice creams at a nearby food outlet. The service was appallingly laboured, so much so that it took

longer to get two scoops and a latte than it had taken us to see the Hare
once we'd arrived in the chalk belt. Normally, such things would drive
me bananas, but not today, not now, not basking in our most important
sighting of the year.

For it was the Hare that finally convinced us that mammal-spotting
can be successful, educational and fun for the whole family. We had seen
the animal so well that everyone, from the youngest to the eldest, had
appreciated it and learnt something. It had got us into the countryside,
defused an argument and set us enthusing again. I wouldn't say that, from
this moment on, we never looked back. But it at least ensured that the
project, like the Hare, was truly up and running.

## February 19<sup>th</sup> – Notes from HQ, Part III

Strangely, the act of sighting a wild animal in a field had an immediate
effect on the deskwork for our project. It seemed as though the Hare itself
had been on the line to the powers that be, and things began to turn in
our favour. Several contacts that had seemed dead ends livened up. I began
to receive emails that, rather than saying a certain professional could not
possibly show us a Mole in a month of Sundays, began to invite us to visit
and enjoy their mammalian treasures. "We've got lots of mammals," they
would say. "Do come and drop in."

Thus I received an invitation from a nature reserve in Hertfordshire to
come up and see Edible Dormice, a very range-restricted animal (found
only within a radius of 50 kilometres (30 miles) from Tring). We were
urged to come and see Badgers and Feral Goats in Scotland, Stoats in
Yorkshire, Dolphins in Wales and Long-eared Bats in Berkshire. We were
grateful for all of these, but probably the most exciting contact was a lot
closer to home. It came from a lady who represented the East Dorset
Mammal Group, and she invited us to take part in some of their regular
events. Now since we live in East Dorset, this seemed the perfect way to
see some of the small rodents and shrews that live almost everywhere
but are hard to see. The group owned a set of humane traps which, once
opened, give children fantastic opportunities to observe these secretive
creatures close at hand. Not surprisingly, I decided to join the group there
and then.

At the same time, the idea of spotting animals serendipitously, hoping to come across them by sighting them from a car or during a walk, a method that had undoubtedly worked with the Hare but was far less successful with the deer species of the New Forest, gradually became less attractive, and less of a focus for us. We had tried on a number of occasions to drive around locally at dusk in the hope that a Badger, Fox or anything else might shoot across the road in front of us, but we had been universally unsuccessful. Well, we had seen plenty of Rabbits, but the vast number of corpses on Britain's roads are enough to tell anyone that serendipitous Rabbit/car encounters are a fact of life, so we were hardly breaking new ground there. On all our trips we saw nothing of genuine worth or interest. The only advantage in all of it was that Emily and Samuel revelled in the chance to stay up beyond their normal bedtime.

After a number of abortive trips of this kind, we subtly began to change tack and throw ourselves, and our emails, into the hands of specialists. In a way, this was our first and most crucial lesson of all in our year-long project. As an inexperienced mammal-finding family, we had discovered that we hadn't a hope of locating 50 species on our own. Even if we visited all the right places, at the right time, we wouldn't just stumble upon the creatures we wanted to see. Instead we would need considerable help from all kinds of experts: with experience, know-how, and – often – the relevant licences. We would need to meet them, persuade them all and charm them into showing us their mammals, species by species.

Bats were a case in point. The mammal-watching book that I did have was full of dire warnings about not going near a bat without the appropriate licence which, of course, I couldn't obtain for myself without the proper training. I soon discovered, though, that there was such a thing as the Dorset Bat Group and that, despite the name, they were actually people rather than bats. And they ran some field visits that were open to all. When I got their newsletter it was a further revelation to discover that, in only a few days time , the Bat Group was going to count some objects of worship at the latter's hibernation sites. I hadn't ever realised that you could see bats during the winter, so this was an exciting prospect. It was also an important lesson – find the people who know.

So, with contacts established at a Bat Group and the local Mammal Group, each within a matter of days, things were definitely going full steam ahead.

# February 23rd – Upside Down in the Underworld

And so today, we nestled ourselves into the arms of real experts for the first time. We were to take part in an official survey of hibernating bats. In every way, this was a privilege. Bats are strictly protected by law and, in theory, the moment you disturb a bat when it's asleep, you are toast. In contrast, you can disturb your human neighbours to a considerable extent: you can camp outside the house of a celebrity and give them hell if you like; with "the Right to Roam", you can even join forces and wander over someone's property. But woe betide you if you so much as make a bat open its eyes without a licence.

Happily, the members of the Dorset Bat Group all had the appropriate pieces of paper, and they were more than amenable to a couple of small children coming along to ogle the sleeping beauties. They went even further than that: the two members that I had talked to, Pete and Nick, were quite taken with our project, and promised that they would be able to help us during the summer, too. We appreciated their enthusiasm. Yet it also made us nervous. The Bat Group were being kind, and we thus determined to be on our very best behaviour, so that they wouldn't have second thoughts.

The trip itself sounded like a mystery tour. The plan was that we would meet in unmarked lay-bys and, moving around quickly, check a wood here and a cellar there. At each site we would need to be careful with our footing, and have only a brief look at each bat. It would often be dark, and we would need to keep the children reasonably quiet. It had all the hallmarks of a strange and sinister undercover espionage operation.

The first lay-by was in the village of Uplyme, not far from Lyme Regis. Slightly to my surprise, when we arrived it was full of cars, and there was also a small gathering of people on the pavement. I hadn't expected the trip to be so popular. To the girls' surprise, many of the assembled enthusiasts were young and some were female; many were distinctly fashionable, and there wasn't a bobble hat in sight, despite the time of year. Now my wife and daughter's general impression of "natural history people" – not necessarily fair or complete – is that, if they are not quite elderly, then they are at least likely to be male. This group was a refreshing contrast, and both girls began to realise that it's cool to be a bat person.

"Right," I began. "Let's get the torches."

"What torches?"

There were blank looks everywhere. We were about to clamber down into a cellar without a torch. We had already made our first mistake.

But the bat people were kind as well as cool, and a lady lent us a light so powerful that, I suspected, it would annoy aliens on distant planets if shone in their direction. It was so robust and manly that it made me rather grateful that I hadn't brought my puny flashlight.

"Let's go," said a tall, well-built man with a friendly, smiling face and a hat without a bobble. This was Nick Tomlinson, whom I later discovered knew more about bats than the animals probably did themselves. He ushered us away from the street to the point where two gardens met behind a group of terraced houses. Here a large, black, heavy Victorian-style gate guarded a concrete staircase down into an abyss. The only thing lacking was cobwebs on the gate, and the spinetingling creak as it opened.

But there were brambles galore, and the steps, which glistened with the grease of recent rain, were quite deliciously perilous. So much so that we found ourselves carrying the children down, Carolyn with Emily, and I with a wriggling Sam, making sure-footedness even more important and even less likely. Carolyn was not helped by the fact that, for some inexplicable reason, she had brought her handbag with her (what did she expect to find down there, a coffee hatch?) Thus, it was with a certain amount of huffing and puffing, and a lot of help from the back markers of the Bat Group, that we made it into the cellar at all. By now we were certain that they were regretting that these tiresome interlopers had joined the bat survey.

A wall of cold hit us as soon as we entered – but it was a sort of enveloping cold, like jumping into an unheated swimming pool without getting wet. Immediately somebody explained that this was exactly what the bats needed. Insulated from the vagaries of the weather outside, the cellar provided a very stable temperature and humidity, which was not too cold or damp for the bats, and not too warm. The latter would make them stir, which is not what a hibernating bat requires (apparently, though, bats are incredibly choosy about their hibernation sites, and regularly shift from one site to another when conditions become less than perfect, even in the middle of hibernation). They were rather like irascible guests at a hotel.

"Who lives in this house?" asked a small, mystified voice in the darkness.

"It's not a house, Emily, it's a cellar," Carolyn responded without thinking.

"What's a cellar?"

It was one of those moments when you realise how much you still have to teach your youngsters. "It's a place underneath a house where you store things," Carolyn replied. "Except this one is empty."

There was a short pause as the synapses connected. Then the half-pleading, half-enquiring voice picked up: "Why haven't we got a cellar?"

Our stammered answer was interrupted. "There are some bats here," called a disembodied announcer from the bowels of the passageway. All at once the torch beams, which had been pointing every which way, merged purposefully in direction. A few steps took us into a small chamber where a dozen or more people had gathered.

"These are Lesser Horseshoes," said a man, and he aimed the beam slightly off three minute bodies hanging from the low ceiling. I'm not sure what I expected, but I was immediately stunned by how small they were, no more than the size of plums. When you see bats in films, they invariably look quite substantial, especially when flying about. In films they also invariably look mean, flying menacingly about and baying for the blood of hysterical actresses. These blobs, however, were tiny.

"Can you see them?" I asked the children.

Their vague responses made it quite clear that they couldn't, so while the kind torch-bearer kept the beam in the bats' direction, we lifted up our children one by one towards them.

"See the tiny feet." That was the most amazing thing. The little toes might have been holding the whole body up, but they looked extraordinarily delicate and thin, apparently borrowed from the nearest mouse, and surely far too weak for their task. Furthermore, the ceiling looked too smooth for a decent grip, leading me to wonder whether these weren't really bats, but actually little models superglued on. They were completely motionless.

"They're amazing," enthused Carolyn.

The bat expert explained to us how it was easy to tell what sort of bats they were. Apparently horseshoe bats hang up differently from all the others. When at rest, most bats don't hang free but hide away snugly in small crevices; furthermore, even when other bats do hang upside down, they close their wings next to their bodies, so that you can see their tummies, whereas a horseshoe bat sleeps with the wings tightly enfolding its body, like a cape or an overcoat. The horseshoes' style of doing things looks a lot more practical, and warmer, too. It was gratifying, also, to know that, should we ever find ourselves in a pitch dark cellar at the bottom of a bramble-covered staircase next to a Victorian terrace, we would at least be able to make a stab at identifying the resident bats.

Suddenly, to everyone's surprise, the nearest bat stirred slightly and, just for a moment, stretched its wing open, twitched and showed its face.

"Ooh," said Emily. "It's real!" Clearly she and I were thinking along the same lines.

It was real all right, and for that brief moment we were given the slightly dubious honour of looking closely at a horseshoe bat's mug. Now I won't say that a horseshoe bat is ugly, but do you remember that game you used to play when you were a child, in which you have a blank face template and have to stick on a selection of ears, eyes, noses and suchlike? Well, imagine what a young toddler would do – the sensory stuff would be all over the place, ears just about on the head, eyes too close together, nose upside down and mouth at a strange angle. Well the mess a toddler makes approximates to the face of a horseshoe bat. The ears are like those of a pixie, the eyes are no more than pinpricks, and the nose – well, it looks as though the bat has flown straight into a window and squashed its hooter against its face.

That unsightly leaf-like nose is very important for its owner. Most bats set off their echolocation squeaks through their mouths, effectively shouting; horseshoe bats, however, use their noses for their electronic radar tracking. I suppose you could say that they sneeze their way to dinner each night.

The bat soon resumed its slumber, but the bat people were slightly spooked at this turn of events. Not because the bat's face had worried them, but because the animal had stirred. The last thing they wished to do was to wake the bat up properly, in case it felt forced to move on elsewhere before it was ready. Everybody was ordered out, and they couldn't have left more speedily if there had been a fire alarm.

Altogether we counted 16 Lesser Horseshoe Bats in the cellar. Emily pronounced that bats were cool.

The next site we visited shall remain confidential. It was somewhere in Dorset, and if I was being interviewed about it on TV, my face would be blacked out, my voice engineered to sound like Darth Vader. It was a manor house in the middle of nowhere, with a large, spacious garden; it, too, had magical cellars full of spinetinglingly rare bats.

Actually, the cellars weren't full. There were only five bats in them altogether. Four were Greater Horseshoe Bats and one a Lesser Horseshoe, and the Bat Group members seemed disappointed and worried with that turnout. It seems that everybody who cares about these animals is edgy. I have already mentioned the laws protecting bats, and it is no exaggeration to say that they are in place to look after what are seriously dwindling numbers. It is thought that the Lesser Horseshoe Bat has declined by 50 per cent in Britain in the last 40 years or so, and that the Greater Horseshoe Bat is now down to 10 per cent of its population figure prior to the Second World War. The actual figures are disputed, but there's no doubt that the decline has been alarming. And the story isn't so different for bats as a whole; most are doing badly.

The decline in bats has many causes, but the change in our countryside over the last century or so is certainly a major contributory factor. Fewer wild places and intensive farming mean that there are fewer insects about than there used to be, and as such there is less food to sustain bat numbers. The Greater Horseshoe Bat, in particular, is a guzzler of large insects like Cockchafers and big moths, and these sizeable meals have become much harder to find.

The very rarity of these bats, although depressing in the general course of things, was nevertheless a boon to our project. To see one of Britain's rarest mammals within our first few species gave the whole undertaking a dose of gravitas. We were still underprepared and under-researched, but – hey, we'd seen some mammals that few in the general population have ever set eyes upon. To acquire that privilege was part of the ethos of what we were doing.

Another part of the ethos was to have fun. And since both kids were now beginning to misbehave, sacrilegiously, in the presence of rare bats, and since Samuel was taking more interest in the hose running down to the cellar (fire engines again) than in the occupants of the same, we decided to cut our losses and leave the Bat Group to survey the rest of their secret locations. They hardly needed us with them and, to be honest, we were probably something of an impediment. But that did not detract from a certain sense of triumph. We now knew that, in some ways, we had stumbled across the best way to see British mammals. Find an expert, lean on their enthusiasm, and let them lead you into the secrets of their passion and their subject.

Just don't stay too long.

## February 24th – Garden Visitors

There are all sorts of different paths that lead to mammal sightings. This one started in a church hall on the Dorset/Somerset border. I had been invited to give a lecture called "Birds Behaving Badly" to a local group of the Royal Society for the Protection of Birds. The lecture, which was all about the intricate details of birds' lives, had gone pretty well, with only a small percentage of the audience passing the time by dozing off. Generally, most of the noises were appreciative.

It was right at the end of the lecture that I had an idea. I briefly explained our family project to the assembled throng and, as much in jest as anything, asked whether anyone who had Badgers or Hedgehogs regularly visiting their garden might care to show them to a couple of young children. I'm not sure if I expected much of a response, but at the end a lady came up to me almost immediately, declared that she had Badgers visiting regularly every evening at seven o'clock, and said that we could come any time, so long as my children could cope with a dog.

Now, as I have explained, I was especially keen to see Badgers early in the year because of these animals' unusual breeding lifestyle. The cubs are generally born in February and, completely bizarrely, the moment this happens the sows become receptive to the males again. Imagine that, girls: you've just given birth, you're feeling flabby and exhausted; you're vulnerable to post-natal depression; your babies (you might have three) demand you all the time; all you want to do is to cry. And then the boys come along looking for sex. It's madness. And it's called post-parturient oestrus.

I digress. There will doubtless be those of you out there who worry about details and are asking yourselves "Do Badgers give birth in the summer as well?" The answer is no – just once a year. A very unusual quirk of their cycle is that, regardless of when the Badgers actually mate – and this can actually be almost any time of year – the fertilised egg inside the female's body never actually implants until the autumn. So births are always at the same time of year, meaning that, once the young are weaned, there will be plenty of food around in the wild, and they can have a positive start to life.

Anyway, with all those hormones sweeping over the sett, February is a hot time to watch Badgers engage in acts of both courtship and aggression. If you can find a sett where the Badgers are active, and the weather isn't too cold and windy, you could be in for a treat of Attenborough-esque proportions. It sounded irresistible.

Then again, it didn't. It's all very well showing squabbling and copulating Badgers to most audiences, but definitely not children. Carolyn and I weren't ready for those sorts of inevitable questions yet, and Emily and

Samuel were absolutely not ready for the answers. Suddenly the idea of a short commute to a garden where Badgers simply came and committed the entirely decent act of munching peanuts sounded a much better option. We made an immediate "booking".

On the night in question we were fresh from our triumph with the bats, and hoped that their stardust might bring out the Badgers on cue, exactly according to their written contracts. But it's just as well they didn't read the small print. We got lost on the dark byways and, by the time we pulled up, frazzled, it was well after seven. We were relieved that the Badgers hadn't already been and gone.

I would have to admit that, of all the black-and-white animals we could have seen that night, one in particular caused a delightfully ecstatic reaction from the children, and sadly it wasn't the Badger. It was Ruth and Eric's dog, which was a spaniel and became excited with the novel attention the kids were happy to lavish upon it, and the Badger vigil became one extended love-in between the two constituencies. One would squeal in delight while the other one jumped up, and it wasn't always clear which was which.

And that does not help much when you are trying to watch "Dancing on Ice". The living room overlooking the garden was dominated by an enormous widescreen TV, which was on. Ruth explained that they had been following the series avidly from the start and if we didn't mind, they would leave it on, even if the Badgers appeared. Well, we were hardly going to sit there and forbid them to watch their own TV in their own house, were we? But it did mean that pre-Badger conversation was a little constricted. We sat on the sofas, the conversation stop-starting as if we were all on a first date, while the children and dog were by now more or less wrestling with each other.

"Would you like to see a Brambling?" asked Ruth at last.

I did a double-take. "A Brambling?" This was a small, Chaffinch-like bird with a neat orange wash to the plumage. It wasn't very common, and I love seeing this species, but as far as I was aware, it definitely wasn't nocturnal, either.

"The cat brought it in. I'll get it," said Ruth. And she went into the kitchen and did, indeed, return with a Brambling, neatly laid to rest upon a piece of paper towel. The people to whom I teach bird-watching skills quite frequently bring me dead birds. It makes me feel that, secretly, they all wish they could be cats.

"It's beautiful," I declared, and passed it to Carolyn, who was still in the midst of munching her biscuit. "Look Emily, Samuel. See this beautiful bird? Emily!"

My daughter took half a second to look and returned to the dog.

By now the Badgers were very late indeed, and at least 78 couples must have slid and double-axled their way across the avidly-watched screen before anything happened. Eric had assured us that, should the garden visitors appear, they would automatically switch on the spotlight, to which the Badgers were completely accustomed. It was really a matter of waiting.

However, I was beginning to feel that strange sense of being made perfectly welcome yet feeling slightly uncomfortable about it. I was worried that we might be spoiling "Dancing on Ice" for our hosts, and even more worried at the prospect of missing out on the reason for our visit. I decided to look out of the sitting-room window.

And there it was, a Badger munching peanuts in the darkness, no more than 3 metres (10 feet) away from the house. I wouldn't have made it out but for the signature black-and-white stripes on the head – and the same signals apply to the Badgers themselves. The pattern is both individually recognisable and hard to miss in the gloaming.

"Oh, is it there?" asked Eric, mystified by the fact that the light hadn't come on.

"Come on kids," I urged, beckoning.

And of course, the Badger is a natural box-office star. The children had known of Badgers through their bedtime stories, and so they were well primed to enjoy this wild one. Which is an interesting point: the Badger doesn't seem to suffer like other animals in the way it is depicted in children's books. A mouse is barely recognisable from the many bizarre images that children see (Mickey Mouse is just weird, if you think about it; Beatrix Potter dressed hers up in ridiculous twee outfits, like her other absurd characters; Angelina Ballerina, agreeable though she is, just doesn't register as a mouse). And much the same applies to rats or squirrels or Foxes (though, oddly, bunnies are usually quite accurate). Anyway, the kids recognised it straight away.

Although it was 45 minutes late, and appearing way after our children's bedtime, the Badger performed a perfect, pre-watershed act. Once under the lights it was so clear and close that we could see every feature, from the neat head-stripes to its well-groomed rug of a coat, black feet, the incidental tail and the rather dog-like nose. It feeding method was almost as distinctive. It just seem to vacuum up its food, nose close to the ground, as if it didn't need to use the mouth or tongue. It reminded me slightly of the Noo-noo, friend and slave of those overly indulged Teletubbies.

Badgers certainly have a mouth and nose, and they also have pretty fearsome teeth. And harmless though they might look, Badgers are seriously carnivorous, as well as enjoying vegetable matter. Thankfully worms don't scream, because if they did, the British countryside would echo to hundreds of thousands of micro-yelps every night of the year (except, perhaps in December when Badgers are relatively inactive). Badgers absolutely adore them, the way children love custard creams, and they can go on eating them every night without complaint – 200 have been recorded in a single night, and 20,000 in a year. However, their diet is much broader, and turns a touch sinister at times. They also eat birds and birds' eggs, small mammals, and frogs and toads. And one of their favourite snacks, believe it or not, is Hedgehog meat – more of that later.

But this good Badger did not harm anything but peanuts during its performance. After a few minutes, on the off-chance that a female suddenly appeared and sent it into a uninhibited lustful abandon, we took our leave of the Badger. Who knows who won "Dancing on Ice"?

We trundled home in the darkness, more than a little triumphant.

"Daddy," declared Emily. "That was lovely."

I just couldn't hide a smile. All this effort to see the mammals was really bearing fruit. Sometimes in life you just have to take risks, but it's worth it in the end. She was right, the Badger was really good value.

"So can we have a dog?"

fox

# March

## March 2ⁿᵈ–5ᵗʰ – Chasing Princesses

You might recall from the introduction that, well before our year of mammal-watching had ever been thought of, let alone begun, we had made a solemn promise to our daughter Emily that we would definitely go to EuroDisney when she was five years old. At the time Emily was only two, and it was one of those classic parental deferments, made in the solid expectation that it would be rendered irrelevant by the passage of time. But we were wrong. Emily determined to make us stick to our promise from the very moment it was made and, by that classic children's method of continual drip-feeding with occasional tantrums, she ensured that we honoured it.

Well, promises are promises, and this one – the one that was the most important ever made in our daughter's estimation – was impossible to break. And let's face it: we were hardly gritting our teeth, packing the alcohol or pencilling in visits to the psychiatrist at the prospect of nipping across to the Paris suburbs and spending a while in the famed theme park. In common with the fictional parents in the TV commercials, we were almost as excited by the prospect as our children. EuroDisney, after all, is designed to be fun.

One thing we hadn't realised on our journey towards the wonderland was that, over the months leading up to the great departure, Emily had formulated an agenda, one that she fully intended to live out during our three hallowed days. In short, she was on a princess-hunt. She was determined to press the flesh with every one of the famous characters, such as Cinderella, whose images covered her walls and toothbrush and waterbottle and books and cutlery and make-up bag and wellington boots and library and cupboard and magazines – and filled her imagination, too. From very early on, we realised that we would need to meet the Disney Princess lookalikes in each of their trademark outfits, and talk to them, and generally catch as much of their stardust as possible to allow our daughter to float back home.

In case you are wondering what on earth I'm talking about, the Disney Princess phenomenon is a recent marketing miracle. A few years ago, with both profits and influence falling, and the company in the midst of internal angst, a marketing executive from the Disney Corporation had a eureka moment and saw the brand potential in some of the cinema's oldest and most traditional characters – namely Cinderella, Snow White and Sleeping Beauty. Despite some of these characters' signature films being made in the 1950s, he discovered that their appeal, along with some more recent creations, such as that of the Little Mermaid, was very modern indeed. Releases of those same flicks on DVD had spawned a constituency of fans who wished to be just like these heroines, and to look like them, too. Thus, within a few years, it became possible to buy everything from spoons to quilts with depictions of princesses upon them, and to buy at least two frocks for every one of the fantastical characters. The branded items have been sensationally popular and, among many thousands of little girls throughout the country, our own Emily had been caught up in the wave of princess hysteria.

Yes, we knew that we and our family had been cynically manipulated by a large corporation into paying large amounts of money for items of little worth except for their branding. But did we care? No.

Now, every visitor to EuroDisney quickly cottons on to the fact that, among the legions of visitors walking around the theme park every day, there are some employees mixing with them who are dressed up, somewhat distinctively, as Disney characters. It isn't very difficult to see them, any more than you would overlook somebody in your own office environment who suddenly decided to come in dressed up as Goofy one day. The only problem is, there are a lot of these fancy-dressers around every day, and they move around the huge site according to a timetable that is almost impossible to fathom. If you are after a meeting with one particular character, you have to be strategic.

On our first day we made the mistake of joining the queue early for "It's a Small World", an attraction full of dolls dressed in various national costumes. As we inched slowly forward, we noticed Cinderella (in her blue outfit) far below on the tarmac, way out of reach, a swarm of little girls crowded around her in awe. Despite Emily's protestations we felt we couldn't just leave the queue for fear of irritating fellow enthusiasts around us and alas, by the time we had floated through the attraction, the notorious midnight party-pooper had left. It was a couple of anxious days before we finally caught up with her.

Eventually we discovered that, if we turned up at a certain spot in front of the Sleeping Beauty Castle at the right time each day, we could join another queue (we soon got used to these) to meet the session's assigned princess for an audience and photo-session. The only time we actually achieved this in our three days, the princess on offer was Aurora. This one is the sneakiest of the princesses, because Aurora is just one of her three names. She's also occasionally called Briar Rose, but the name everybody really knows her by is Sleeping Beauty. And just to add to the confusion, she has two costumes, a pink one and a blue one, which mean that, if your progeny is an Aurora fan you have to buy both. And today, as the lookalike was dressed in electric blue, I was darned if I could tell the difference between her and Cinderella. Throughout the day I kept on getting it wrong, asking Emily: "What did Cinderella say to you?" when I actually meant Aurora, thus inviting looks of derision from the female side of the family.

Nevertheless, Aurora herself was charming. And much as I might want to declare that it was totally absurd and pointless to queue for 40 minutes to meet an actress dressed up as a completely fictional character for a half a minute of small talk, the look of wonder in my daughter's eyes suggested otherwise. And yes, we have the photo: it captures a moment of joy and shy deference.

We had another great moment of glory in our princess-hunts, too. Once we had sussed the daily gathering by the Sleeping Beauty Castle, a little detective work and surveillance led us to the source from which the princesses were coming (they switched every half an hour or so) in order to reach the stage. We realised that, if we cunningly placed Emily outside the gate which led to the changing rooms, then it would take a stone-hearted lookalike indeed not to say hello to my daughter at the start of the short walk to the stage. And I'm happy to say the strategy worked a treat. After a few minutes of nervous anticipation the Little Mermaid herself, who is actually called Ariel, appeared, and the actress, having switched with commendable speed into character, stopped, bent down and gave Emily a chat and a hug, with not a five-year-old rival in sight. Carolyn and I high-fived, tears in our eyes.

But that slippery creature Aurora had the last word. Emily told us that, during their conversation, the princess had told her that she would give her a wave during the afternoon's parade (lots of characters on floats, with loud music). Since Aurora was a princess, Emily declared, she was bound to keep her promise, so it was perfectly essential that we should be there. Well, by now, I would have to admit, the sheer magic of the place had totally engulfed us. We resolved to be at the parade so that Aurora, a 20-something actress, who had met at least 50 five- and six-year-olds that afternoon, would duly wave at Emily, recognising her among the thousand-strong crowd. It was barmy, but we fell for it.

Well, the parade duly began and, as float after float passed, none of us could see Aurora. It was only after the last one had gone by that we caught sight of her, right on the other side of a large float that was cast into the shape of an old galleon. She was with a prince and, to all appearances, none too in touch with her rabid fan-base. She made a few rather wan waves towards the crowd on the other side, then frolicked up towards the stern of the boat, exchanging places with Belle, the beauty from "Beauty and the Beast".

For a while we played cat and mouse with Aurora. We kept behind the float, but could never quite get on the right side to cross the lookalike's line of sight and receive that all-important wave. Emily began to fight back tears, so I lifted her on to my shoulders for one last attempt. We knew that the parade would make a circuit of the Western-style shopping mall before finally disappearing through the theatrically large gate that led to the EuroDisney staff's refuge, so I ran almost to the very last viewing point, fighting the crowds and, eventually, stood up on a bench so that, if she happened to turn in the right direction, Aurora would at least be able to see us. And yes, on the very last turn, just an hour before we were due to leave the theme park for the last time, the float turned perpendicular to us and Aurora, with a few dainty steps, leapt up to look towards our part of the crowd. And then, to a missed heartbeat from daughter and father, she waved.

Emily's confidence in princesses was thus preserved, and an important stage in growing up was safely negotiated. It was a close thing, though.

You might possibly be wondering what Sam was up to for all this time. Well, he had no truck whatsoever with the princesses, I'm relieved to say. But the trip was also a rite of passage for him. He began to eschew fire engines and, for the first time, the reign of Bob the Builder, so reassuring up until now for both boy and parents, began to crumble. Buzz Lightyear, the character from "Toy Story", was the leader of the revolution, while Lightning McQueen and the characters from "Cars" made up the rest of the legions conquering the peace of Sunflower Valley.

And of course you will be wondering what all this stuff has to do with wild mammals? Well, nothing really, except that, when it comes to the sheer drama and unpredictability of the chase, you can learn a lot from three days of racing around trying to fulfil a little girl's dreams.

# March 20th – Notes from HQ, Part IV

After a good February, March just never got going for our project. There were two reasons for this. Firstly, dull though it might sound, we were all leading our normal lives. Secondly, and most importantly, there just didn't seem any rush. Spring was imminent and then, gloriously, the summer. I envisaged loads of trips for small-mammal-trapping in the long, halcyon days, lots of time and room to plan, and a steady progression towards our target of 50. It was one of many errors of judgment I made during the year. I should have made more effort with common and widespread species early on – it led to months of relative panic later.

But now was the time for spring cleaning and taking stock. And for asking ourselves: where were we on our project, and what might lie ahead? What mammals did we still have to see, and what could we reasonably expect to see? Those were two very different questions. As I have mentioned elsewhere, Britain's mammals are a pretty poorly known lot: go beyond the usual Otters and Foxes, and you enter into a fog of half-remembered names, or indeed into total ignorance. We were still learning what some of our targets would be. We had barely heard of half of them.

So, how do you plan to see 50 wild mammals in Britain? Well, you start with a list of the possibles, the species that have actually occurred in Britain before. That rules out giraffes and hippopotami and elephants. Actually, it doesn't, because all these types of mammal have been found here as fossils but, short of going back a long way in time, they can all be reasonably discounted for now (though it does make me think what an exciting, and potentially dangerous family challenge this would have been if Carolyn and I had been a Stone Age couple – "Daddy! Look, there's a Woolly Mammoth!") Then you whittle these down to the realistic possibilities, and from there pick out those that require a bit of effort, those that are highly probable, and the bankers mentioned earlier. With such a list, you plan your year.

We had, of course, seen nine species of mammal so far and, much as I would have liked to see them all again, I had an inkling that, in order to approach anything like our target, going back to indulge in previous sightings was an unaffordable luxury. Seeing the remaining 41 would be hard enough. So, much as the kids might pine for another view of a Greater Horseshoe Bat, they would have to do without. I know, I know, it's cruel.

So what was on our list of targets? Well, just to give you the list printed here would be dead boring and meaningless. So instead, I'll lay out a very brief overview of all of Britain's furry creatures, and at the same time give you an inkling of what challenges each group poses to those who might search for them. If you get bored, you can always skip to the next section, or try a book by Anthea Turner. If that doesn't work, you could always try the washing up (Anthea, incidentally, has some useful advice on this).

Actually, the first furry creatures to mention among Britain's mammalian population don't have any fur at all. If I told you that there were 106 mammals on the British list, what group would you think would constitute the largest set of species? Your starter for 10? You don't know? Well, incredibly, it's sea mammals, such as whales, dolphins and porpoises, which constitute a whopping 29 species. More sorts of these have reached Britain than any group of land animals, although a goodly number of them have done it somewhat clandestinely – such as the odd Blue Whale spotted zillions of miles from land, but just about in our waters – and quite a few unintentionally, such as the various beaked whales that are occasionally stranded, tragically landing up on a beach, flailing and desperate, like lorry drivers misdirected by sat navs. On the whole, these animals collectively represent both a headache and an opportunity. No mammal-watcher can afford to ignore them altogether, but actually seeing them means going on dedicated sea-mammal trips, and these can be both expensive and somewhat unsatisfying if all you see is a distant fluke. And watching sea mammals from land, as we discovered with the Common Porpoises, is very much a hit-and-miss affair. So, while it could be possible to collect a decent set from among the more regular species, such as Bottlenose Dolphins and Minke Whales, there are few creatures that are more unpredictable than these. We would need to be well organised, and spend a good deal on time looking on the surface of the sea.

The second largest club of British mammals are bats, a fact that probably wouldn't surprise most people. A total of 22 species have been recorded in Britain, and of these, 16 breed and are therefore quite possible to see somewhere. As far as bats were concerned we were fortunate to live in Dorset, one of the best places for them in the whole country. And, by being in touch with the local Bat Group, we were hoping for more great things from the flying mammals besides the two species we had seen – the Greater and Lesser Horseshoe Bats. By the way, talking of bats, the natural inclination for most people, even quite keen natural history types, is to assume that one species seamlessly merges into another, and that the different sorts are somehow characterless and samey. We soon found out that this was not the case at all.

Another species-rich group are the rodents. Now, although you might see the word "rodent" and think "Oh, how dull!", these small animals actually rouse some very strong feelings in many people. For example, it was a rodent, the Black Rat, which allegedly helped to cut Europe's human population by a quarter or more between 1346 and 1350, with the onset of the Black Death. The House Mouse and the Brown Rat remain pest species of profound importance absolutely everywhere in the world – even Antarctica. Yet Jerry, foe of Tom, must be one of the world's most loved cartoon characters, and Tufty the Squirrel taught thousands of British baby boomers to cross the road (not that squirrels themselves seemed to have learnt the lesson from their fictional colleague, so many squashed bodies does one see on the road). So the point is, rodents are important and I have to confess, personally, to a sneaking affection for them.

Aside from those mentioned, we are moderately well off for rodents here in Britain, with several voles to our name and a couple of mice, including the delightful Harvest Mouse, which is one of the smallest of its kind in the world (a small mouse – heavens, that's small). Meanwhile, we have two squirrels and two dormice to complete the set. To somebody searching for mammals, all these species, except the Black Rat, which only occurs in the wild on an island group off the Outer Hebrides, and the Common Vole, which only occurs on the Orkney Islands, should be reasonably easy to find.

The next group to consider rouse strong feelings, too: the carnivores. Just think of the Fox and the Badger. Some people adore them, some loathe them, and there aren't many sitting on the fence. Extremist views are rife, and the sheer differences of opinion sometimes even ignite violence among people – I'm sure if the animals knew about this, they would be baffled. People have lived on the land alongside Foxes and Badgers for centuries, so it is no surprise that there is both enmity and mutual respect. Yet if you think about it, the sheer abundance of both these medium-sized carnivores in our modern world is truly a marvel, and testament to their adaptability. The Fox is a winner almost worldwide; the Badger's success is perhaps more surprising. It so happens that Britain has the highest density of Badgers in the world – really, we should be proud of them.

Seeing both of these species is not too difficult, but the rest of Britain's terrestrial carnivores are an absolute nightmare. They are invariably scarce, unpredictable and secretive – and that's the easy ones. By far the most widespread are the Weasel and Stoat – but how often do you see those? A handful of times a year, at the most, if you spend a lot of time outside? And as for the Wildcat, Pine Marten and Polecat – the first two restricted to Scotland and the latter, at least formerly, to Wales – have you seen any of them? Of course not. Oh help – hand me those tranquillisers.

One might have better chances with the aquatic carnivores, the Otter and the American Mink. Both are widespread, and the Otter is making a widely welcomed comeback to the British heartland. Yet neither are in any way guaranteed anywhere. The Mink is probably slightly less reluctant to show itself, but the Otter is probably the easiest to find, not because it is conspicuous or amenable, but because it is revered. Good Otter sites simply become known.

Talking of aquatic carnivores, many people don't realise that seals are, in their own way, every bit as predatory as terrestrial carnivores. The difference is that fish don't scream – or at least, they don't sound distressed in the same way that a Rabbit reacts when being dispatched by a Stoat: truly, that is a sickening sound you don't want to hear too often. All the fish do is probably look a bit more wide-eyed than usual when being grasped in those formidable jaws. Because the seals, of which there are two sorts in Britain, the Common Seal and the Grey Seal, have at least as impressive a set of teeth as any British meat-eater. It's just as well that their tastes don't stretch to people; they could swim rings around us and do a great deal of damage with a single nip. Swimming would be dangerous all around our coasts, because both species are ubiquitous.

At the other end of the scale, you are highly unlikely to be eaten by a deer, and especially when you're swimming (boy, that would be unlucky). That's not to say that deer are completely inoffensive, as a certain invading king might testify, but they are vegetarian and normally aren't very threatening to people. That said, if they are male and imbued by lust in the autumn rutting season, they do get a bit crazed and single-minded (nothing unusual there) and can be dangerous to approach. There are six sorts at large in Britain, unless you count a semi-tame herd of Reindeer found in Scotland. Of these the hardest to find is the Chinese Water Deer, which is found in a few places in East Anglia and the Midlands. But really, deer shouldn't present any major problems to mammal-watchers.

That isn't something that can be said of a small group of fascinating mammals that were formerly called Insectivores, which was nice and easy to remember, but are now called Eulipotyphla (this new, tongue-twisting epithet is presumably installed just to give the scientists intellectual space between themselves and the masses). Anyhow, this group of mammals contains the Hedgehog, the Mole and the shrews and, while the spiny character shouldn't present any problems to see, the three species of shrew and, in particular, the Mole, are specifically designed to make life difficult for mammal-watchers – small, sneaky and, especially in the Mole's case, living under the earth. Realistically, you won't see a Mole except in a trap, and shrews are so minute and hyperactive that they present a difficult challenge too.

Well, that's about it except for a few bits and pieces. In addition to the Rabbit and Hare we had seen, there was the upland version of the latter, the Mountain Hare, found in Scotland, the Peak District and Ireland. And then there are a couple of slightly bizarre hoofed mammals to add to the roll call, the Feral Goat and the Wild Boar, the latter a previous inhabitant of Britain in years gone by, but now reintroduced.

Perhaps a word is appropriate here about what we wouldn't include. Familiar domestic animals such as sheep, horses and cows would not be acceptable – not even the New Forest Ponies that dwelt nearby. Neither would animals in zoos, of course. And there was also one entirely legitimate species that, despite living and breeding freely in Britain and having arrived here by entirely natural means, we just felt we couldn't count. It was a primate – mankind.

Unless, of course, we were on 49 mammals come December 31$^{st}$…

# March 21$^{st}$ – Notes from HQ, Part V

Now I know what it will be like when people finally make contact with aliens. I have experienced a deep shock to the system and felt a profound and unexpected vulnerability. My world has been shaken, my presuppositions ditched. It's unsettling.

We are not alone. There is someone else out there besides us trying to see as many mammals as possible in a year.

Or at least, he did last year. And the year before. He claims not to be trying this time round. His name is John Dixon, and I discovered him on a website called BirdForum.

If my wife came across me using a website with a name like that, you might think she would ask for a divorce. But in fact, BirdForum is more than legitimate and not remotely pornographic: it is designed for bird-watchers and, it turns out, all sorts of other wildlife-watchers, too. There are thousands of discussion forums and, among them, browsing innocently one day, I discovered one with the giveaway title of "John's Mammals 2008".

So my idea wasn't so new after all.

And, to make matters worse, John was evidently a much, much better mammal-spotter than any member of our family could ever be. Or you. Or anyone else. Judging by his blog, this man just sees mammals everywhere. He sees them when he goes shopping, when he goes to work, when he walks to the shops – he probably sees them in the shower ("I had just switched the water on when I noticed a Polecat in the garden…") He is just incredible. A typical entry in his blog might read: "Made a short visit to the canal last night. Not much about in pouring rain. Only seven of the Badgers were showing, along with 287 Wood Mice and three Yellow-necked, the latter being pursued by a Weasel…" Or perhaps: "There was a Sperm Whale recorded fifty miles north of Shetland yesterday afternoon at three o'clock. Hopped on to motorway and made Aberdeen by midnight; just managed to arrange helicopter, and by daybreak was delighted to see the side-shooting blow of a group of a dozen, way out in North Atlantic. Marvellous sight. Finally got in to work in Hampshire at nine-thirty, half an hour late, a bit tired…"

And so on. All right, I'm exaggerating a bit, but clearly John was like a cross between Superman and Doctor Doolittle. His blog was funny, informative and full of great tips for mammal-spotting, and it quickly became essential reading for me. However, it also made our project feel a bit inadequate. By now John had more than double our total of mammals, and he himself had only just broken the 50 species mark in the last two years, which didn't exactly fire off too much optimism. At least, though, he wasn't trying to drag kids along with him, so our aims weren't entirely identical. There was also one other major difference. He was trying to see everything absolutely in the wild, whilst I was more than happy to catch some of our mammals in traps – otherwise, as I have explained above, the kids just wouldn't be able to appreciate them.

I soon contacted John himself and, quite naturally, he was completely helpful, enthusiastic and charming.

Don't you just hate some people?

## March 21st – Current Affairs

It was time to get a move on. If John Dixon could see 15 species of mammal before breakfast every day, then there was no reason why we couldn't do much better than we were (actually there were a host of reasons – children, incompetence etc., but that's not the point). You could say that we were spurred on, given a kick up the backside and generally shamed into trying harder.

We decided to do battle with the local Otters. As you probably know, Otters were once an extremely scarce sight on Britain's lowland waterways. They had virtually disappeared from almost all of England by the late Seventies, mainly because poisonous insecticides, such as dieldrin, were leaching off agricultural fields and into the river system, eventually building up in these animals' tissues. Once the poisons were banned, the decline halted and, little by little, the Otters have recovered their populations to what is now a remarkable extent. Now they are everywhere. They haven't just returned to wild, unspoilt places, either, but also to seemingly unremarkable urban and semi-urban waterways, living cheek-by-jowl with dogs, fishermen and abandoned supermarket trolleys. Their comeback is remarkable, and so it no longer has the same resonance as it once did when you use the phrase "local Otters".

Ours dwelt just a mile and a half down the road, where a waterfront hotel nestled beside a roadbridge and weir. We knew they were there because I had seen them myself on several occasions, often close-up. They obviously weren't excessively afraid of humans, because both the hotel and towpath were busy areas, and surely Otters of less robust constitution would have been permanently riddled with nerves and avoided the place? It thus seemed a good plan to drive down once or twice at dusk, park so that the car headlights lit up a stretch of river, and wait.

So that's what we did. There is no doubt it was an excellent plan. The trouble is, kids are not very fond of waiting around, and anyone who has been a parent for longer than 20 minutes knows this. But you have to grit your teeth and try, don't you? Carolyn and I endured the kids climbing over us and settling on our laps; we tolerated them shouting and laughing every few seconds; we coped when first Samuel, and then Emily, played with the controls on the dashboard, turning the car radio on high, switching on the hazard warning lights, flicking the indicators, changing the clock and threatening to put their little fingers in the cigarette lighter. I even remained tight-lipped when Emily started fiddling with my precious Barry Manilow CD (only joking)! We found that we could deal with each one of these things with serene indifference; it was all of them happening at once that drove us mad.

And as all parents forlornly do – at least all parents who have listened to children's agony aunt Tanya Byron – we tried to distract them from the situation, by making positive comments and shifting the balance of conversation. Oh all right, we told lies. We would suddenly shout: "Oh, hold on, what's that over there?" knowing full well that the nearest Otter was probably in Stockton-on-Tees. It didn't work for long. (Actually, I am from a generation of fathers whose kids' early lives were shaped by that same Ms. Byron. We used to be glued to programmes like "The House of the Tiny Tearaways", not for the wise counsel it offered, so much as to the cruel pleasure of watching flailing parents try to handle ferocious children much worse behaved than ours. As a result, plain-speaking Tanya is a heroine to my wife. And for me, one look from her would make me go into a corner and bow my head, even if I hadn't yet done anything wrong.)

Anyway, you will have gathered that the Otters were not forthcoming on this trip. We tried again several nights later, and it was no better. The third attempt just made the exercise seem futile. All my previous Otter experience came to nothing.

But we watched the river flow by, and, in a way, we began to realise that, metaphorically, that was what we should be doing too. Why all this fuss about achievement and sightings anyway? We were meant to be taking it all in and relishing the process, not the results. Emily, for the first time, learnt what a current was, and I did my best to explain the full moon (you try doing that to a five-year-old). And, as we did so, an enormous stormcloud crept towards us, looming like a monstrous wave, and heavy rain was soon tumbling theatrically against the windscreen, cutting off our view of the river. It was magical.

# April

## April 7th – Lost in a Sea of Reeds

Today we had hoped to see one of the most extraordinary wildlife spectacles Britain has to offer. It is a freak of timing, weather and the sometimes foolhardy ability of animals to push boundaries. Few people seem to know about it, but if they did, I could imagine that the relevant coast of Cheshire where it occurs would gather a crowd to rival the opening of a new Ikea (OK, I'm being wistfully optimistic). But it is up there with the killing of a Wildebeest on the African plains for sheer drama, although on a much smaller scale. The setting – a dreary saltmarsh near Liverpool – isn't quite as spectacular, either.

For a few momentous hours on the highest tides of the year, though, animals on the saltmarshes of the Dee Estuary can find themselves in serious trouble. The muddy creeks and ramshackle grassy tussocks that provide them with a rich supply of food throughout the year are usually safely above high-tide level, but during the highest springs this can change suddenly. If there is a northerly wind, even a short-lived one, a sudden surge of water can flood these small animals' homes and make them refugees. Many diminutive creatures, such as Moles or shrews, can barely run at the pace of the advancing tide, so their escape is by no means guaranteed. In their dash towards dry ground and up the seawall, all caution is abandoned and usually secretive species break cover. This is often fatal. Many predatory birds know what is coming and ruthlessly pick them off.

For the human observer, standing on the seawall at Parkgate, I had heard that you should expect the bizarre. Small mammals such as Water Shrews and Field Voles find themselves floating by on rafts of flotsam, lethal water all around; Weasels and voles, predator and prey, scamper away side-by-side; Moles take to swimming. At times dozens of small mammals, one after the other, can be see running away from the deadly tide, like lemmings in reverse. I am told it is both spellbinding and horrifying, and, at the same time, a bit like a Japanese gameshow, just without any volunteers.

For our project, the idea of easily seen Weasels, Moles and Water Shrews made a visit to Parkgate a must – at least in the right conditions. I knew that our children would not understand the desperation of the situation for the animals, and the excitement of the other visitors would be infectious. The hubbub of excited wildlife enthusiasts might even drown them out if they decided to be noisy. But Parkgate was also at least a five-hour drive away and, to complicate matters even further, I had just arrived back from a conference in Ireland late the previous night. I didn't want a long trek up north to witness nothing else but a harmlessly rising tide.

Happily, our new friend John Dixon, he of the Doctor Doolittle-like ability to see wild mammals, had decided to make the trip anyway and combine it with an attempt to see Polecats in the Cheshire area. The night before the potential great event, he wasn't optimistic about the wind being right, and cautioned against coming.

We took a chance on his advice and, for the next 24 hours I couldn't help but imagine vast hordes of small, tricky-to-see mammals appearing to enthralled throngs of admirers at Parkgate.

That left us with a day to fill down south and, since there would be no Ikea opening today anywhere near us, we opted for a mammal-hunt instead. It wasn't hard to choose a target. The Otter business had now become personal. We had missed our aquatic neighbours enough on our local river to feel let down by them. Today, however, we would get revenge, nailing them in their own backyard, watching from the famous Decoy Hide on the Somerset Levels, reckoned by many to be the most reliable place to see wild Otters in the whole of Britain.

So we set off in our Vauxhall Zafira battle-bus with adrenaline pumping and enthusiasm set to maximum. How was I to know that the postman had parked his bicycle in my way as I reversed out of the drive? It clattered to the ground, our neighbours' precious deliveries spewing everywhere.

And throughout the remainder of the journey both Emily and Sam kept on repeating "Daddy hit a bicycle!" every few minutes, their voices mixed with glee and sheer wonder.

Nonetheless, it was the kind of day when the spring, in brash and confident form, can banish even wounded pride and seize your attention. Its influence was everywhere. It would have shamed a despotic dictator in the sheer impudence of its overwhelming street-side exhibitionism – greening trees and thickets, loud daffodils and unsubtle wafts of Blackthorn blossom. For once the children were awestruck – and no wonder; they had probably never noticed a spring before.

I had spoken to the Somerset Wildlife Trust's Otter expert a few days previously about the current hot locations for our nemesis. Sure enough, the lake in front of the Decoy Hide at Shapwick Heath had been hosting two adult Otters for weeks, and he assured us that they were likely to show during the day. "But don't go too early in the morning," he warned. "The Otters will feed at the end of the night and won't be hungry again until lunchtime."

From the road through the Somerset Levels, a straight drive through a flat landscape dotted with huge, black piles of peat blocks, some 10 metres (30 feet) high, like poor men's pyramids, it turned out to be a long way to the fabled Decoy Hide. For normal, tuned-in mammal-hunters the mile-long walk would have been a small inconvenience. But for us, such was the slow progress, we might as well have been queuing to get Cinderella's autograph at EuroDisney. Every few metres we seemed to be lifting the children over the dark, peaty, gooey mud. The novel landscape, with its imposing, forest-like reedbeds, wide skies and patches of bright blossom on the wayside trees, was equally a distraction. For the children there were sticks to pick up, dozens of small passageways into reeds or thickets to explore, and two hot, tormented parents from whom to escape. We made several wrong turns. It felt as though we were stuck in one of those modish mazes constructed in large fields of crops.

As we came to yet another featureless crossroads, it seemed as though we might never find our way out to civilisation again, let alone make it to the Decoy Hide. In desperation, I checked the condition of the path-side dandelion leaves, pored over the bushes for any leftover berries, scoured the ground for hazel nuts and checked my mobile phone for Ray Mears' contact details, just in case we found ourselves without food for the next few days. Then, in an effort to work out where we were, I left the family at the crossroads and ran ahead down yet another anonymous path.

After a couple of turns and a distance of about 400 metres (1,300 feet), something moving along the track caught my eye. In an instant its bounding gait, chestnut brown coat and long, lithe body suggested the possibility of something good – something really good. After being completely distracted by our family's predicament, I suddenly froze, heart thumping. The animal was scurrying confidently along, with a sense of purpose and no little menace. This was a predator, no doubt about it. But which one?

The animal was decidedly preoccupied, working its way along the raised path between a reedy ditch on one side and a flooded thicket on the other, approaching more rapidly and daringly than it probably intended. At once it was obvious that it wasn't an Otter; it was far too small. Furthermore the bi-coloured pattern, with white chest, removed the possibility of Mink. We were down to two: Weasel and Stoat. And whichever one it was, it was a huge bonus for our project.

These two mini-predators are notoriously similar and many people, even experienced naturalists, seem to have trouble telling them apart. Yet I can never quite understand this. Every Weasel I have seen has been minute, no more than an elongated mouse, and nothing but a wisp, disappearing in an instant. Stoats, on the other hand, are a size larger and very much more confident – the old adage is right, they are "Stoat-ally different". Even before this one turned around and showed off its diagnostic black tip to the tail, I had nailed the ID.

The Stoat, caught up in a world of its own, eventually approached up to a distance of about 10 metres (30 feet). Then it saw me and, without any sense of panic, simply turned to its left and leapt into the flooded woodland with a pretty impressive splash. Stoats have conquered the world, occurring in much of Eurasia and North America, and right up into the depths of the Arctic, where their fur turns white in winter. Among their many talents is the ability to swim.

Much as it was exciting to observe the Stoat, the key snag, of course, was that I was separated from the family and thus the sighting would not count towards our goal. Sod's Law, it seemed, had struck – surely one of the chance encounters of the year had revealed itself to only half an audience. I knew that the Stoat wouldn't reappear. The only time that Stoats ever repeatedly show themselves is when they are chasing a particularly large, juicy Rabbit, during which time they will follow their target across fields, under cars, through the undergrowth and whatever else they find in their way. A Stoat latched on to a Rabbit is like a determined cop keeping up a chase in a movie: the goodie never gives up the pursuit, whatever the collateral wreckage of tipped-over carts, cars crashing and extras diving out of the way. This Stoat, however, was probably after bird chicks or mice, and it had been so serene it could have been perusing an art gallery. My curses rang out across the reeds, which caught a breeze and seemed to whisper disapprovingly.

But amazingly, the Stoat did reappear. It really did. And incredibly, the kids were with me. I had obviously run back to tell the family of the encounter and, as we retraced my steps, there was the Stoat again, covering the same ground. This time it was a little more reticent, disappearing much more quickly, and as far as we could tell, of our kids only Emily got any kind of view of the animal. "It's got a long body and it's brown," she said, a little five-year-old walking field guide.

We had harboured better than tentative hopes of making it a double carnivore day but, although we did eventually make it successfully to the Decoy Hide, I shall have to admit to you that the Otter remained elusive. Despite plenty of excited references to Otter sightings in the logbook ("there was an adult terribly close, enough to obtain its dental formula and see that it had half a whisker missing on the left side of its nose…"), we never got a sniff. To the children's credit, we remained in the hide for two hours, just eating lunch, gazing over the lake and enjoying the sun. When the kids began to get truly bored we passed the time by making up stories of greater and greater absurdity, and I can tell you from experience, it's pretty hard getting both a Disney Princess and Buzz Lightyear into the same plot again and again.

But although the Otter failed us, you might be surprised to learn that, in the context of a year's attempt to see a fixed number of species of mammals, a Stoat sighting is much more significant than an Otter sighting. Otters attract a following, and reliable places to see them simply get known and are fairly repeatable. Stoats, on the other hand, are far more fickle. Aside from Mount Grace Priory, in Yorkshire, a National Trust property where Stoats have been studied, encouraged and followed for years, there are no places where sightings can be guaranteed.

So a Stoat it was, our tenth mammal species of the year.

Meanwhile, up in Cheshire, John Dixon was living the dream – or the nightmare. It turned out that he had been perfectly correct about the weather; the wind wasn't quite right and the tide never reached the seawall. Not a single furred refugee was seen.

John did two nights of hunting the minor roads for Polecats, too, hoping one would run across in the headlights, but unfortunately he was unsuccessful with these, too.

We felt sorry for him but, in this year of searching for mammals, it happened to be the last time that we would.

## April 26th – A Glass Half Empty

I don't wish to give you the impression that, in 2008, mammal-searching was dominating our lives. We made sure that we remained the same normal, hard-working, church-going, nuclear family that we had been before, with kids at school and preschool, for whom searching for furry creatures was merely a temporary subtext. Just to prove it: on April 26th 2008 we went shopping for a pair of sandals.

It so happened, though, that instead of checking out our nearest footwear outlet, we chose to go the 40 kilometres (25 miles) or so to Salisbury. That was because just to the west of this sumptuously lovely city is a chalk stream that, I had been told, was a sure-fire bet for seeing Water Voles.

Considering that they are rodents, related to rats and mice, Water Voles enjoy a remarkably high degree of affection in the hearts of the British public. This can almost entirely be put down, of course, to the character called Ratty, from the much adored *The Wind in the Willows*, the children's story written by Kenneth Grahame in 1908. Ratty is actually not a rat at all, but a Water Vole, which is made clear by the description in the book, but when Water Voles were common, in Kenneth Grahame's day, they were frequently called Water Rats. It so happens that Brown Rats also like the water and are more than capable of swimming along rivers and in streams, and they are frequently mistaken for Water Voles, despite having much longer tails, longer faces and longer ears. So if you see a water rat, it might be a Water Vole, or quite possibly a Brown Rat in the water. However, if it's in a miniature rowing boat, escorting a Mole, it's definitely a Water Vole. (Incidentally, the link between Water Voles and Moles is greater than that concocted by Grahame's imagination. Water Voles often live in Mole tunnels, and on some parts of the Continent, Water Voles live far away from water, in burrows beneath fields.)

But while we might love Water Voles in our hearts, we haven't acted like friends in the way our society has treated them. We have destroyed and polluted their habitat and, worse still, have introduced an enemy that, although we didn't expect it to, has decimated their population. Only 21 years after *The Wind in the Willows* was published, American Minks were brought into Britain for the first time for the purposes of fur-farming. Small numbers of these importees escaped and, by the 1950s, several parts of the country held wild-living populations. Nowadays these sleek predators are everywhere and, surprise, surprise, Water Voles aren't. It is estimated that the latter have disappeared from a whopping 94 per cent of the sites that used to hold them, one of the worst population declines recorded for any mammal in Britain, at least since Medieval times. The Mink is largely to blame.

So to see a Water Vole in Britain is now quite difficult, and even sustaining their fragile existence is a matter of hard conservation management, involving the maintenance of riverbanks and the control of Mink. However, one excellent outpost that we were told about is the River Wylie, in south Wiltshire. This was to be our destination to see this little character and add it to our list of 50 mammal species.

As it turned out, we could hardly have started our mammal – sorry, shopping – trip in more spectacular style. No matter about the Water Vole, before we had even arrived in Salisbury we managed to see Fox, Badger, Hedgehog and Polecat, all from the car. What a boon they would have been to the project. But the trouble was, every one of them was squished on the road, a mammal-watcher's heaven made hell. If nothing else, it did prove that the area was exceedingly rich in wildlife.

The area for the Water Voles was rich all right. It was exquisitely, gloriously rich. It looked like an improbable exhibit from the Chelsea Flower Show, replete with Bluebells, marble-white Cow Parsley, pink Cuckoo Flower, snappily dressed Red Campion and full-volume buttercups, this whole set of blooms set off by the glinting river and set snugly below a toothpaste-white chalk escarpment. While we got out of the car, the birds were singing at full force, yelling, in fact, like market traders, their chorus probably enough to cause a settler from the city to complain to the local council.

Together with the delicate, somewhat intoxicating scent of the rape field nearby, the overall atmosphere overwhelmed us, and for a while we were punch-drunk on spring countryside.

The Water Vole site was, unsurprisingly, along the river. However, my contact hadn't told me which way to go when we arrived, so we meandered west as only families with children can when skirting the water's edge: kids peripatetic, adults apoplectic. We soon settled upon a spot where a tributary was clogged with Watercress and waited there for a while, enjoying the sun and the outdoors.

It's funny whom you meet in a fresh-air idyll. Very soon a group of three people came along who gave the impression of being both professional and knowledgeable. They were dressed in the right gear: green clothing, binoculars and very large, expensive-looking cameras attached to huge, heavy tripods. I was certain that they would know where the Water Voles were – they probably knew the individual Water Voles' names. So I enquired this of them in a casual and, I hoped, friendly manner.

The people looked at me and my children as though we were escapees from a chain gang. It was obvious that they didn't like the idea of children at their favourite nature reserve.

"I've been coming here for twenty years and I have only ever seen a Water Vole once," said the man with the largest camera. He scowled as Emily placed her hand on a tree trunk and swung herself around.

I was taken aback my his abrupt manner, and there was an awkward silence. Somewhat unhelpfully, Sam dropped a pebble into the river.

"You'll only see one if you wait very quietly," he added coldly, with heavy emphasis on the "very quietly", and with that the entourage of unhelpful wildlife snobs strode off.

Oh, sod you, I thought. Although I was unaware of it at the time, this man was the first representative of a group of people that were to become familiar to us throughout the year. These were the doomsayers, the folk who took it upon themselves to be actively discouraging of us and our project, who thought it petty and absurd, who spoke volumes by their disdain but were never honest enough to come out and say so.

The man's discouragement produced its desired result, though. Within a few minutes we decided to leave this spot and try somewhere else, although we weren't sure where to go. As we returned to the car park, however, another man walked past, younger and less "professional"-looking than the previous visitors, with nothing more to weigh him down than a camcorder.

There was nothing to lose, though, so I made the same Water Vole enquiry to him.

"Oh," he said, with interest, fumbling with the camcorder. "Is that what this is?" And he showed me the most perfect footage imaginable of a Water Vole chewing contentedly on some waterside grass.

"Where did you see it?" I asked, suddenly excited.

"Oh, just a couple of hundred yards along there," he said, pointing to the east. "About ten minutes ago."

Fancy that. Only the second sighting in 20 years!

I shall have to come clean and admit that, much as we obviously rushed off to the spot that the second man directed, we didn't see his Water Vole, nor any other along that stretch of river, despite searching for some considerable time. But the story didn't end there. As we were flailing around scouring the Water Vole-less river bank, a small party of students walked past. It turned out that they were on an Ecological Habitat Management course, and one of their number had a hot tip. "You should go to Harnham Meadows, on the very edge of Salisbury," she instructed. "There are loads there."

So we did. And within a short time we were standing on a tarmac path, watching a delightful Water Vole standing protectively at its hole entrance like a rotund rodent bouncer outside an exclusive club. It was chewing away at a grass stem, holding it up to its mouth with both paws in that endearing way that some small mammals have, a manner that appears both quaintly fastidious and over-polite. We half expected the vole to produce a napkin at the end of its meal and wipe its lips.

And do you know? While we were watching the Water Vole, dozens of people walked past within 3 metres (10 feet) of it. Some of them had dogs; some of them were manoeuvring pushchairs; plenty showed curiosity. All of them were living daily life, nobody was showing the least discretion towards the rodents in their midst. Certainly, not one of them had heeded an instruction to be "very quiet".

For the record, we also saw a Brown Rat by the riverside almost in the heart of Salisbury, and thereby scored a kind of "rat double". This second animal, which we didn't watch for long, was only about 400 metres (1,300 feet) from the shoe shop.

wood mose

May

## May 10th – Seeking Sika

This is the story of what was undoubtedly our dullest mammal-spot of the year. There was no suspense, not a lot of effort, and the animals concerned weren't doing anything interesting at all. Sorry. If you decide to go to the next section, that's fine by me. You bought the book, after all.

The trouble is, you were probably raised on watching wildlife programmes. You get the introductory shot of the animal, and then 10 seconds later it is either dead, or fighting, or *in flagrante*. Another couple of minutes and you'll witness all three. All the many hours of frustrating nothingness when the camera-person was tearing their hair out, hoping for some action, swearing under their breath and probably reviewing their choice of career, are edited out.

But in front of us was the reality: Sika Deer simply…standing around. To see them we had intentionally driven the half-hour to Arne, on the Purbeck peninsula, where there are hundreds of Sika, in almost plague proportions. It is impossible to miss them and, for once, we didn't. We saw a group by the roadside and got out of the car, under-whelmed.

I tried to summon interest with a little identification lesson. "Sika Deer are mid-way in size between Red Deer and Roe Deer, and they've got a round whitish rump patch with a small amount of black on the tail," I announced. But I bored even myself. Even the deer seemed to yawn, and mumble dolefully to each other, "I do wish everyone wouldn't always compare us to Reds."

After two minutes we upped and left and went for fish and chips. Poole Quay was riveting in comparison, full of bustle and the excitement of a seaside weekend. We wandered past the new marina, the shiny pride of the redeveloped quay, where we stared at the million-pound cruisers, and Carolyn and I briefly and privately flirted with longing meditations on a rich person's life. We watched the famous Yellow Boats fill up with visitors to leafy Brownsea Island. And we stared spellbound as the sea-scouts and volunteers tied up the sails of a traditionally decked-out schooner on the harbourside. They skipped up the narrow mast ladders like professional circus acrobats, and dangled fearlessly from the sails like primates in the rainforest canopy. They were high enough for a false move to produce an epitaph. Watching them made you purse your lips and shift slightly away from their shadows.

Samuel, for his part, was a little more nervous than most. Throughout the time we were standing next to the schooner he was holding on tightly to my trouser leg.

"What's up, Sam?" I asked at last.

He looked up anxiously and spoke almost in a whisper. "Where's Captain Hook?" he enquired.

It is likely that Poole Quay itself has a strong connection with Sika Deer. Certainly the nearby harbour does. The Sikas are not native to Britain, but are found in east Asia, including China and Japan; the first ones were introduced to Regent's Park from the latter in 1860 and to several parts of the British Isles thereafter. But the first group that really began to thrive in the wild were introduced to Brownsea, the largest island in Poole Harbour, in 1896. They evidently adored Brownsea Island so much that a large proportion of the released herd promptly jumped into the water and swam off to the mainland, not even staying for the night. In the nearby acidic heathland and woodland, dotted with desirable bog and shelterbelts, the animals spread all over the Poole Basin and beyond. These days they have made their way as far as Devon.

It was easy to imagine the Sika Deer being herded on to the boat to bring them to Brownsea, a place that we could now see from where we stood. Perhaps the operation was performed right here? Who knows what the scene was like? No doubt the boatman thought the whole idea was bonkers, and the Sikas just temporary playthings for the idle rich. I doubt anybody supposed that it was the start of something big for the Sika Deer, a new life that is still going strong over a century later.

All in all, it must have been quite a drama. A far cry from the uninspiring meeting we had had with the same animals an hour or two before.

# May 15ᵗʰ – The Toy Box

Christmas arrived in May in the household this morning. A large, important-looking box found its way to our doorstep, containing all sorts of treasures for the avid mammal-watcher.

I had been working on some sponsorship for our project, and came across a company called Alana Ecology. In every way I was impressed by their operation because, apart from anything else, they sold some of my own books (authors are at once both paranoid and absurdly grateful creatures). And their catalogue was a revelation. Aimed partly at professional researchers and ecologists, the catalogue listed almost any kind of trap you can imagine: Mole traps, Mink traps, bat traps, rodent traps. All of them were humane and, thus, temporary holding ports for various mammals prior to processing for scientific study and, in most cases, immediate release. The company also stocked an enthralling range of other equipment, from pond-dipping nets to moth traps and from GPS devices to microscopes, weather stations, microphones, binoculars, nest boxes, data loggers, hides, and much else besides. To be honest, it was Gadget City.

I contacted Alana Ecology and, to my utter delight, they took enough interest in our project to agree to donate some equipment. Today was the day when, after great anticipation, it arrived.

Deep down I am a gadget man. I think most boys are. Sam certainly is. The moment we got the parcel he was almost beside himself with excitement (as was Emily), and it wasn't just the act of opening the box that turned him on. It was the packaging and all the new and shiny stuff inside, the adrenaline-rushing fresh-out-of-factory smell everywhere. He got giddy with the polythene, the foam coverings, the wires of all colours, the instruction books, the LCDs, the switches and the buttons. He fingered them all lovingly, rapt with curiosity. Soon wires and equipment were strewn everywhere around the living room. He and I could have been on laughing gas. It was sheer delight.

Sam was particularly taken with our new spotlight. As it was he was already obsessed with torches, and this was a torch to change the world. I had begged Alana's entrepreneurial Chief, Andrew McLeish, for exactly such a powerful lamp, since I was anticipating trying to find some elusive nocturnal creatures over the summer. The spotlight had the wonderfully masculine name of the Clubman CB2, and it was big and black, with a large handle and an imposing xenon lamp that was on a movable head. It was the sort of light you could, if you wished, use for interrogating some hapless human captive – a traffic warden, perhaps. The instructions claimed – in that no-nonsense language that understates sheer wonder – that it gave out one million candlepower. One million! And lo, that one million candlepower was gleefully shone upon every member of the family until finally we could prise the Clubman CB2 away from Sam's fingers. It was returned with strict instructions not to blind anyone.

We also received a night-vision scope. I had coveted one of these for quite some years but, as a bird-watcher, I had never really needed one before. Yes, some birds, such as owls are nocturnal, but trips after dark looking for birds are very rare indeed, as the vast majority of birds go dutifully to roost at night. But with mammals, the situation is reversed; the list of diurnal mammals is almost as paltry as the roll call of nocturnal birds. Some 60 of our targets would either be essentially animals of the dark, or they would be active both by day and night. I figured that, to enter into the mammals' domain, a night-vision scope could be indispensable.

It wasn't until the evening that we were able to try it out, and only then during the gentle winding down of the day around a child's bedtime, when its wonders weren't yet truly apparent. It was a surprisingly light piece of kit, even with the batteries fitted, and looked like a normal pair of binoculars, except that, while there were two objective lenses (i.e. the lenses by which light enters the viewing chamber, the ones that seem to point away from the eyes), there was only one front lens, through which you looked, with the other eye shut. The device also had two control wheels, one to focus the image, the other to regulate the intensity of light. For the children, simply to see their world magnified twice, and a lot brighter than usual, was revelation enough. The opportunity to turn knobs and switch on buttons just added to the stew of pleasure.

Trying the night-vision scope out in total darkness, I found that you had to practice quite hard to get the hang of it, but once you did a whole new world indeed did open up. I had seen this monochrome reality many times in wildlife films, but to see it at the end of your own scope is actually far more special that you might imagine. The experience is equivalent to snow unexpectedly covering your local landscape, making the familiar instantly unfamiliar and the humdrum wondrous. In the total darkness I could read, from 6 metres (20 feet) away, the manufacturer's trademark on our garden swings, and see flower heads in black-and-white perfection, and amazed myself with the straight lines and pits of bricks and earth, our under-used spades and brushes. It was a good reminder that wonder can be nothing more than a new look at what is already well known.

Further rummaging through our lucky dip unveiled a set of four metal small-mammal traps. The idea of these would be to catch some of the various creatures, such as mice and voles, that we would have trouble appreciating in any other way but close up in the hand. You might be surprised that we had decided to do this. You might even think it cheating to accept animals caught in traps towards a list of animals seen in the "wild". If you think this, it's a perfectly valid opinion. But then, this was a family challenge, and how can you excite a child by, say, waiting in a hide and pointing at a tiny shape rushing by for a millionth of a second and claiming it to be a Field Vole? It just wouldn't register. The core of our project was, after all, to enthuse our children towards an appreciation of mammals, and any rules that we made should defer to that aim. Thus we had decided that, if we were party to the opening of a pre-set trap in the wild, or if we caught any animals in our own traps, this would be valid enough.

You might also be surprised that we were happy to catch wild animals at all. Well, of course, it isn't as simple as that, and we didn't take the idea of capturing wild creatures lightly. Although it is legal to catch some small mammals on your own property (or elsewhere with the agreement of the local landowner) we were anxious to do so responsibly. And bizarrely, you are not allowed to trap shrews without a Shrew Licence. To cover all our bases, I was about to undertake some training so that I would be able to set the traps and handle the captured animals properly.

So, for the moment, the traps remained in their boxes, ready to be unleashed in the next few days.

Besides, there were quite enough toys to play around with for now. Everybody was exhilarated with those we had already opened. We all went to bed excited, unable to sleep, as if it were Christmas Eve once again.

# May 16th - Breathing Space

There are some events within any year which are no pleasure at all to recount. They normally enter the private fabric of our lives and safely remain there, never to be spoken out loud. But this little incident, unpleasant though it was, is slightly different, because it led directly to an encounter with a mammal. I only write about it because it happened, and this book is a faithful recollection. A mammal-watching year is, of course, no more a buffer from pain and worry than any other.

Our precious daughter Emily has viral asthma. It means that, when she gets a cold, she develops breathing difficulties that are often quite serious. As a result, she has ended up in hospital a good many times in her short life. Actually, she loves it there. She loves the attention, and perhaps she likes the drama, too. But we don't, and we fervently hope that, one day, she will grow out of her condition.

On this day she began to get symptoms in the evening and, pressured by mounting concern, we eventually decided to take her to the out-of-hours doctor. Actually, only Carolyn did this, whilst I remained at home with a slumbering, carefree Samuel. Apparently, as Carolyn recalls, once the doctor saw Emily he went into crisis mode, immediately calling an emergency ambulance, which henceforth whisked mother and daughter at high speed to Poole Hospital. Emily, who had never been in an ambulance before, was thrilled to bits, especially when the driver switched the siren on.

Once the usual oxygen and steroids had been given to Emily and her condition stabilised, the hospital discharged her into the spring night. Called to fetch the girls, I awoke Sam and took our second increasingly excited youngster on a journey through the deserted early-hours streets.

And that's the thing. We had searched for Foxes several times during our mammal year up to now, but always without success. The Fox's mainly nocturnal habits make it a tough animal to show kids who have early bedtimes, and these fleet-footed animals, although common, have wide territories over which they can feed. But this night we were deep into the Foxes' most active time, and on the journeys to and from hospital we saw no less than three. One was sleek and fit and sharp-witted, another was mangy and not so aware of its surroundings, the third disappeared too quickly to tell, ghosting into a back garden among bins and potted plants.

Thus, for a brief time, we entered the world of the Fox, one of Britain's best known mammals. But it was still a night to forget.

## May 18th/19th – Buzz-Lightyear-Cinderella-Gingerbread-Man

The introduction of a mouse trap into a household is usually a rather sorrowful and negative affair. Infestations of mice are no fun, and removing the bodies one by one is a little sordid – certainly not something that you wish to show the children.

To our household, however, the prospect of mouse-trapping was nothing less than joyful. Happily, our house itself was free of rodent trouble, and only the garage and the garden provided a likely habitat for whatever unknown feet were treading our land. And we simply couldn't wait to catch one of these resourceful rodents. For us, a mouse wouldn't just be a mouse – it would be a vital link in our race to 50 species of mammals.

The generous people at Alana Ecology had provided us with no less than four humane small-mammal traps, of a type known as a Longworth. Made of light aluminium, these traps consist of two parts, a detachable tunnel and a housing unit. In between the tunnel and housing unit is a little tripwire that closes the door of the tunnel, trapping the visitor inside. The idea was to bait the unit with something edible (we used hamster food), leave it for a few hours, or overnight, and await the results.

Although trapping a wild animal might seem a rather upsetting experience for the tenant, the truth is that these traps are more like hotels than prisons. For one thing, they always hold plenty of food inside (many trappers provide water, too), upon which the animal can gorge itself. Secondly, procedure dictates that you should always put a copious bundle of hay within the housing unit to keep the animal warm and comfortable, and in the course of their studies many workers find their animals fast asleep when they check the contents. Apparently, once they have emptied and processed their catches, some of those workers swear that they find little questionnaires filled out by tiny hands, gushing with glowing customer comments.

So just before bedtime the whole Couzens family assembled outside the French windows for the official inauguration of our own Longworth traps. Samuel was the designated hay-stuffer, pulling out huge lumps from the bag of pre-packed meadow hay and placing it ceremoniously inside. Emily poured in the hamster food, filling each trap with enough to feed a veritable army of rodents. Once set, the kids between them chose where to place the shiny contraptions: one in the garage, one along our perimeter wall and two within our herbaceous border. Very soon the Longworths were ready to unveil any hidden visitors in our well-trodden garden.

In bed that night Emily, in particular, kept calling out from her darkened room, way beyond her normal bedtime: "Have we caught anything yet?" It made a pleasant change from her signature five-year-olds' mantra: "Are we nearly there?"

Not surprisingly, it was early morning when we were inveigled into undertaking the first trap-round, in dressing gowns and slippers made wet by the dewy ground. I was still in mid-yawn when Emily, working at her usual running pace, completed her check of the outside sites. No, she said, there was nothing in the herbaceous border traps and nothing under the wall. She was right: the traps were exactly as we had left them, with door open and not a sign of life.

In the garage trap, however, the tunnel door was shut.

Exciting though this was, it presented something of a problem. The previous night I had devoted all my attention to setting the traps properly; in my enthusiasm I hadn't ever planned what to do if we actually caught something. You might call it my Bush and Rumsfeld moment. I knew from my brief training that the next stage would be to open out the trap inside a large, strong see-through bag, around which the rodent would obediently run around and we would be able to identify it. The only problem was, we didn't have one.

Eventually, after much searching, Carolyn eventually uncovered a polythene bag that, with a bit of stretching, we thought might just about accommodate a mouse. Gingerly, holding the trap over the open rim, I tried to ease the two parts of the Longworth apart.

In retrospect I can easily imagine the rodent inside must have been thinking, sniggering to itself and saying, "What a bunch of amateurs!" Certainly, we were no match for its opportunist professionalism. The moment it saw a glimmer of the outside, our overnight tenant bolted through the gap in the trap and leapt for freedom, landing effortlessly after a short drop and bounding across the paving stones and under our garden gate. In that three-second manoeuvre it must have qualified for several Olympic events.

Carolyn squealed, in splendid wife-afraid-of-mice style. Emily laughed. Samuel made for the inside of the house. I was left wondering what species it was, thoroughly frustrated that we couldn't add it to our challenge list until it was properly identified. Thus, in the crisis, we all reverted to our respective personalities.

"Whatever it was, it can certainly run fast," noted Carolyn, her usual poise restored.

"It was like the Gingerbread Man," laughed Emily delightedly, recalling the nursery rhyme: "Run, run as fast as you can, / You can't catch me, I'm the Gingerbread Man!"

"It was more like Cinderella, running away from the palace on the stroke of midnight," said Carolyn.

"It was Buzz Lightyear!" declared Sam, for no genuine reason.

And so our mouse was christened Buzz-Lightyear-Cinderella-Gingerbread-Man, and as it turned out he became quite a prominent character in our garden over the summer, being shown to various interested guests as well as turning up regularly in our official trapping.

The problem for Buzz was that he simply couldn't resist any kind of handout. Later on that day I set the Longworth in the garage again, just in case we caught him upon Emily's return from school. Sure enough, the door to the tunnel was slammed shut and, had we put our ears close enough to the trap, we would probably have heard him munching and belching and urinating with a signature lack of decorum.

This time we had procured a decent-sized polythene bag and could open the Longworth within its confines, cutting off any escape. This isn't to say that Buzz didn't try. When finally disgorged from his temporary nest he tore around the bag with impressive, turbo-charged athleticism. He persistently jumped up towards the rim of the bag and made several attempts to bite my finger. He was a big mouse. One way you could not describe his vigour and strength was "mouse-like". Actually, I began to worry that he was more psychopathic than anything else.

Buzz's aggression was a little puzzling and I hadn't expected it. His large size and very smart colouration, with bold white belly and pleasing nut-brown upper side was also not quite "right".

And then I realised. This was no average mouse.

I checked his chest and, yes, there was a broad band of bright chestnut across it. I couldn't believe it. Buzz was a Yellow-necked Mouse. Not a

House Mouse or a Wood Mouse – those are easy to see and both common and widespread. No – here in our garden was a species that I thought might cause us a major headache in our family project. This mouse was going to save us a lot of trouble.

So pleased were we with Buzz that we let him go right back into our garage. When released from the bag he didn't hurry out at all. He acted as though he knew the place only too well.

Delighted, I went straight up to my office to celebrate the event with a little research. The book was reassuringly certain about the Yellow-necked Mouse's scarcity. For your information, it is virtually confined to the south of England, and mainly occurs in mature deciduous woodland.

And garages, too.

# May 23rd – A Mammal-watching Holiday

If our attempt to see 50 species of mammals in a year hadn't already become serious by now, the next week would certainly prove our credentials, if only to ourselves. We were about to invest real time and real money by embarking upon our first ever dedicated mammal-spotting holiday. We would be spending a week in a remote part of Scotland in a self-catering cottage, with no TV, no friends nearby and a distance of 80 kilometres (50 miles) to the nearest McDonald's.

If you happen to be an expert in mammal-watching, I won't have to tell you precisely where we were going. For, just as Covent Garden is the best place in the UK for opera, Glastonbury the best place to get dirty and Glasgow the best place to die young, so the Ardnamurchan Peninsula, the westernmost point of mainland Britain, is universally regarded as the best place for wild mammals on our islands. Its roll call of possibilities is mouth-watering: Otters compete for attention with Wildcats, Pine Martens blithely visit bird tables and, at times, it is said to be hard to get into the sea without bumping into seething masses of whales, dolphins and porpoises. It sounded irresistible.

So it was that we loaded up our Zafira with provisions and drove north the moment that Emily ran excitedly out of the school gates for her half-term break. After the recent successes with Foxes, Sika Deer and the Yellow-necked Mouse we had cause to feel optimistic. The sense of delight was compounded by the weather reports, which promised fair weather for at least the start of our visit.

By the time we arrived at our half-way hotel near Lancaster we were all punch-drunk with exhaustion and excitement. The children, normally reliable sleepers, were overtired, still jumping up and down on their mattress beds and giggling late into the night, doubtless drawing curses from the other side of the thin walls of our Premier Inn room. The following morning we took breakfast late, and sheepishly.

## May 24th - Stag Cottage

You know instinctively when you've reached the Highlands of Scotland. It's not when you find yourself overawed by the sheer grandeur of the scenery, nor when you see the first signs for a whisky distillery. You know it when you stop loathing the caravan driving in front of you. Scotland calms you down.

For our three-year-old and five-year-old, the long haul to the West Coast was a real proportion of their lifetime. For the dedicated Carolyn, who read them stories and encouraged them every mile, it must have felt the same. Still, we did what families do. We sang, we bickered; the kids asked for the toilet the moment we hit junctionless stretches of motorway; the adults took prescription coffee. To smooth things along for the junior passengers, we played a CD of classic Disney songs again and again and again, although by the end I wished I could have grabbed Uncle Walt by the throat and thrust him into the eight strangling arms of the evil sea-witch Ursula. No, no. I'm calm, I'm calm.

Our first real introduction to West Coast life – indeed, the first time we were thrust into contact with the Scottish locals – was when we took the Corran Ferry across the narrowest point of Loch Linnhe. For those out there who need parenting advice: take your kids on a Scottish commuter ferry. They are fascinating. For one thing, you can see the vessels gliding importantly across the water towards you, tall and whitewashed, steady and unrushed, somehow theatrical, casting an enormous wake. Equally, they hold you spellbound by disgorging an improbable quantity of vehicles from the other side, apparently from the unseen bowels of the ship. Then the loaders somehow squash huge lorries nose to tail with cars, bikes and foot-passengers, and follow the rule of locals in the middle, visitors towards the treacherous edge. And finally, to compound the thrill, a real person comes to take your money, with an under-the-breath, "I'll take twice the fare from yea, ya Sassenach bastards."

The ferry ride didn't just take us across the sea-loch. It marked the transition between journey and holiday. We were in the same car, in the same cramped conditions on the other side, but it felt different somehow. If you fly to a foreign country, the plane and the airport are drearily similar to everywhere else in the world, but the ride from the airport to your destination – that's the beginning of your adventure. It was the same for us. Suddenly the surroundings for our last few miles weren't just novel, they were refreshingly relevant. We left behind the last town, Strontian, surprisingly neat and leafy, and took a daringly narrow road out into the wilds, up to the summit of a hill clad in moorland that was littered with shattered fragments of rock. The road then twisted sharply down, in rollercoaster style, past a sharp corner with a waterfall and through a thrillingly gloomy conifer forest. At the valley bottom glinted Loch Doilet and, a few hundred metres from its shores, a small whitewashed cottage was tucked into the shelter of a posse of impressively tall spruce trees. This was Stag Cottage, our temporary home.

Here we almost had Scotland to ourselves. Apart from a single neighbouring house across the forestry track, Stag Cottage, a converted gamekeeper's bungalow, was completely isolated. We opened our car doors to be greeted by what might be called homely solitude. The cottage looked inviting and comfortable, and was set within a square garden with pleasing lawns and a well-kept wooden plank fence. Above and around it, the bright, friendly sunshine accentuated all the nuances of the all-round view – forestry trees, earth, bracken and rocky hilltops – and the wind, while not very strong, made that deep, almost contented sigh on the tops of the trees that it seems to give only when coming from far away, unhindered by the human world. Just across the track, a stream added a gurgle to the soundscape. The kids, finally unshackled, ran and skipped across the lawn and, within a few moments, had hidden themselves behind the trunk of a giant spruce.

We all raced to the front door to take a first peek inside our temporary home, Emily winning, as usual. It opened into the sitting room, where a large sofa dominated the space, covered in a veritable family of cushions, varying in both size and pattern, and with a tartan blanket over the back. Below it was a hairy white rug, basking on the floor like a dozing Old English sheepdog. There was a wood burner in one corner, while dotted elsewhere were an antique dresser, an armchair and a magazine rack, the latter full of periodicals and leaflets containing exciting details about the local area. Carolyn enthused about the kitchen, which included that symbol of modern rural comfort, an Aga, while the kids jumped up and down upon their adult beds, which were equally replete with cushions, the youngsters thrilled that they would be sharing their sleeping quarters. At the far end of the kitchen was a drying room, which I quickly made my own, storing away mammal and bird books, our mighty torch, the night-vision binoculars, the telescope and our Longworth traps. Within an hour or two, the car was unpacked, the children were in bed and Carolyn was lying back in the armchair, getting to grips with a glass of wine and some serious Scottish contentment.

With the long evening still light and full of possibilities, I decided to take a walk. Despite the delicious peace that had fallen upon us all, this was no serendipitous perambulation. I was curious to size up Stag Cottage's trump card, the reason we had been drawn to this precise location in the first place. The neighbour's garden, you see, was a sure-fire hot-spot for Pine Martens, a large and rare relative of Weasels and Stoats; people came from all over the country to spot these arboreal predators as they took jam sandwiches from a bird table. The animals had even been featured in that yearly mass-market TV jamboree "Springwatch".

I hadn't expected to see anybody on this private jaunt, so I got something of a surprise when the owner of the neighbouring cottage, an elderly gentleman, came out to say hello while I was unsubtly training my binoculars on his front garden. It soon became obvious that the owners of Stag Cottage had primed him for our arrival. We shook hands.

"I'll be putting out the food at seven o'clock," he said. That was 15 minutes' time.

I thought about Carolyn, settled in paradise, and my pyjama-clad children, just sinking perfectly down to sleep. With a week ensconced here, we had no panic about Pine Martens.

"Oh, but…"

"I'll just show you round the side. If you park there and stay reasonably quiet they should turn up very soon," he went on. I followed him round to the forested side of the garden and, in that very precise way that many people develop in later years, he showed me exactly where I should leave the car. "I'll move my van so you can fit in easily," he added. It was clear that Tony, my new friend, was taking a great deal of trouble on our behalf.

"There you go. All right, I'll see you and your family at seven," he called cheerily, returning indoors.

It felt important not to upset our neighbour the moment we arrived. There was nothing for it but to whisk sleepy children and a profoundly reluctant wife into the Zafira for a short drive.

"But I don't want to see a Pine Marten tonight. I'm happy, the kids are happy. We've got a week," complained Carolyn. She's frighteningly logical at times.

"Well, let's at least see it tonight, then we won't have to worry about it later on," I entreated. "I feel we ought to. Tony is really being very kind to us, you know."

"I was so totally settled. Why did you have to go for that walk?" Feeling guilty and embarrassed for loading the family into the car once more, I manoeuvred us the short distance into the parking bay overlooking Tony's garden, and we watched the hallowed bird table in an atmosphere poisoned with exhaustion and discord. To make matters worse, Emily and Samuel were soon no longer sleepy; they were overtired and complaining. Both Carolyn and I knew it would take ages to get them back down again. In my mind I pleaded for the Pine Martens to turn up quickly so that we could all go to bed.

But they didn't. The sods didn't show up at all.

## May 25th – Seals, Beaches and Muck

At 9:30am the next morning we found ourselves at Laga Bay, some 10 minutes to the west of Strontian, our nearest town. Here we had a very important appointment with a company called Ardnamurchan Charters. We were going out to sea.

I would have to confess that, personally, I felt profoundly excited about this, like a schoolboy in a sweetshop. I love boat trips and always have. For a landlubber, they inevitably represent something out of the ordinary, a turn away from the mainstream of life. So even a short ferry journey of a few minutes gets my heart skipping. Now the whole family were to spend an entire day out on Loch Sunart and the Sea of the Hebrides, landing on a couple of islands and searching for sea mammals as we went. What a prospect this was.

The weather looked promising, too, as we boarded the *Laurenca*, our 10-metre- (32-foot-) long motorised yacht. The light was as radiant as it had been the day before, and the wind did not seem interested in stirring the waters of the loch. We set off in high spirits and on a negligible swell, eagerly scanning the waters waiting for a fin to stir. I had read that Common Porpoises had been seen regularly on the inner part of the loch, and that this species was hard to miss in the general area.

You might remember that we had something of an issue with Common Porpoises, having missed seeing them on our very first mammal-watch of the year, almost six months before, off our local stretch of coast. Now, 15 species into our quest, it seemed entirely right that we should catch up with them in these most commanding of surroundings, here in a sea-loch set between barren hills of green, gold and purple, almost as far away from the South Coast as it is possible to go in Britain, whisked away by the adventure that almost never got started because of the non-appearance of these animals. It would be strangely satisfying to spot a Porpoise and stick two fingers up at it.

Porpoises are, on the whole, peculiarly poorly known sea mammals. I bet that most people, even if they had heard of one, would not know the difference between a Common Porpoise and a dolphin, or even if there was a difference. Porpoises are actually more numerous around our coasts than dolphins or whales, and yet many people would not recognise one even if they saw one. These sea mammals, which, at less than 2 metres (6½ feet) long, are the smallest in our waters, seem to keep a low profile – and in fact they do so literally, since usually all you see sticking out of the water is a near apology for a fin on the middle of the back – a long way from the high, impressive and stately curved fins of Bottlenose Dolphins. Porpoises rarely stay long at the surface, they almost never make those attractive free-spirited leaps that dolphins make, and they seldom take any interest in vessels, never riding the bow-wake in the manner of their more boisterous relatives. They are harder to see and, to cap it all, they are much less sociable than dolphins, rarely gathering in groups of more than two or three. Perhaps they are a little embarrassed by their appearance – small and dumpy, with a short, blunt head that lacks the beak of a dolphin, and a body that somehow lacks the grace and elegance of their more popular cousins.

Here in these waters, though, Common Porpoises were apparently easy to see, seeking out the plentiful fish supplies in the loch during short, shallow dives. However, during the first hour of our trip, we hadn't yet seen one.

"Sometimes Minke Whales come in this far up the loch," said Andy, our skipper, encouragingly. A man in his thirties who clearly had saltwater in his blood, he showed a youthful certainty in his voice, at least as far as the potential success of our trip was involved. I envied him the hundreds of cetacean sightings he must have enjoyed in his life, and hoped that he would be true to his certainties and be able to show us at least a few of these special creatures in the next couple of hours.

My pre-trip excitement was entirely justified by the list of possibilities for the voyage. Besides the Common Porpoises and the Minke Whales, the rich waters hereabouts had a habit of turning up the sort of cetaceans that dreams are made of. Mine, I have to admit, mainly featured Orcas, those giant black-and-white dolphins that used to be called Killer Whales. It so happened that, just prior to our visit, a small pod of them had been sighted off the Point of Ardnamurchan, exactly where we were now. The roll call of possibilities also featured Common and Bottlenose Dolphins and, towards the wildly optimistic end of the spectrum, such spectral specialities as Risso's Dolphins.

Andy was in communication with other vessels in the area, and would be told if anything exciting was within reach. But, as we ploughed out of Loch Sunart, spotting a Golden Eagle flying over almost the last crag along the Ardnamurchan Peninsula, we ran into something of a snag. After the calm of the sea-loch, out on the waters of the Sea of the Hebrides, it was now becoming decidedly choppy. Either the wind had just got up, or we had previously been sheltered from it, or perhaps the water was always like this. The boat began to pitch and roll so that it became increasingly difficult to keep our footing; the waves were now enthusiastic enough to soak anyone sitting near the stern. After 45 minutes of this, the colour of our small band of whale-spotters began to turn increasingly green. Emily and Samuel just huddled next to Carolyn on a seat next to the wheelhouse. It was clear that they weren't going to see a thing.

My own tummy was beginning to agree that an all-day whale-watching cruise had been a bad idea, when salvation suddenly arrived for everyone. We floated into the lee of a miniature archipelago of low, rocky islands. We had made it to the northern tip of the island of Coll and a channel known as Acairseid Mhor, where, mollycoddled by the islands, the sea was completely calm. This area also happened to be a paradise for seals. They were hauled out on to just about every available rock, peering at us, as seals always do, from a reclining position. Most were Common Seals, which tend to adopt a head-up, tail-up posture, like one of those red Chinese Miracle Fish toys you sometimes find in Christmas crackers, which shrivel when you put them in your palm. But there were Grey Seals, too, meaning that we had seen two new species for our mammal-watching year within a couple of minutes.

Seal haul-outs remind me of a mass of human flesh crowded on a beach in a Bank Holiday heatwave: lots of bodies, most of them immobile, a high proportion showing more flesh than they really should, and many carrying more flesh than they should. At least none of the seals were reading *The Sun*. Nobody is actually sure why seals spend so much time hauled up on land, when they are such confirmed sea creatures and don't have any actual legs. Studies show that Grey Seals spend about 40 per cent of their entire lives up on land like this, apparently doing nothing. There is some evidence that it helps them to conserve energy, and other theories suggest that they do it for their skin – so, not much different from people, then.

The haul-out is rather like a harbour, a place to which the seals return after a spot of fishing, and individual seals usually use the same haul-outs year-round, provided they are not breeding. The individuals on these rocks would normally spend two to five days on fishing trips before their return, going out about 50 kilometres (30 miles), and sometimes more, looking for patches of sea with sandy or gravely bottoms. The faces of seals can almost look human, with their forward-set eyes, but these are alien animals, for sure. They go to places people have never seen, and, on their foraging trips, they spend at least 80 per cent of their time underwater, kept warm by their blubber and possessed with eyesight especially evolved for the sub-surface viewing world.

A good number of seals were in the water and taking a much more lively interest in the *Laurenca*. They swam around us, popping their heads up every few moments to get a closer look. It began to feel as if they were lining the watery streets to applaud our arrival. They were experts at taunting photographers, however: the minute you got a seal head in your viewfinder, it disappeared, leaving merely a perfect shot of open water.

Distinguishing between Grey and Common Seals is by no means easy. Andy tried to guide us through it: "There's no point trying to separate them on the basis of colour or pattern," he said, "since it all overlaps. But look at the shape of the head. See those seals on the water?"

We peered as he pointed.

"The head looks a bit like that of a dog. There is an obvious muzzle coming away from the top of the skull, leaving a sloping forehead. OK? That's a Common Seal. Now, look over at that big bull seal sitting on that rock?"

All heads turned in unison as if we were watching a tennis match.

"See the Roman nose? And the flat forehead? Well that's a Grey Seal. Got it?"

Well, probably. I looked in my mammal field guide, and it was a lot easier to see in a picture than it was out here, in the wild. After a while I think I got the hang of it, but I'm not sure that the children ever did.

"The Common Seals will give birth soon," Andy went on. "But the Grey Seals are very different. Their pups aren't born until September or October, so they can just lounge around for months. Right, would you like to spend half an hour on this island?"

The opportunity to walk on land again, of course, was completely irresistible. And perhaps it was the glory of being reunited with our natural surface that sent us all into raptures, or perhaps it was the warmth of the sun, or simply the peace of the island, with nothing but the gentle, insistent breaking of the waves, and the shrill piping of the Oystercatchers that flew past in black-and-white packs, but this place felt like heaven on earth. The grassland centre of Eilean Mor was dotted with wildflowers, especially the subtle pink of Thrift and the more confident white of sea campion; there were even Bluebells here. They gave off a mixed fragrance that jostled with the smell of the sea. Over the moorland there was a beach inlaid around a shallow bay; but the sand here was not the conventional stuff that you find on most British beaches, but instead made entirely from fragments of seashells. It was such a brilliant white that, in the strong sunlight, it actually hurt to look at it. And it was hot to the touch of feet, too.

I have always poo-pooed the idea of Scotland having some of the finest scenery in the world. It felt like an insult to more stupendous places, such as the Grand Canyon and the Alps and any tropical rainforest you could name, or the Skeleton Coast of south-west Africa. Yet here, for the first time, I could sympathise with such sentiments. The islands looming in the distance – Rum, with its towering mountains, and the much lower Muck, and the distant profile of the Outer Hebrides 40 kilometres (25 miles) away, just seemed to combine perfectly with the blue of the sea and the stark white of the sand in front of us.

Our passage to Muck was across some further "high-spirited" seas, and it was clear that, even if we were to come across some cetaceans during this part of our voyage, they would have to be pretty close for us to see and identify. Carolyn and I were beginning to question how suitable this trip was in terms of our children's viewing possibilities anyway. They were having a great time, but not seeing a lot. At their tender age, their ambitions were limited to trying to stay on their feet… Or not – both of them broke free from parental grasp at regular intervals, evidently relishing the feeling of staggering around and falling down. Emily, in particular, found the obstacle course of running from one parent to another across the heaving deck irresistible. More challengingly, she also descended the stairs to the cabin several times, beaming mischievously as we tried, and failed, to stop her.

Our misgivings about sea-mammal-viewing were confirmed a few moments later. The call of "Dolphin!" came up, and while Andy cut the engine and everybody scanned the water surface, a dolphin actually jumped out of the water about 100 metres (325 feet) away. The trouble was that not everybody saw it and, as far as I am aware, that included both of our kids. This was especially frustrating because it was clearly a Common Dolphin – it had a sort of "hourglass" pattern on its side, with two stripes of different colour, one grey, one yellowish, narrowing and meeting each other in the middle of its body – so it was a species that was relatively hard to see in Britain, and very unpredictable. We were unlikely to encounter it again for the whole year. A few times some fins surfaced to give extra glimpses, but the dolphin show only lasted for a few moments. Andy said we had been unlucky. These animals are often attracted to vessels and take time out to play in the seas ploughed up by their forward motion, a behaviour known as "bow-riding".

To make matters worse, somebody spotted some Common Porpoise fins shortly afterwards. These were further away and even fewer people caught sight of them. Another exciting opportunity lost. This was doing my head in.

Still, everyone's mood lifted when we reached Muck, an island only 3 kilometres (2 miles) long and 1.5 kilometres (1 mile) wide. It wasn't the island's intrinsic beauty that so captivated us, however; that had been trounced by the islets off Coll. It was the sense that we were entering a confined community, physically cut off from the rest of the world. With an official human population of "approximately thirty-eight", whatever that meant, plus 50 Cows, 430 Sheep (of two breeds), four Highland Ponies and three pigs (to hell with people, let's get the animal totals exact), everything on Muck felt exclusive. We visited the only café in the only settlement, Port

Mor – all neat, white and tidy – and saw cups and keyrings that could not have been bought anywhere else in the world. We climbed the highest hill and admired the view from next to the island's wind-powered generator, and main source of electricity. Everywhere else seemed to be a long way off.

It always seems amazing that people can live in places like this, especially in the dark and draughty winter months. But the people on Muck are permanent residents who lease their cottages and smallholdings from the estate that owns the island. Most of their money is made by selling lambs or calves or foals, plus a few crafts. The children have a local school that they attend until they are 12, and then they have to go to boarding school on the mainland at Mallaig. In former times most of the residents were local West Highlanders who spoke only Gaelic, but nowadays the demographic has changed completely. Muck-dwellers come from all over the British Isles, overdosed, perhaps, on reality TV programmes that promise them a better life in the country. They find isolation and yet, at the same time, a community – and perhaps that's just what they are searching for.

Isolated though they are, the islanders haven't been forgotten by the rest of us. In the last few years the kind British taxpayer has funded a new and magnificent pier for Muck, so that ferries can dock here and avoid the pesky business of using small boats to ferry from ferries. Andy told us that the pier cost five million pounds to build, just in case you were wondering where your money had gone. Doubtless the (approximately) 38 residents are mighty grateful.

By now it was late afternoon, and after the previous hours of searching, enthusiasm for watching out for sea mammals aboard the *Laurenca* had dwindled almost to nothing on the return leg from Muck to Laga Bay. If anything did swim by, we missed it and, as we chugged back to our landing pontoon, a full nine-and-a-half hours after we had set off, the reality of missing all the sea mammals we had hoped for began to sink in.

Oh dear. No Orcas, no dolphins that the kids could see, nothing. And there was no chance for a repeat trip – we simply couldn't afford it.

It was the Minke Whale that bugged me the most. Dolphins are fun, but also quite widespread; we could expect to catch up with at least some of these later in the year. But whales are really special, and we had desperately wanted the kids to see one. Although pretty small by whale standards, full-grown adult Minkes are still 7 metres (23 feet) long, and the idea of sailing past one of these beasts of the deep, as it surfaced regally, offering up its

2-metre- ($6^1/_2$-foot-) high blow, had been a dream that I suppose we had expected to become a reality. The kids had known about whales from their earliest childhood, and to see one in the wild would have been, in words they were beginning to use, incredibly cool.

*red squrl*

It had been a curious day – fantastic in every way except in contributing much towards our project. Whaleless, Carolyn and I felt flat. And completely knackered. We put the kids to bed and sank into the armchairs at Stag Cottage, wine glasses in hand.

By force of habit I glanced out of the window.

I could see a movement.

Obviously the bird table had a customer.

It did. A Pine Marten.

Cue pandemonium.

Within seconds all four of us were looking out of the window at this gorgeous animal – a relative of the Stoats and Weasels – helping itself to peanuts, evidently without the least concern about anything in the world, particularly its enraptured audience. It remained on the bird table, stuffing itself for such a long time that we had to put the kids back down to bed before it had finished.

The Pine Marten has the design of a very large Stoat, with the same arrangement of four limbs at the corners of a sausage-like body. But this animal is clearly much larger, and the limbs are longer than those of a Stoat or Weasel, as befits an animal that climbs trees for a living, coping effortlessly in the forest canopy with its strong grip and the ability to leap like a squirrel when necessary. Its tail is also mush bushier. But the most obvious difference is in the colour; although it is a rich chestnut-brown above – slightly darker than a Stoat – the colour of the underside, from the throat downwards, is a very distinctive brownish-yellow, whereas in both Stoats and Weasels, it is white.

Given its carnivorous kinships, you might be surprised to hear that it was eating peanuts; well, despite its relatives, the Pine Marten is very much an omnivore. It eats voles and other rodents, plus a small number of Red Squirrels, and a wide variety of other foods, from birds to berries, fish to crustaceans. Over much of its range in Britain it has also become famous for being unable to resist strawberry jam put out for it on bird feeders.

And this Pine Marten was indeed jammy – as far as we were concerned anyway.

Back in our armchairs, we made a toast to it. The last sips of wine were immeasurably better than our first.

## May 26<sup>th</sup> – The Point of No Return

It might sound a little ungrateful, but the Pine Marten couldn't entirely cover over the disappointment of a catastrophic lack of hard-to-see sea mammals from the whale-watching trip. In short, we hadn't legislated for missing absolutely everything. In the context of seeing 50 mammals in a year, even one would have made a difference, and two would have set us well on our way. But none… Oh dear. It was a serious setback.

Ruefully, we mused on this, over the course of what should have been the most perfect Scottish morning. The sun wasn't just out, it was blasting down its rays as if trying to distract our attention. The wind, curse it, had dropped still further, leaving the treetops still. The view from Stag Cottage was no less mind-blowing than it had been the day before. But failure thwarted our ability to enjoy it properly.

A Bank Vole, bless it, tried to make life better. We had set our four traps in the garden overnight, and now, for the first time north of the border, we had enticed a client in. It was our first close-up view of this animal, and also Carolyn's first of the year anywhere. We admired the rich chestnut fur, and the Bank Vole's signature small eyes and ears – features which, to many, slightly undermine this rodent's charm. But not to us. It was still small, cute and cuddly, and, after it had done a few laps in the bag, we released the little vegetarian back on the edge of the garden to terrorise the seeds once more.

So, what to do?

I should by now have mentioned that, of the two people involved in our marriage, Carolyn is by far the better organiser and plan-maker. I flail, she works it out. She is the one who, when the chips are down, simply picks them up again, while I am more likely to call an emergency meeting about how we are going to deal with these infuriatingly prone chips.

"Well, let's rest in the morning and then drive west to Ardnamurchan and see if we can see any whales from the Point," she suggested casually. "And look for other stuff on the way. Then, if we have a late tea at the Point, we can try for those Wildcats you mentioned near Glenmore as it gets dark."

For a commonsense assessment of our situation and its possibilities, it was nothing short of brilliant. If Carolyn had been a military commander, I would not like to have fought on the opposing side. What a woman!

Thus it was that, after a lazy lunch, we set out to the wild west to nail all those pesky missing varmints. Our first port of call was a hide just beyond Strontian, which, we had been assured, was a reliable place from which to watch Otters carousing in the food-rich waters of Loch Sunart. Besides whales and dolphins, Otters were one of our main target animals here in Scotland. While English Otters tend to be exceptionally shy and elusive (and didn't we know it!), Scottish Otters were generally reckoned to be much easier to find. Part of this is no doubt because they occur here in the safety of the sea, rather than in the cramped confines of a river or lake system. People often refer to them as Sea Otters, but that delightful animal, famous for floating on its back and using stones as tools to dash shellfish to bits, is only found in the Pacific Ocean off North America. British "Sea Otters" are simply sea-dwelling Eurasian Otters.

The stake-out was a large, spacious hide affording a wide view over the loch and a nearby island. The tide was low, making the whole coastline a contrasting clash between dark rocks and pale, exposed sandy ooze. This marine stew was lavishly seasoned with patches of blackish seaweed, as if there had been a volcanic eruption of the stuff nearby, and the beaches, sand-bars and water had all been covered here and there with fragments of algal mash, each clump resembling a discarded, matted wig.

We were looking for a dark-coloured animal at long range, among black rocks and glistening black seaweed. It didn't look easy.

But the logbook left us in no doubt that Otters occurred hereabouts. In fact, almost every entry referred to one, not always in the reverent terms you might expect:

"Another Otter today…"

"No change today. Otter appeared at 12.10…"

"Disappointing to see nothing except Otters…"

Indeed, you might say the animals were barely appreciated.

"Today I saw what I suspect might have been a Woodpigeon. Unfortunately, however, my view was obscured by an Otter and I wasn't able to be sure…"

The logbook might as well have said: "Quite frankly, if anyone fails to see an Otter from here, they really ought to reassess whether they are making any meaningful contribution to society."

But even with a telescope and all the determination we could muster, we just couldn't see one. The loch was full to the brim with perfect furnishings, but the tenants weren't at home.

We didn't do any better at Glenmore Natural History Centre, further along the coast. The staff there almost fell off their seats when we told them how elusive the animals had been. And when we asked them where we might find Otters in their vicinity, they replied thus: "You could try looking in Port na Croisg – that's the next bay along. Or Camas Ban, the next bay to that. Or, failing that, there have been plenty of sightings at the one next to that, which is Camas nan Geall. Then there's always the next and the next and the next and the next and the next…"

And they suddenly dashed back into the room behind the counter, where there was not enough soundproofing to muffle the hysterical peals of laughter.

What was it about us?

Actually, to set the record straight, the staff were actually genuinely helpful at the centre, if a little bemused by our project. We had a superb cup of tea in the light and airy surroundings there, and our search for carnivorous mammals wasn't completely blank: Emily made friends with the incumbent cat.

Nearing the Point of Ardnamurchan we actually scored a new mammal for our year's project, making 19 altogether. Grazing some way off the roadside was a herd of Red Deer. This is Britain's largest land mammal, the Monarch of the Glen, here living rough and wild, rather than being cosseted in a soft southern deer park among traffic and picnickers. And a magnificent sight they were, too, among the Highland heather, their hides shining rustily in the sunlight, the single stag, shaggy on the neck, fussing about like a flustered wedding planner, the slimline does trying on the odd skittish attempt to run away in the grass, just to wind him up. There must have been 20 animals in all.

Now, I must confess that I have been a bit rude about deer so far in this book. I'm a sort of reverse Simon King in this respect. Where he raves endlessly, I yawn. But these creatures were a different matter. Where most of the deer species we had seen were standing around looking as bored as teenagers in a geography lesson, these animals deigned to run around a bit, and show a smidgeon of character. We must have been spellbound for five minutes, a record for us in a six-deer year.

We rolled on to the Point of Ardnamurchan. For those out there who occasionally don anoraks, you might be interested to know that this is the westernmost point of the British mainland – no, that's not Cornwall, nor St. David's in Wales, but Ardnamurchan. It stands at the end of the eponymous peninsula, jutting confidently out into the Sea of the Hebrides with only islands for close company: Mull, Rum, Eigg and Muck. In such a position, it is not surprising that the Point delivers a panoramic view of the rich waters around the Inner Hebrides, and it was here that we felt sure that, with a lot of hard searching and a small amount of good fortune, we should be able to spot the spout of a whale or the leap of a dolphin.

But it was the lighthouse that commanded our attention at first – particularly Samuel's. He had found these buildings irresistible ever since our visit to Portland Bill on January 1st, when, inevitably, we were also looking for dolphins. Once back home from that early trip he laid claim to a corner of our living room, behind an armchair, and called it "The Lighthouse". This important part of his territory is where he had stored his current favourite playthings ever since.

No wonder he was awestruck. Ardnamurchan Lighthouse was tall and manly, with an imperious granite tower and a shiny black top. Samuel begged us to climb it, something we had foolishly promised we would do the next time we got the opportunity. Infuriatingly, however, this accessible lighthouse had closed a few minutes earlier, and so, short of breaking in, and citing temporary insanity caused by the high-volume tears of a small child, we had to contend with standing at its foot and admiring its stark magnificence. It was hardly compensation.

The teashop, catastrophically, was also shut. Ardnamurchan, always a remote place, was feeling just a little too much so for comfort. Carolyn and I glanced at each other and rolled our eyes. Deer apart, nothing much was going right.

Hoping to turn things around, I scanned the water with naked eye, binoculars and finally telescope, working unusually hard. Quite what

I would do if I managed to see an insignificant fin a way offshore I hadn't quite decided; perhaps I would lift each child up to look through the telescope and hope they somehow managed to make something of it. Really, I was hoping for a Minke Whale up close and unmissable. But whatever might be out there, it seemed almost treacherous to check small fields of surface water without taking in the scenery as a whole, equivalent to admiring mere brushstrokes in a corner of a great master's canvas. The gorgeous juxtaposition of deep blue sea, pale sky, dark rocks and white sand on the beach, together with the looming olive green islands offshore, should have been a sight to drink in and cherish, but, to be entirely honest, all I wanted to see was a dark, fin-shaped blob of no beauty or aesthetic merit whatsoever. I followed the advice of the guidebook that suggested you should check aggregations of seabirds to find cetaceans, but the seabird masses I could see were all so far off that I couldn't make out anything large and mammalian among them. After a half hour or so, all I had to show for my efforts was the dull overture to a headache.

Not entirely surprisingly, Carolyn, who meanwhile had been indulging in the unglamorous task of minding children near a cliff edge, soon became edgy herself as my vigil stretched on. She suggested, without any allowance for dissent, that we should descend to the beach immediately and eat our tea. Frustrated after my fruitless scanning, I was not about to demur.

The afternoon gave way to evening without much dulling of the light. Up here at these high latitudes, close to the middle of the year, there wouldn't be much night today, more an incredibly long semi-twilight, painting the landscape ever darker in infinitesimally small increments, a few wavelengths at a time. Delicious and mollifying as this was, it was also a problem. Later on we hoped to look for Wildcats 25 kilometres (15 miles) down the road, but since these were normally too shy to come out in anything lighter than gloaming, we knew it could be a long wait before conditions became suitable.

We amused ourselves with rock-pooling. We crept down an embankment on to the beach, finding ourselves in the company of some Sheep that, judging by their ease with this peculiar habitat, could well have been taking Marine Biology qualifications. Happily, the children had not seen many sea creatures before, so they reacted full-bloodedly when I held a diminutive crab by its carapace and let the pincers wiggle threateningly towards them. We chased fish with our hands and discovered some astonishingly indomitable shrimps that evaded all our attempts to capture them, even when cornered. I showed Emily and Samuel the different colours of seaweed, and the alluring red "blooms" of sea anemones. Carolyn and I drank tea from a flask while the kids sucked Fruit-Shoots; and for a while we forgot, sweetly, about the task in hand.

Eventually, however, after several more unsuccessful attempts to spot that all-important swimming mammal  ve deemed that it was time to go. Semi-darkness was in reach and with it the chance to see what is perhaps Britain's most elusive and difficult mammal, the Scottish Wildcat.

The Wildcats of Britain are a far cry from the familiar moggie that shares countless centrally heated homes the length and breadth of the country. The domestic animal is seen as something of a hedonist, relishing open fires and warmth and the good life. The wild version could hardly be more different, living in Scottish woodland and moorland throughout the year, with all the ferocious and unpleasant conditions that that may bring, often struggling to scratch a living. The Domestic Cat all too willingly uses human beings as its slaves, feigning affection to get easy meals; it also lives completely at ease in a man-made environment, feeding on mice and Blackbirds and other garden inhabitants. The Wildcat, on the other hand, shuns people fanatically. It is only found in remote country, and clearly regards contact with humans as something to be avoided. Its Scottish population is kept from expanding further south by the broad swathe of dense human settlement across Scotland's central belt from Glasgow to Edinburgh.

Some things don't change, though. A cat is a cat and, at heart, this is a predator. Even in domestic situations we struggle to contain its predatory personality, fattening it up and fitting it with a bell to give the birds and rodents a chance, but Domestic Cats still manage to kill millions of birds a year. With Wildcats, at least nobody pretends that they are anything but professional carnivores. They live mainly on mammals, including Rabbits, voles and mice, but also eat a lot of birds and diversify into frogs, snakes and even insects at times. And while everyone would recognise the way a

Wildcat feeds, sometimes stalking through dense vegetation, sometimes jumping down from above, and sometimes waiting at the entrance to a burrow in preparation for a strike, perhaps less expected is that the Wildcat will eat carrion at times, making the odd daring visit to a roadside to feed on squashed flesh.

The Wildcat's relationship with people is no less fraught than that of almost every other British predator, despite the fact that Domestic Cats are so enormously popular. The animal became extinct in England and Wales a century and a half ago, and the Scottish population is still kept low in some areas by forms of intense illegal persecution such as shooting and trapping. This is caused, as ever, by a complete misunderstanding of this animal's true self; although a confirmed predator, it mainly deals in small stuff, and there is no evidence to support the theory that it takes significant numbers of important gamebirds, such as Red Grouse or Pheasant. But hey, when you're prejudiced, who cares about facts?

This persecution, together with a whole load of other problems, including habitat loss, road traffic and diseases borne by escaped Domestic Cats, has made the Wildcat one of the rarest mammals in Britain. There's another problem, too: when is a Wildcat a Wildcat? It isn't unusual for Domestic Cats to escape and turn to a life of living rough, which may bring them into contact with true Wildcats. When they meet these big, tough, outdoor-living strangers, relationships blossom and lead to hybridization. Little by little the genepool of the true Wildcats is diluted, leading to problems in the definition of the real thing. Recent estimates of the total population of pure Wildcats in Scotland have ranged from as little as 400 to 3,500 animals – still not very many, even at the top end of the scale.

As far as we were concerned on this May night, however, all we wished to do was see one. We would gladly forego the remaining 3,499, just for a single representative to cross the road or somehow afford us a view of its distinctive, black-tipped tail disappearing behind a rock. To see a real live Wildcat would be a real boon to our project.

We knew that we had a chance, at least. For along one particular stretch of road on the Ardnamurchan Peninsula, there was a large scree slope which these animals were known to frequent. Indeed, this was probably the best place in the whole country to see Wildcats and now, with a great deal of effort, we had arrived on site. We had the hide, in the form of the car; we had a spotlight; we had reasonable weather. And now, at last, we just about had dusk, which during the summer months is the most active time of day.

However, there was conflict aboard our vehicle. It was past 10 o'clock by now and the children were overtired and pretty much out of control. Equally overtired, the parents were not much better. All the talk was at maximum volume, because nobody was calm any more. The children chattered constantly, no longer sweet or enquiring or polite, but silly and trivial and full-blown annoying. We yelled at the kids to behave, they yelled back, they yelled at each other, Carolyn and I were seething. My headache – the result of hard driving and scoping the sea – had now developed into an absolute stinker. Furthermore, we had other practical difficulties: the windows in our "hide" steamed up with our tempers; the scree slope was difficult to see, as it loomed above us on a steep mountainside; and we were in a small lay-by, so passing traffic made the car shake. The spotlight wasn't very effective, either, because we needed to open the windows to illuminate the hillside, and that meant that any Wildcat for miles around would hear our vociferous disharmony and avoid the area.

It was sheer, undiluted, irredeemable, mammal-watching hell. And we couldn't stick it. Angrily, after saying things to the children we always promised we would never say, we set off on the 90-minute journey home, and into an abyss of despondency and irritation.

It was unbearable. We had missed Otters, Wildcats and every cetacean we had tried for. What was the point of all this?

Mercifully, almost immediately the children went to sleep. Now at least we could live our joylessness in peace. The drive back was very quiet indeed.

Close by to Strontian, almost on the stroke of midnight, a mammal ran across the road in our headlight beam. At first we thought, from its size, it was a Fox, but even with the most fleeting of views we couldn't miss the rings on the tail and the broad, blunt, black tip. It was a Wildcat, for sure.

I checked behind, just in case. Yup, the kids were still slumbering all right. We couldn't count it.

# May 27ᵗʰ – We're All in this Together

In every way, today was a watershed.

Despite everything, we decided not to give up on our mammal-hunt. We had had a couple of excruciatingly unsuccessful days, that's for sure, but they were only two among the 365 originally available for the year. Besides, we couldn't give up now, not after all the efforts we had made. And you know this anyway, because you're only halfway through the book.

Another watershed was our twentieth mammal of the year. Yet again we were grateful for our small-mammal-trapping campaign, which this time yielded not a Bank Vole, but a Field Vole.

"Oh no", I can detect you thinking. "Not another vole. What is this book – *My Family and 50 Voles?*"

But wait a minute, please. I promise you, this is positively the last vole in the travelogue. I've told you about Bank Voles and Water Voles and, despite the fact that there is another vole species on Orkney, I assure you that our year's mammalling didn't take us anywhere near the Orkneys. Honestly.

The Field Vole was bigger than the Bank Vole, and much paler in colour, a rather disappointing brown-grey. It was even further away from the mouse spectrum than a Bank Vole, too, with even smaller eyes and almost invisible ears hidden by its fur. Its tail was also shorter, making it rather satisfyingly distinctive.

And I was more than a little chuffed with it, actually. Having caught the Bank Vole in a semi-wooded section of the garden, I deliberately placed a trap in the long grass next to a field, in the hope of attracting – yes – a Field Vole. Complete genius really.

These creatures seem mainly to subsist on grass and leaves. They are found in open areas, less typically in the "edge" habitats, such as the woodland margins and hedgerows favoured by their darker-furred relative.

There you are. That didn't hurt, did it?

The final, and most important watershed today occurred in the life of our daughter. You won't be surprised to hear that, after all we had been through, we dedicated ourselves mainly to resting and part of our rehabilitation was to play a couple of DVDs, in the absence of a workable TV.

One of the DVDs was *High School Musical*.

Need I say more? Our five-year-old was hooked. For the rest of the year, Cinderella and Aurora quickly gave way to Troy, Gabriella and that foxy creature, Sharpay. Emily never looked back. Her lunchbox, writing pads and affections switched brands. She was growing up.

As we watched the film, I ruefully reflected: there was only one set of Wildcats we were going to see this year, and they were on screen in front of us.

# May 28th – What's the Story in Balamory?

After three days of missing practically everything that couldn't be caught in a small trap, the Scottish leg of our yearly adventure was lurching close to disaster. We had scored just five new mammals in four days, and none of them especially difficult to see. Otters, Minke Whales and Wildcats had all kept out of scoring sight.

But, rather than inducing a state of mild panic, as perhaps it should have done, the failures had lulled us all into a pleasing state of irrational calm. The children were quiet as the car seemed to float over the straight road to Lochaline, and Carolyn failed to have her usual panic attacks about my driving. I even began to muse how it was such a privilege to be in the Highlands, on our way to Mull, wild countryside all around, the whole family together on an adventure. Somehow, I was bathed in a mood of contentment. It's amazing what headache pills can do.

My mood darkened considerably, however, during what should have been a harmless visit to the coffee counter by the ferry terminal. The burly lorry driver ahead of me, the sort of man-mountain whom you might imagine could have loaded his stack of logs with his bare hands, surprised me by enquiring politely about our holiday and, then, the subject open, began to drool about his latest Otter sighting.

"Och, I wass watching a mother and cubs at twenty-past-four this morning," he declared. "Just east of Strontian where there's a white hoose baside the loch."

"How marvellous."

"On the east end of Loch Sunart…"

"Oh, yes."

"They were playing in tha watter, couldna missum. Best view I've ever had. You should try there."

"Thank you. Yes, we will."

He went on to describe his sighting in glorious detail, but I regret that my frustration scrambled out his message. How was it that this man was falling over Otters without trying, when we had embarked on several sustained special missions for them and seen nothing more than rocks and surf? And a lorry driver, too. Don't get me wrong, I've got nothing but respect for lorry drivers, especially very large ones. But being told about the Otter by such an incongruous source was a bit like hearing from your binmen that you had missed an excellent episode of "Panorama". It was unexpected, and thus strangely unwelcome.

My face must have told a story as I brought the coffee to the car. "Why don't you watch out for dolphins by the jetty, darling?" suggested Carolyn, making protective glances towards the children. "We'll stay in the car until the ferry arrives."

I consoled myself that Mull, looming across the water from us, contains the densest population of Otters in Great Britain. *Canna missum.*

In fact our first mission on Mull was potentially an exciting one, and nothing to do with Otters. Since March, Loch na Keal, in the centre of the island, had played host to no less than a Bearded Seal. Now, in case you are not yet saying, "My gosh that's amazing!", a word of explanation is required. The Bearded Seal is a denizen of the very high Arctic, where it is most at home among the pack-ice and no doubt spends much of its lifetime avoiding Polar Bears. Mull must seem pretty dull by comparison, like moving from Brixton to Dorset, but this one, inexplicably, had found its way south and was now, potentially, just a 10-minute drive away. According to *The Handbook of British Mammals*, there had been only about 10 previous records in Britain, so to get one on our family list would be a huge bonus. It was incredibly rare. I found myself feeling so giddy with excitement, as we turned off from Salen on the Ulva Ferry road, that I felt almost guilty.

Breathlessly, we arrived at the campsite that I had been told about during a phone call to the Hebridean Whale and Dolphin Trust. Even more encouragingly, it was thronged with people with binoculars and waterproof gear in shades of green.

"Any sign of the Bearded Seal?" I asked the nearest enthusiast.

He shook his head. "No, but there's a Sea Eagle nest just over there. The adult will be coming to feed the youngsters soon. It's fantastic."

Well, any other time in my life it would indeed have been fantastic. It was a great sight to see, and I'm meant to be a bird-watcher. But I was crestfallen. The Sea Eagle was a bird, confound it, and I was after a mammal, and I had a car full of children.

"We saw a Hen Harrier a few minutes ago…" the enthusiast went on.

"Splendid."

"Look! Oh my God, it's a Pterodactyl!"

All right, he didn't say that, but he might as well have done, for all the attention I was giving to his sightings. After a few moments he did confide that the Bearded Seal had been seen three days before, but no-one he knew

had been lucky since. It seemed as though the gloom pervading our trip
was beginning to take a liking to us and stick.

We watched from the campsite for a short while, but it was impossible
to see a seal at all from there, let alone a Bearded Seal. For the first time
in our holiday, heavy rain also began to fall. Carolyn and I looked at each
other in resigned fashion and sighed.

Well, there was always Tobermory, Mull's multi-coloured north-eastern
port and capital. After three days in the wilds we had decided that a bit of time
in civilisation would do us all good. Walking down a real street, for example,
something all too familiar at home, had become a novelty, and the coffee
shops were giving their siren call. The children also deserved a rest from all
the driving. Oh, and Bottlenose Dolphins were a possibility offshore.

Tobermory, happily, turned out to be a delight. We approached through
heavy rain and mist, entering the town in the most depressing conditions,
the sort that could easily have switched every scene to monochrome and
emptied the streets of life – a tourist officer's nightmare. But there was no
dampening of this town's vitality and colour. From the judiciously sited car
park, set beside the brewery – an imposing, confident building theatrically
spewing out smoke – it was possible to admire the famous seafront, lined
with three-storey buildings all painted in different bold colours. Tobermory
wasn't just thriving, it was teeming. Every tourist bus on Mull must have
been here, each coughing out eager pensioners in plastic macks, to wander
the streets and yield to the pull of Scottish-themed tourist traps, as helpless
as wasps on the trail of sweet things.

There was another kind of tourist, here, too, albeit a much more retiring
type. These were "Balamory Tourists". To those who have never heard
of it, "Balamory" is, or was, a children's programme for the under-fives,
distinctive for its appalling political correctness and wooden characters. It
was set in the town of Tobermory, but the makers, for reasons presumably
of brand, changed the name. Two years ago they pulled the plug on it,
but for a generation of parents Balamory was a staple part of their early
evening's viewing, the time when the only salve for tired parents and
hyperactive kids would be aspirins and a dose of CBeebies.

It was Carolyn, in particular, who was seized with enthusiasm for the
Balamory Tour. Several local shops stocked a modest map showing the
locations of the landmarks of the TV series and, despite the rain, it was she
who led us all, post-coffee, from one to another with an earnestness that, I

noted, seemed to exceed her regard for Bearded Seal-hunting.

"Oh, here it is – Miss Hooley's house," she exclaimed bright-eyed, as we hauled up to what was now a B&B. "And if we turn left, we'll find Spencer's!"

Spencer was a bright-dressing, black American who had been drafted in by the BBC's Casting department to get the racial mix right for a kids' show based on a remote-ish Scottish island. What's the world coming to?

What they don't show you in Balamory is just how precipitous the place is. You will find out if you search Tobermory for the hotel where Josie Jump stands on the balcony (don't ask). From the main street it was a pretty stiff climb and Sam, in particular, was complaining loudly.

"We're going to see Josie Jump's house," I said, trying to encourage him. He looked very blank.

"Who's Josie Jump?" Emily pitched in.

And then it occurred to us. Having been off the air for two years, Balamory had vanished from our children's consciousness. Carolyn and I were really doing this tour for our benefit.

And so, it seemed, were most Balamory Tourists. Creeping shiftily along the streets, pointing to otherwise unremarkable buildings, were a stream of 30-somethings with guilty looks on their faces, their children bored and complaining. Which, in a way, was quite reassuring: we weren't the only ones. Several times we exchanged glances with other sufferers, silently noting a shared history with complete strangers, a history of which we were all, it seemed, a little ashamed. It seemed that the town was diffident, too. Many of the distinctive houses had been painted a different colour to those featured on the TV, as if the townspeople were trying to wipe out a painful chapter in their past.

But a few hours in Tobermory had undoubtedly been a tonic for us and, despite the fact that the mist and rain had now settled on this part of Scotland, a dose of fish and chips had given us the will to do battle with Loch na Keal once again. The short drive took us back to the campsite, where the inclement conditions had even forced the Sea Eagle-watchers to worship elsewhere. There was nothing onshore and the beach was deserted by people and seals alike. For the next two hours or so we scanned the northern rim of the loch, driving this way and that, stopping a few times for a spot of rockpooling in the rain. I'm sure we checked every possible point at which a seal might haul out, but the shore was just shore, and none of the rocks moved their heads. The only long haul, to be truthful, was ours. We saw nothing on land and just a few heads in the water, none of which belonged to the Arctic wanderer. It looked as though we were going to be returning home empty... again.

But the tranquillity of our morning's drive returned and settled. The rockpooling had been fun – the thrill of adventure and education in the exotic Scottish mist. The change in the weather was both refreshing and magnificent, a welcome dose of cool and damp that added a melancholy edge to the scenery's loveliness. Now hidden from the sun, the islands in the loch were darker and more forbidding than they had been before, while to the west the mist covered the offshore, rendering the coast unseen and mysterious. Our days of sun had been unsubtle, but now Scotland was really expressing itself.

Late in the afternoon our admiration of the scenery was interrupted close at hand by the sight of people with binoculars and telescopes, clustered at the roadside. Considering they were all looking in the same place and that the rain was coming down quite hard – conditions that keep all normal people in their cars – this could only mean one thing: good wildlife.

Somewhat breathlessly, I enquired as to the source of interest.

"Otter," said a man under the hood of his raincoat, and pointed.

And there it was, a moving shape just offshore. Even with my initial view through raindrop-splattered binoculars, I could tell it was an Otter straight away. The flat head peered over the waves before the animal quickly submerged. When they dive Otters are a bit like whales, rolling slowly down, the tail disappearing last. I called the family.

It was a moment of relief as much as anything. I set up the telescope and, one by one, everybody managed a view as the animal went about its business 100 metres (325 feet) offshore. Samuel, for his part, marched out of the car, had a quick look, declared that it was raining and returned to the dry interior – a little bit of three-year-old amateur dramatics.

The great advantage of this Scottish Otter was that, not only was it perfectly visible now in the daylight, but we could also stand on the shore watching it without scaring it away. In fact, in contrast to the shy creatures we had been searching for in Somerset a month ago, this Otter seemed to be completely inured to any audience. Instead it simply swam around in the seaweed, occasionally chewing on the fish that it had nimbly caught. We could hear the chewing from shore, almost enough to remind our children that this sort of thing is bad table manners. Otters always give the impression of having a great time, revelling in the water, like human swimmers who have been working hard in a lesson and are now given free rein, and this one was no exception.

Spellbound as we were, it was now very wet, and the last ferry back to the mainland was not long due. We made a dash for it, driving a little too fast, worried that we might not get a place on the vessel. But astonishingly, despite the fact that this would be the last opportunity for anyone to get off Mull by public transport tonight, there was not a single other car queuing. We checked the timetable several times. Yes, this was the last ferry, but all we had for company at the slipway were a few Chaffinches feeding from crumbs at the tables of the long-closed café. And so it remained until the ferry lumbered into view and disgorged a similarly paltry load of arrivals.

Just before the ferry left, at the very last moment, a large lorry loaded with logs appeared and clanked on to the vessel, doubling its number of fare-paying passengers. The engine stopped and let off its burst of steam just as, presumably, its harassed driver did the same. As our family huddled on the upper deck to enjoy the breeze off the Sound of Mull, without a Bearded Seal but with a memorable Otter tucked into our consciousness, I bore the driver only good cheer and hoped that he, too, might enjoy a superb wildlife sighting in the early hours of the morning.

## May 29th – Resting on Top of the World

It's funny how one sighting of an eagerly awaited animal is so often followed by a second, that is both effortless and unintentional. In bird-watching it happens all the time; you see your first ever Lesser Spotted Woodpecker and – lo! – along comes the second less than a week later. I have never understood this rule of multiple sightings – I presume it is similar to the one that determines the inevitable arrival of three buses at once after a tiresome wait for just one – but it definitely holds good for all kinds of animal-watching.

For us, it happened with Otters. After yesterday's begrudging appearance in the wet weather, we were not subsequently overrun with Otters, but we did see two more. Both were doing exactly the same as the first – swimming just offshore in a kelp haven full of crabs and other sea creatures. Both kept us amused by diving, then reappearing some distance away, sometimes just a head in the water, sometimes appearing as an elongated, almost banana-shaped floating animal with a lithe tail.

What made these Otters a bonus – and perhaps a lesson – was that we weren't even looking for them. We had decided to take another day off, and devote tomorrow to the serious business of trying to spot sea mammals yet again (a result of Carolyn's military-style planning). So they were serendipitous sightings, or perhaps more significantly, they were non-pressured sightings. We enjoyed them all the more because we hadn't tried. Could we somehow employ the same lack of needfulness on future trips?

On this rest day we decided to visit the nearest large town, Fort William, and then go on to the Nevis Ranges to allow the children to experience the famous cable car that runs up towards Britain's tallest peak, Ben Nevis. Our view of the former was undoubtedly coloured by the fact that we got caught in one of the slowest and most irritating traffic jams that I can ever remember suffering – isn't it strange that small or medium-sized conurbations can so often produce absolute stinkers? Perhaps it was my mood, but it made Fort William look like a grey, shallow place, with little of an identity and even less love bestowed upon it, in the sense that its tourists were all off somewhere else (in the hills, or on a local distillery tour) and nobody seemed to give the shabby town itself a second thought. Thus ensnared, we stopped at a McDonald's in desperation, finding it peopled by witless teenagers and slightly embarrassed parents with young children – so in this respect at least Fort William was like the rest of the United Kingdom.

But our experience at the Nevis Range was simply breathtaking. It helped that the cable cars, all smoothly crafted and airy, were each named after famous mountain bikers, and one of these was called "Sam," leading to much reflected glory in our three-year-old. But our mode of transport could have been a hellhole and we would still have enjoyed the experience. The sun had burnt every scrap of cloud from the sky, so we could feast on the most minute detail of the panorama, as we rose upwards gradually, passing the treeline and even, to the children's excitement, bringing snowfields into close proximity. Emily, for her part, just drenched herself in the view, stating at regular intervals, "Whee, this is wonderful", and giggling, and reminding us both why we pay to give our children memories and delights.

A strange thing happened at the top of the cable car run, where there was a restaurant and shop complex and, either bizarrely or brilliantly, depending on your point-of-view, a children's outside play area with rugged swings and a slide. Carolyn, whom I thought might rail against the cold wind and rough walking hereabouts, experienced a sort of eureka moment. She had spent many of her childhood holidays walking in the Lake District, and sometimes in the Alps, and it never seemed to have rubbed off on her; here, on Ben Nevis, she discovered that it really had entered her blood all those years ago. Unexpectedly and irrationally, she felt an overwhelming desire to walk and walk and walk. Despite the fact that Emily and Samuel would probably have preferred a weekend on the naughty step than share this sudden passion for bipedal progression, the rest of us did as best we could, crawling upwards, aiming for a patch of snow where we might actually be able to touch the magic stuff. But the kids were slow and reluctant. They preferred to play at the bottom of the chair-lift or simply to dangle their legs over a stream rather than making an attempt on the summit of Ben Nevis. And, in spite of our best attempts at bribery, we just couldn't get them excited by the prospect of being cold, tired and slightly higher above sea-level. Carolyn was frustrated, yet also slightly high on adrenaline. For a moment I thought she was going to look up to the heavens, open her arms, swing round and round, and burst into song, Julie Andrews-style. But happily, despite being caught by the mood and altitude, she refrained.

Emily turned to me conspiratorially. "Why does Mummy want to walk up the mountain?" she enquired with bewilderment, as her mother tore on ahead of us.

I shook my head in wonder. "I really can't explain now," I replied.

Recovering over a high-altitude latte, I took the opportunity to ask the man in the shop about Mountain Hares. I suspected that these elusive animals might occur somewhere hereabouts.

He wasn't very encouraging. "The best place is really the Cairngorm Range, if you're going there," he replied.

We weren't. It was 100 kilometres (60 miles) to the east.

Once he knew I was genuinely interested in seeing these animals, however, he began to open up. He quoted me several sites, which, sadly, all involved long walks or very long drives. Despite my protestations that I had two children under six, and a wife under the influence of altitude and long-forgotten memories, he seemed oblivious to these impediments and detailed sites that became ever more extreme.

"Well, if you stop at the loch here," he would say, pointing at an alarmingly detailed OS map with incredibly tight contours and lots of those suspicious-looking scribbly rock-face markings on it, "you only have to ascend fifteen hundred feet, run under the waterfall here (mind that the river isn't in spate, by the way), jump this crevice (of course, you never look down at this point), and then descend the scree slope *there*. There's a little mountain hut where you can stay overnight and then, if you wake in the dark before dawn you only have a ten-mile section to get to this plateau, where you really can't miss the Mountain Hares…"

After a while, I began to think it might be easier to find a Yeti.

Actually, the truth is, the man probably had far too much knowledge about this part of Scotland locked inside his head, and not enough people to share it with.

We descended by cable car, this time enjoying watching several mountain bikers who appeared to be undertaking time trials down Ben Nevis's rump. Several actually beat us down. We marvelled at their bravura and skill. They were only kids, too, some of them barely into their teenage years. Yet they tore down what looked like a perilous slope replete with fearsome corners – a possible broken limb at every turn – at speeds that ensured that any mistake would be punished severely. Several times they vanished from view behind trees and, our hearts in our mouths, we waited for their colourful helmets and tops to reappear, undamaged. Thankfully, they always did. Sam, in particular, was profoundly impressed, especially since it was possible that one of these lads shared his own name.

As we reached the bottom I began to feel suddenly grateful for something. I was glad Carolyn's parents had never taken her mountain biking.

## May 30ᵗʰ - Points Mean Prizes

This morning, for the first time, we met a mammal that was to become our "friend". Not that the feeling, from the mammal's point-of-view, would have been reciprocated, since it is a bit difficult to get warm and cuddly with somebody who keeps catching you in a trap and generally manhandling you (well, each to their own…). But for us, the rest of the year would be marked by continual encounters with Wood Mice, and I would have to admit that we adored them from the start, and grew ever more fond of them as the months went by. In some ways, this small-change rodent was our "mammal of the year".

Wood Mice really are cute. Male Wood Mice would probably object to this description, if the reaction of my son to being called "cute", which he sometimes is, is anything to go by. They often fight other Wood Mice, they urinate with improbable frequency (I wonder whether, like human men, they stand adjacent to one another and have competitions to see who has the strongest flow?), and they probably snarl at each other, make high-intensity insults and think they are hard. But the fact is, they just look sweet and cuddly and gorgeous, and irredeemably lovable.

We caught our first one in a trap set out opposite Stag Cottage, in the most woody place I could find within reach, close to our stream, which, after the rain a couple of days ago, was beginning to take on a healthier flow. The Wood Mouse was small and coloured in a winsome pale brown, its eyes were big, its ears were huge and it had a long tail to give it a pleasing, balanced look. Everything about it was appealing – and that makes you wonder – what is it about mice that makes women stand up on chairs and scream at the sight of one? (And don't ever doubt that this occurs, because I've seen it happen.)

By now the mere act of setting and emptying small-mammal traps was becoming more and more perilous. In fact, the mere act of doing anything remotely outside-ish was fraught with hazard. Since the rain had fallen and made the landscape lush, it had unleashed hordes of infamous Highland midges, which now danced around every cubic centimetre of Scottish air, ready to make our lives hell. In the spot in the garden where, just three days ago, we had enjoyed sunbathing and playing games of tennis, we couldn't even spend five minutes without considerable discomfort. We came to understand why some of our friends had emphatically told us that they would never have a holiday in the Scottish Highlands.

Midges are curious torturers. Their bites don't hurt or annoy you in the same way that a single mosquito bite can. It is the cumulative effect that really gets to you. The midge bites feel like tiny pinpricks at first, then you realise that they are all over you and that you are itching everywhere. It's as though the air has sprayed you with slow-acting itching powder, and by the time you are flailing around trying to brush it off, it is too late. The midges get your ears and eyes and fingers – and then they work their way inside your clothes.

We stopped at Strontian to buy some repellent. Noticing our swollen faces, the lady immediately reached for an evil-looking potion behind her.

"I think you'll be needing this. It's organic."

We coated every millimetre of exposed skin. It didn't work, of course. The midges hadn't read the label.

Or had they? When I did check, it said: "Organic liquid to sell to gullible tourists who harbour the ridiculous notion that anything on earth can stop the insect hordes. God bless Scotland."

Carolyn, as I had mentioned earlier, had prescribed a return trip to the Point of Ardnamurchan today in an attempt to cure our acute lack of sea mammals. It turned out to be a masterstroke. Since we were now cured of Otter frustration, and we knew what to expect of the Ardnamurchan journey, the extraordinary length of the drive (1 hour 50 minutes for about 40 miles) no longer fazed us. Instead, we all enjoyed the journeytrip, buoyed by a CD given to us by the Scottish Tourist Board. Entitled something like "Games to Play in the Car with Bored Children", it combined jingoistic reminders about road safety with jolly songs and the eponymous games. Hilariously, however, the people that produced the CD clearly ran out of game ideas almost at once, and the only one they had much clue about was "I Spy".

"The next game," the voice would say, "is 'I Spy'."

"Not again," we would say in chorus.

"The idea of this game," continued the voice, unfazed, "is to guess how many things you can see from your car window that begin with the letter G. You've got one minute, starting... *now*."

"Grass!"

"Er, gorse!"

"Garage!"

"Where? There's no garage."

"Lorry!" yelled Samuel at the top of his voice. He is only three, though.

"We'll return to this game in a wee while," said the tape. "Now let's have a song..."

When they finally, inevitably, nominated the letter X, we swapped over to a CD of the *Veggie Tales*.

wood mose

If the Point of Ardnamurchan had been stunning and frustrating in equal measure on our last visit, this time it was just stunning. The sea was glinting in the strong sunlight; the surface was flat and calm across to Rum and Muck, and promised much. The lighthouse seemed even more imposing than it had before, and mercifully, it was open to visitors. There were quite a few other tourists about, to suggest that we weren't quite so far off the edge of the earth than we had felt previously. The feel-good nature of the day remained with us.

Sam was almost exploding with anticipation, so we made for the lighthouse first. Surprisingly, entrances were staggered, with just a few people allowed up at any one time. We soon discovered why; much as the lighthouse looked huge, by the time you reached the top there was only a small balcony, which soon got very cramped. Reaching the top was no mean feat, either, especially if you were only four, but Emily helped Sam count the steps – 129 in all – and we all hauled ourselves up eventually.

The moment we arrived at the balcony, however, Carolyn froze. Although the sheer drop was protected by a tall and strong railing filled in with a network of wire, over which the kids couldn't possibly have hurled themselves, the problem was that the balcony, quite naturally, went all around the building, so that with a few quick footsteps it was possible for the children to run away completely out of sight, 30 metres (100 feet) above the ground. Coupled with this, looking down was enough to make anyone with a slight fear of heights dizzy, and so Carolyn, whose fear of heights is only exceeded by her fear of missing children, turned into something of a nervous wreck.

Going back inside, we took a ladder and climbed somewhat gingerly to the light room, where an impeccably dressed, elderly man was holding court. He had a severe face and a less than soft manner, and his whole mien was somewhat melancholic. Actually, in looks and voice he recalled the dour Scots character, Fraser, in *Dad's Army*.

It turned out that he had been the last full-time lighthouse keeper before mechanisation (and the Point of Ardnamurchan was one of the last lighthouses in Britain to change over), so you couldn't possibly argue that he had a right to be there. But he wasn't the most child-friendly of guides.

Despite everything, I decided to ask him how the sightings of cetaceans had been in recent days. "Any Minke Whales in the last week?" I enquired cheerfully.

He looked at me as though I had just asked whether his wife could pose nude for a Women's Institute calendar.

"They're very, very scarce here," he replied, shaking his head and casting his hand dismissively over one of the richest stretches of coast for cetaceans in Europe.

He was completely wrong, but I pressed ahead.

"Did you see the Orcas last week?"

"I've heard the rumours."

Oh, for goodness' sake. I had always thought that being a lighthouse keeper must have been a romantic, if not inspiring job, but clearly the hardship and long hours must have got into this guy's bones.

He might as well have said: "You're doomed!"

Shoo

But we weren't doomed. Not a bit of it. From the lighthouse I had seen a couple of aggregations of feeding birds, much closer in than a few days before, and I was eager to get down to the low cliff and set my telescope to search the sea.

And this time, it worked. It really did work. The adrenaline kicked in when, scanning across a mass of kittiwakes and guillemots, I finally noticed a couple of fins. At last, real fins, real sea mammals. It was a great moment.

"I've got some Porpoises, everybody," I announced.

A pretty nervous few minutes followed as I tried to get the family on to them. This wasn't easy at all because, being Common Porpoises, their fins were quite low in the water and, like most sea mammals, they never showed themselves for more than a few moments at a time. However, it was to our advantage that the animals were too excited by the concentration of fish around them to worry about making life difficult for a foursome of humans. Emily, at least, got on to them with no problem at all – little black fins that made all the difference in the world.

We celebrated in our signature style, with two cups of coffee and a pair of Fruit-Shoots at the local café. In fact, Carolyn and I were pleased enough to buy the children a souvenir each. Emily chose a necklace made out of local seashells, while Samuel opted for a water pistol – they can be deliciously gender-definitive, our offspring. Within minutes, the latter gift had been put to disreputable use, when Samuel fired a little overenthusiastically and drenched the leg of a passer-by.

We left Ardnamurchan in disgrace.

Wood mose

It was the evening before our departure and, for this reason, or another we couldn't fathom, none of us could sleep. The children went to bed fairly late, at around eight o'clock, but by nine were still wide awake, talking and singing and messing about with the cushions in their room, which was still lit up by the lengthened day. This was hardly ideal in advance of the long journey home tomorrow.

"Oh, let's go for a night drive," suggested Carolyn. "Maybe they will fall asleep in the car, and maybe we'll see a Wildcat."

Well maybe. But we didn't.

We did see a cat, though. It was a tabby, and our hearts missed a beat as it slunk across the road, just as its wild relative had done a few days ago. But it was clearly much smaller and, on its journey to escape our approaching headlights, it took refuge beneath a caravan parked on the roadside. Somehow, the idea of Wildcats and caravans didn't fit.

We saw a Roe Deer, too – our first on this trip – dashing away into the deep, dark conifer forest uphill from Stag Cottage; literally a deer in the headlights, making quite a to-do about its escape from sight. Honestly, these fleet-footed drama queens do go in for a touch of the theatricals.

The light eventually gave way to proper evening. The stars came out, the moors were thrillingly lonely, the roads were almost completely devoid of traffic. We stopped and listened in silence and smelt the moorland grasses and the fresh air. We would miss this place.

## May 31st – The Island of the Wallabies

If we had enjoyed a mammal bonanza on the West Coast of Scotland, we would not have contemplated stopping at Loch Lomond to see the colony of Red-necked Wallabies. Had we seen such delights as Minke Whales and Bearded Seals, we would have motored by without a second thought. But this, as you know if you have read the last sections, is not what happened at all, and it made the eccentric possibility of us looking for Australian animals among heather and bracken, rather than in their natural eucalyptus-dominated surroundings, a reality.

Our hesitancy was not caused by an unwillingness to see the Red-necked Wallabies – they would have been fun at any time. Our hesitancy was based on economics. In order to have any chance of success, we had to get to the uninhabited island of Inchconnachan, and since this island was off the tourist route, preventing any easy way of getting there, we would need to charter 50-quid's-worth of boat.

Still, we made the decision to go, and soon found ourselves on the jetty serving the village of Luss, on the western side of Loch Lomond. It commanded a splendid view across a network of small, thickly wooded islands dotted across the broadest part of the loch, and it was extraordinarily busy. People were making the most of the fine weather by crowding along the adjacent beach; a good few, mainly teenagers, were also amusing themselves by jumping off the jetty into the water, right next to a large, imposing "No swimming" sign.

It turned out that our pilot was a lady by the name of Mary. She ushered us on to the small motorboat, fitted Emily and Samuel into garishly bright yellow lifejackets, and then proceeded to throw cold water over all of our plans.

"You want to see the Wallabies?" she enquired.

When we replied in the affirmative, she frowned. "Well, you've come at the wrong time of year. If you really want to see them, you ought to come in October. They will have bred by then and there isn't so much ground vegetation."

I checked my watch. Yes, it was still May, and we were right here, now. Not in October.

"You'll be very lucky indeed to see them," said Mary, shaking her head and turning the ignition. "Now hold on while we manoeuvre out here."

As we chugged at moderate speed through the dark blue water, enjoying the refreshing breeze, Mary frowned again.

"I must say, you've really come at the wrong time of day. Usually the Wallabies rest now after their morning feed, and they are very difficult to see. It's the late afternoon when they are most active. Then, I would say, at least you've got a chance."

I began to worry about wasting our precious money. Still, the kids were enjoying the voyage – they couldn't stop smiling. The green, curvaceous hills that rose up from the loch-side looked spectacular reflected in the water, and the broad lake, together with its forested islands (some of them populated by conifers), gave the landscape a slightly Canadian feel. In the distance, one of Loch Lomond's famous sea-planes, all gleaming white in the sun, was making a pass over the northern edge of the loch. The boat was going fast enough to be mildly exhilarating. This was good stuff.

"I must warn you," Mary went on. "There are ticks on the island, and there is Lyme's Disease present, which is very nasty if you get it. So you need to wear boots, and the children must tuck their socks in. When you've finished, make sure that you check yourselves very carefully in case you have any on your clothes."

Mary was beginning to sound like a health-and-safety manual.

"Did I tell you," she went on, "there are no paths, so you'll gave to do quite a bit of scrambling? It won't be easy and you might get cuts and bruises."

I was dying to ask her whether she felt we had much chance of getting out of Inchconnachan alive, but held my tongue (not literally, of course – that would have been potentially dangerous.)

Besides holding unseen hazards behind every corner, the island also lacked a jetty, so Mary coaxed our motorboat into a sheltered bay where, with a nifty piece of steering, she beached the bows enough for us to jump out. Somewhat to my surprise, there were two other boats in the bay. One was inhabited by a stripped-down man who was sleeping blissfully in the stern of his expensive-looking cruiser, his chest impressively hairy and his eyes covered by glasses so large and shiny that, for all we knew, he could have had a TV monitor fixed inside them. The other, equally ostentatious vessel was unoccupied.

"There's a small group camping on the west side of the island," Mary told us. "That's their boat. But you will need to look in the eastern part, which is that way." She pointed up towards a low hill, which, admittedly, was covered with impenetrable-looking vegetation.

"How do we get around?" asked Carolyn.

"There isn't a map," said Mary. "Sorry. But there is an abandoned holiday cottage a hundred or so yards uphill. I suggest you use that to orient yourselves. Once you start up the hill, keep going right."

Mary returned to her favourite subject. "You'll be very lucky to see anything," she replied. "But give me a call when you want to be picked up. I'll see you here when you've had enough."

"I'll call you as soon as we've seen the Wallabies," I said, impishly. Mary waved. She was probably off to attend a bridge afternoon, or something similarly time-consuming.

Well, perhaps we had more chance of seeing the Loch Ness Monster than a Red-necked Wallaby, but being left here on this uninhabited island, 1,200 metres ($^3/_4$ mile) in length and covered in heavy brush and thick woodland, on a warm day in late May, was simply inspirational.

We walked the short distance to a sandy beach and sat down to have lunch. We could have been on a deserted tropical island somewhere near Fiji, for the thrill of isolation we felt. It was for precisely this sort of adventure that we embarked upon our year-long mammal-hunt in the first place.

The Wallabies of Inchconnachan form one of the very few viable colonies of this species that exist outside Australia (there are a few in New Zealand and some on the Isle of Man). They have been here since 1975, when a certain Lady Arran Colquhoun, who owned the island (and from whose surname the island derives its name), introduced two pairs from Whipsnade Zoo. The idea was to turn Inchconnachan into a safari park. The plan fell flat, but nobody told the Wallabies. They thrived and continued to breed, and, there are still at least 30 individuals on the island today. Occasionally the animals have a bust-up (well, they *are* Australian), and one or more goes Swimabout, making it across almost 1,600 metres (1 mile) of water as far as the mainland, but these pioneering attempts to colonise the rest of Britain are usually squashed under the wheels of a car. Thus the colony is something of a backwater in Red-necked Wallaby distribution terms, making it an interesting curiosity to give tourists a few moments of thought, and mammal-watchers a strain on the wallet.

Now, whether it was because Mary was merely enjoying a well-honed joke with us, or whether we were lucky, or whether we are just naturally good at observing Australian mammals as opposed to English ones, I cannot say. But we found the Wallabies without any trouble at all. We aimed for the highest part of the island, where there was some uneven ground and moderately open scrub dominated by heather and bilberry (the two main components of the Wallaby's diet here), and there they were, two or three of them, standing still and watchful. They were decidedly handsome animals, only about the size of a Fox, with exactly the long tails, springy hind legs and short, boxing hands that you would expect of Macropods (the marsupial family to which wallabies and kangaroos belong). Predominantly grey-brown all over, they had a pleasing reddish-brown patch on the neck and shoulders, and a very distinct white line running from the black muzzle to just below the eye. The hands were black, as if duly kitted-out for a fight.

But far from being in fighting mode, this lot were half asleep. If we went too close they shuffled off with their unmistakable two-footed hop and disappeared into the brush, but otherwise they just stood and watched us in that classic, disinterested way that grazing animals so often seem to adopt when their heads aren't down at the grass. One thing's for sure: they wouldn't have paid 50 quid to see *us*.

We saw the Wallabies so easily that we had plenty of time to enjoy the rest of the island. We climbed up slopes; did some bird-watching; turned over a few logs to see whether we could find an isolated colony of Inchconnachan Wood Mice; played a special game of uninhabited island hide-and-seek; found a deep, dark grove of Douglas-firs in which to feign terror; and finally came across the abandoned bungalow that Mary had mentioned in her fight-them-on-the-beaches instructions. It was a large, wooden structure, with several outhouses and was tucked away in a small clearing. Apparently it had been built in the 1920s by an admiral, who, having moved to Scotland from the Far East, decided that he liked the taste of solitude, and lived there until he ran out of money. Other owners took residence until Lady Arran began to use it as a holiday cottage in the 1970s: presumably she needed to take occasional refuge from her exploits of the waters of the loch – she was the fastest woman on water for many years and a demon in powerboats. Presumably it was from this building, now sadly abandoned, its windows broken and beams decaying, that the mad plot to fill the island with Wallabies was originally hatched.

Naturally, Mary wasn't available when we first tried to call her on the mobile phone, giving us a little longer than we expected to enjoy our treat on this island. Once she did pick us up again, she kept up the same tone as she had before.

"You really were very, very lucky," she went on…. Though I think I detected just the hint of a knowing smile as she steered us back to the port of Luss.

June

## June 24ᵗʰ – Sinking In and Dropping Off

There comes a time during a family-based project such as ours when you do wonder how much the children are getting out of the endeavour. We knew that Emily and Samuel had had plenty of fun, and that was part of the point of what we were doing. But had it really been much of an education for them? Had they actually appreciated spending time outdoors looking for animals and, when they had seen them, had the experience impressed anything upon them? And even though they had each seen more than 20 species, and thus undoubtedly already held their respective ages' record for seeing wild mammals in Britain in a year (and would probably hold it for ever), did this actually make a jot of difference in their lives?

Well, today I had part of the answer.

Carolyn, being a devoted mum and, today, a devoted daughter-in-law as well, had taken my children and my 76-year-old mother (of whom more later) to a picnic at Furzey Gardens, in the New Forest. It was just a bit of recreational time to get everybody out of the house while I was preparing some work on Nightjars prior to the shooting of a TV programme.

When they all returned, I asked them, somewhat casually, how they had got on. I expected Emily to talk about the enchanted nature of the place,

Carolyn to enthuse about the teashop and Samuel to tell me nothing at all. But that's not what I got.

"Daddy! Daddy! We saw a Wood Mouse!" exclaimed Emily, almost exploding.

"Wood Mouse," repeated Sam. And Carolyn. It sounded like the highlight of the visit.

"It ran away from the bottom of a tree where we were having a picnic," yelled Emily.

Wood Mouse. Get it? Not just a mouse, a Wood Mouse. My daughter, wife and son could now differentiate between several sorts of mouse.

"Emily," I asked. "How did you know it was a Wood Mouse?"

What did I expect her to reply? "Well, the pelage was largely grey-brown, but warmer above than a House Mouse, lacking any russet across the chest like a Yellow-necked. It had whitish underparts, characteristic large eyes and was clearly not so heavy-bodied as a Yellow-necked."

"Oh, Daddy, I've seen one before," she replied, groaning.

Later in the day, I went on a reconnoitre to the extreme western edge of the New Forest with a wildlife film cameraman, called Graham, to find Nightjars. Next week there was to be a state visit to this site from Mike Dilger, filming for *The One Show*, and we needed to know that the birds would be co-operative.

The Nightjars were fine, and we also acquired a trophy. Film cameramen get themselves into some strange places and, during one trudge across the heathland, probably placing his feet where no man had probably gone for years, Graham almost stepped upon a deer antler. I was so excited by this discovery – having never found a deer antler before – that I probably slightly overreacted. I blurted out immediately how interesting they would be to show to the children and Graham, being the mild-mannered and gracious bloke that he is, said that I should have it. Considering that it was he who had found it in the first place, this seemed disingenuous of me, but it was also too late. It soon found its way back to our living room, where it still is today.

The children were suitably impressed, and no wonder. The antler was almost half as tall as the kids, strong and with extremely sharp points. Several times while we were handling it there were near-misses to eyes and other parts of the anatomy, and eventually Carolyn and I had to ban the children from playing with it altogether. But feeling the antler and seeing it up close certainly demonstrated that, when fighting, deer have formidable weapons, and they don't mess about.

Identifying the antler was intriguing, because it took us into a completely new world, with terms that we had never heard before. Apparently the pointy bits at the end of the antler, the points that probably do the most harm to rivals, are known as "tines" and, as you doubtless know, some males have more elaborate antlers than others and therefore more tines. This antler was very large, as I've mentioned, and it also had a bottom tine that skewed away at an angle of more than 90 degrees to the main branch, indicative of Red Deer. This lowest point is known as a "brow tine". This antler had another branch half way up, known as the "trez tine"; other Red Deer may have two points before the top tines, the lower one being known as the "bez tine". None of this was especially significant to our project, but it certainly helped Carolyn and I to improve our chances at Scrabble.

We are all so familiar with deer antlers that it is easy to forget what remarkable things they are. They are, essentially, both weapons to keep other males at bay, and a form of bling to make the does throb with desire. Antlers serve little, if any, survival purpose – if they did, the does would have them too; but no, apart from in Reindeer, they are exclusively buck kit. Besides, the males don't even keep them all year long. Incredibly, after going to all the trouble of growing their formidable weapons, once the antlers have served their purpose, they are shed during the months of autumn and winter. All that bony growth, put together by a good deal of munching minerals and consuming earth, just one day suddenly falls off, like a limb in a *Monty Python* animation. And then the antlers grow back again, surrounded by skin known as velvet, which itself falls off when its function of fuelling growth is not longer required. It all seems incredibly wasteful.

Mind you, boys, how many times have we bought clothes to look hard and horny? Us bucks, we're all the same.

## June 27th – Going Batty

It was late June, and high time for a bat walk.

Bats are the small currency of British mammal-watching. There are 16 breeding species, which means that, for anyone trying to see a good number of mammals in Britain, these remarkable flying machines require serious attention. Up until now our family's only bat encounter had been with the horseshoes in February, a good four months ago, which might lead you to suppose that, with half the year gone, we were being a bit negligent about the critters. But the truth is that bat-hunting before June is a bit of a lottery; midsummer is only the beginning of the "bat season", when bats look and act like they should, jinking actively about in the twilight and scaring anyone with a vivid imagination.

If you take a year and squeeze it into an imaginary day, the behaviour of bats mirrors that of human students: they get up late and stay late. Whilst most hibernating creatures stretch and yawn in early March, when the sun is first showing its strength, bats remain torpid for at least another month and a half. Once roused they don't necessarily come to and start their day with any enthusiasm, either; they may continue dozing periodically well into May, depending on how many insects are around in the night skies. Bats have to be active in June and July, when the females are suckling young, but in some ways they really come alive in the autumn, when the evening of the year induces a certain mellow friskiness, and social interactions are charged with excitement and lust.

Thus it was that we were entering the bat household only once the inhabitants were finally all up and active. The skies had finally filled with flying insects and their hunters, and we were free at last to cash in on the increase in bat numbers. At least in theory.

But bat-watching, as anyone who has tried it will tell you, is a highly specialised craft. It is not at all easy to tell the species apart, even if you see them well. These are one of the hardest casts of lookalikes in the whole field of natural history. A bird-watcher, for example, would never start with the premise that all birds are similar; even a novice distinguishes many of them easily. A potential fish-watcher might begin with the assumption that all fish look alike, but it won't be long before he or she is familiar with the different shapes or characteristics that quickly and decisively set the species apart. But bats are quite another matter. It is almost impossible to distinguish the different ones with a quick view in flight, even with a great deal of experience. They are tricky enough in the hand. And indeed, even if you idly flick through a series of pictures or photographs in a book, I defy you to see many differences at all. "Oh yes, that's a bat," you would say. But you cannot look at a picture in a book and then ever be sure that the secret shape that flickers over your garden is a Common Pipistrelle or a Serotine. You need to study much harder, and become a specialist.

Bats, therefore, need experts and, for our family, that meant meeting up once again with our friends from the winter horseshoe bat-hunt, Pete Banfield and Nick Tomlinson. Nick, tall and jovial, was clearly in summer plumage, stripped down to the enthusiast's essentials of T-shirt, trousers and bat detector, while Pete looked just the same as he had earlier in the year. He still had a long-sleeved shirt and jacket with myriad pockets, plus torch and detector, notebook, pen, and who knows what else. And while Nick watched the skies and chatted with us, Pete constantly perused his bat detector with the same implacable concentration that a teenager would reserve for an Xbox. They were a perfect pairing.

We did not have their services exclusively. This was a themed walk run by the local authority entitled "Go Batty at Radipole Lake" (that's the walk, not the authority), which had attracted a goodly set of participants including, to my surprise, several kids as young as ours. We were surprised because, at this time of the year, bats come out very late, way past the bedtime of any non-obsessive parent's child. By the time the walk started it was already 9:30pm, and Emily, for her part, had had a short doze in the car. Sam, meanwhile, was up for a Personal Lateness Best and proud of it, still awake and raring to go. But we worried for both of them, uncertain as to whether they would cope with the walk ahead.

Radipole Lake is a curious anomaly, a large area of prime marshland right in the middle of the extensive urban part of Weymouth, one of Dorset's largest seaside towns. There is a smart, well-equipped visitor centre at one end of a large, inspector-infested car park and right next to an array of tacky fast-food joints. Walking along Radipole's trails, which are all public footpaths, is an eclectic experience, during which you can see ugly buildings looming over whispering reed tops, and pass a retired couple with expensive binoculars one moment and a down-at-heel, blank-eyed drug-user the next (Weymouth, despite its pleasing seaside persona, has a serious drug problem). Radipole is every bit the jewel in Weymouth's environmental crown, except that you might say the crown is a little tarnished.

Mind you, even for anyone used to Radipole's eccentricities, our ragtag band of bat enthusiasts young and old must have made for an unexpected sight as we bobbed between the reed heads going Batty. We might even have looked alarming. Prior to setting off, Nick had pulled off the impressive feat of providing almost everyone with a bat detector to use (impressive because these bits of equipment cost about £120 each). Bat detectors look a little bit sinister – they are hand-held black boxes with dials and switches, the sort of thing that was always used as a prop in science-fiction TV series, such as "Blake's 7" or "Doctor Who". Anyone walking past us might have wondered whether they would be monitored, searched or otherwise abused in some way.

It is bat detectors, however, that have revolutionised the study of their eponymous subjects. It was once thought that bats were almost mute as well as blind, but actually they are neither. They are perfectly capable of catching small insects on the wing by sight, if there is enough illumination. More usually, however, bats use echolocation, shouting out ultrasonic signals that rebound off hard objects, including prey, and paint a radar-like pattern of echoes in the night sky that is so up to date and clear that bats can chase and catch fast-moving moths or flies. Most of what a bat yells out is far too high-pitched for us to pick up (if we did, it could literally deafen us), so the bat detector acts as a kind of interpreter, converting the echolocation pulses into audible and palatable equivalents well inside our hearing range. Happily, different bats have different voices and speak in different patterns, allowing many of the species to be identified while they are flying around. And even more happily, since the pulses are converted into sounds below the bats' spoken range, they don't interfere with the animals' activities.

However, in order for a detection to be made, there have to be bats. It doesn't matter what equipment you have, or how hard you try, you can't find what isn't there.

Our walk started badly. Tonight was not a typical June night. It was warm and muggy but, unusually, it was also windy, and the bats didn't appear to like the wind.

Nick was the designated leader of our party, and it was his job to find us the quarry. "I'm pretty confident tonight," he had said at the beginning. "We have five species of bats here at Radipole…"

"Look for noctule first," he suggested as we wandered the early yards. "Noctules come out earlier than any other species; about now, while it's still quite light. They fly the highest and have the longest, most pointed wings. We usually see one here."

No noctule showed.

"It's June. Many female bats are suckling and they must find food for their young, so they should come out tonight, even in these conditions," he assured us, looking around with a degree of agitation.

The dusky skies remained blank.

"There's a sequence of species," Nick began after more fruitless minutes. "The pipistrelles and Daubenton's Bats should be out soon." He was almost beseeching now.

His voice began to rise slightly as he aimed his detector into the gloaming. "Normally some are showing by now," he accosted the ultrasonic silence.

We had reached a bridge over the narrow end of a reed-fringed lake. We all stood there in silence, thoroughly enjoying the unusual delight of spending a midsummer night on a bat walk, and amusing ourselves with Nick's obvious, but entirely unearned discomfort. "I've never done a trip like this without seeing something," he said dolefully, shaking his head, as if claiming mitigation to a High Court judge.

But it was time for the bats to take pity on him. At that precise moment one zoomed over us. I yelled and pointed.

"Daddy's seen a bat!" announced Emily to the crowd, as everyone looked in every direction and missed it. No matter. Soon another appeared, and another. The bat detectors were switched on and Nick visibly relaxed. We were in business.

"These are all pips," remarked Pete – the sort of thing you might say if you were examining an apple core. We were still in the process of learning bat jargon, and it was only after a moment or two that I realised that he meant "pipistrelles". The bats that were flickering past were pipistrelle bats.

The pipistrelle bat is the smallest and by far the commonest of the British bats, and although it often looks diminutive in the wild, as we were finding out, that's nothing to how minute it appears when settled. It can literally fit into a matchbox and, by extension, that allows it to crawl through the smallest cracks to get into warm places, such as roofs and the gaps between tiles, making it a familiar sight around houses and in gardens. It is also the bat most often found in church belfries, and old buildings, such as churches, suit it perfectly. There are records of small roosts being found behind church noticeboards, and you can imagine the shock that such a discovery might have caused for anyone who doesn't like bats. This midget feeds on gnats and is reputed to take more than a thousand in the course of a night. By extrapolation, that approximates to a human being eating a thousand chips in a night, which shows just how quickly these animals must burn up fuel.

In recent years, there has been a discovery concerning pipistrelles that has rocked the bat world to its very core. As long as bat detectors had been in use, it had been noticed that pipistrelle bats seemed to give off two distinct echolocation calls, one with a peak of energy at 45 kilohertz, and one at 55 kilohertz, but never anything in between. This is not the sort of difference that you or I would notice, but using different frequencies is pretty fundamental to the bats themselves – they would equate to different languages. The thing was, there seemed no clear physical differences to go with the different languages. Gradually, however, it was noticed that bats grouped together according to their calls, and even seemed to use slightly different habitats. In the last few years, the suspicions of some were confirmed by DNA analysis – Britain has two common and widespread species of pipistrelle bat! After hundreds of years of thinking we just had one, the public of Britain were delivered a new pipistrelle, unveiled as a "cryptic" species. It was like suddenly discovering that we have two capital cities, not one, or that Elton John is actually two people, or that there are two Millennium Domes, one hidden under the other.

The same two-for-one deal was duly delivered to our group of bat lovers.

"Some of these are Soprano Pipistrelles," said a man called Iain, referring to the higher-voiced 55 kilohertz speakers. "But the first bat was a Common Pipistrelle. Nice to have them both. I would expect mainly Sopranos here in this wet habitat."

And thus our family total for the year clicked from 24 to 26 species almost in a blink.

By now there were plenty of bats flying past us, quite high over the reedbeds and scattered willows and brambles. Most people in the group were now conversant enough with the detectors to have put the setting to 45 kilohertz, and every time a bat went past there was a chorus of emissions from the different machines. Considering that the volley of clicks emanating from the pips made a sound that could politely be described as flatulent, the overall sound from the machines amounted to one enormous raspberry. Quite what the onlookers must have made of this I can only speculate.

"Here's a Daub," shouted a bat worker above the din.

"At last," replied Nick, almost unhealthily relieved by the appearance of a third bat species, the Daubenton's Bat. "This one is a distinctive little blighter," he said, beginning to enthuse. "It hunts much lower to the water than any other bat, running little transects fractionally above the surface. It can fly so low that it will actually go beneath this bridge..."

On cue, the bat did exactly this.

Emily inspects Beaver field signs in the Cotswold Water Park – in this case the rodent's been gnawing at the foot of a tree.

Pointing out Chinese Water Deer at Woodwalton Fen – or at least, trying to.

Phoebe Carter shows Emily
the Beaver pelt.

Those famous Beaver teeth
are made for gnawing.

Rockpooling at the
Point of Ardnamurchan.

Bat workers need to be
well-protected. This bat
worker is holding a bad-
tempered Noctule in the
Savernake Forest.

The Mink trap at the Cotswold Water Park.

Our nemesis for much of the year, the Otter. It took a trip to the Hebrides to nail this one.

Penny Rudd checks the contents of a Longworth Trap near the grounds of Chester Zoo. Sam doesn't seem to be concentrating.

Emily admires one of our favourite mammals of the year, a Water Shrew.

The easiest place to see Mountain Hares in Britain is the Cairngorm Range in the Highlands of Scotland.

"Isn't that Simon King over there?" Fallow Deer contemplate their easy lives in the New Forest.

One of our star mammals of the year, the sleek and beautiful Pine Marten.

Looking up at bat boxes in the Savernake Forest.

Although Red Squirrels are in retreat over much of Britain, we saw them easily on Brownsea Island, Dorset.

Risking life and limb to see the Red-necked Wallabies on Loch Lomond.

We never quite got to grips with sea mammals. After many attempts we finally saw Bottlenose Dolphins on December 22nd.

"Any bat you see just above the water is likely to be this species," Nick went on. "It eats a lot of caddisflies and mayflies. The water surface is a good niche because it's just crammed with flying insects. So the pips fly at head-height and the Daubenton's fly just above the water. And, as we've seen, here the Daub usually comes out a little later in the dusk, about half an hour after sunset. But it might be later tonight."

Revelling in its glory, the Daubenton's performed another pass under the bridge, showboating like a model on a catwalk, only one in a severe hurry. Under the guidance of our experts, this bat was no longer just a flying shape; it began to acquire a character and identity. Moreover, its clicks were not as "wet" as those of the pipistrelles, they were drier and more regular, like machine-gun rolls. Interestingly, however, they also showed a peak of 45 kilohertz, just like the Common Pipistrelle.

Our lesson in bats was beginning to demystify these creatures. Up until now, I had always viewed flying bats with suspicion and defeatism, always suspecting that I would never "crack" them, in the sense of understanding the different species. It felt like learning a new language. Now I knew some of the characters and could, metaphorically, say "Oui" and "Bonjour" with confidence. I hoped that some of this would also have rubbed off on the kids.

Mind you, Samuel had almost dropped off by now, having long sunk into the luxury of the old pushchair that we kept for special occasions. After the finery of the bats' eventual performance, most of the party started back on the short walk to our respective cars, deliciously satisfied by the evening's entertainment. I'll assure you, it beat any episode in the history of "EastEnders", as far as this commentator is concerned, and it was real life, too.

Once we reached the bridge next to the Visitor Centre, it was quite dark, and a nearby streetlight shone brightly under the still-murky sky. We were about to say goodbye when, suddenly, Pete's bat detector sprang into life once more. Immediately we could tell that it was something quite different to what we had heard before. This was a very loud "chip, chop" that seemed almost to burst the detector; it was like a lick-smacking sound from an animal at least the size of a Pterodactyl.

"That's a Noctule," said Nick. "There's so much energy in that call that it could blow your head off."

We believed it, too. But where was the monster in the skies? We looked up but, since it was dark and we were looking for a brown bat high above us, we were pushing our luck, to say the least.

There were more sounds, and another excited announcement from Pete. "Serotine, over the top of the Visitor Centre." This was yet another species. I knew that this was quite a big bat, too, although smaller than a Noctule, but out here, in the field, it was hard to tell.

"How do you know that it's a Serotine, Pete?" I enquired.

"Less regular calls than Noctule, not as loud," he replied. "They sound more like hand-claps."

They probably did, but, by now, most of us, I suspect, were beginning to get confused. It was though we had been learning French in a classroom, and now had been unleashed into a market full of gabbling voices, too numerous to decode individually. We had just about managed the pips and Daubs, but that was enough for a night. Even so, the leaders did manage to find a spotlight and follow some of the bats in the sky. And now we could see that the flying insect-hunters, having teased poor Nick into submission, were all over the sky, despite the strong breeze.

"You were lucky," said Nick to us. "You've managed to see all five of the common species here in one night. In fact, anywhere you might go in southern Britain, these are the species you are most likely to see flying around." By now his voice verged on the triumphant.

I felt like saying, "Not half as lucky as you, Nick. For a long time, we thought we wouldn't see any bats at all. And neither did you!" But that was hardly fair on a man who had tried his very best to help us see the nocturnal mammals we so desperately needed.

Nick will be interested in the derivation of the Serotine's name, though. Basically it means "late" – aptly for this particular bat, and its colleagues.

## June 28th – The Mother of All Bat Box Checks

You might think that one bat-chasing day in a weekend would be enough for any normal human being. You might think that two trips would be going well over the top, leaving you to use the word "obsession" to describe the perpetrators. Well, if you think that (and you have a point) ask the Dorset Bat Group. It was they who organised today's bat-box checks in mid-Dorset, hot on the heels of the trip to Radipole. It was they who must have sorted out their weekly shopping, their bills and their DIY and set the video to record their favourite programmes. It was they who summoned the energy, after staying out late, to get up again and think about bats, load ladders into their cars, and make the sheer effort to make contact with their favourite animals again.

They are the people who turn out through much of the year, year after year, usually unpaid, fuelled solely by curiosity and love for their subject, to climb up those ladders, to count and identify bats that might or might not be roosting in the boxes that, in previous years, they spent money upon and spilt sweat to put up. These people are sheer enthusiasts. Perhaps they are obsessives, but I prefer the company of obsessives to most "normal" people any day. Obsessives are a privilege to meet. They break down frontiers, they challenge orthodoxy, and they allow that most basal of qualities, curiosity, to allow them to rise out of the day-to-day blandness for which the rest of us settle.

God bless them.

And it was these same folk who persuaded us, despite a few misgivings, to come along today on this bat-box check.

"You should see some bats very close up," they told us, coaxingly. "And you might even find a new species for your project." It was they, frankly, who made the temptation to join them all but unbearable.

One misgiving we had, however, was the presence of my mother. She was staying with us, having come over from her home in Australia, and, with only two weeks in the company of her youngest grandchildren, we weren't sure how much she would want to spend an afternoon at the bottom of a ladder in the middle of a wood, waiting to find out if a number of boxes half way up a tree might be housing some small mammals that scare less indomitable people half-witless. Especially when she was 76 years old. It's not the sort of thing that people do.

But we needn't have worried. My mother was delighted at the prospect. She has always had an adventurous spirit. And besides, the idea was hardly novel to her. My childhood was chock-full of wildlife-hunting. It was defined by it. And my mum wasn't necessarily the passive encourager of her wildlife-mad son, she was often the perpetrator of trips and adventures. It was she who first showed me the ducks in a London park, and the beetles in a pond and the squirrels in the garden. It was she who always made sure that holidays had a bird-watching element. It was she who fed the pets that I loved but hadn't a clue about looking after. It was she who watched wildlife programmes with me and tried to listen to my endless lectures about birds. It was an upbringing that, she realised, was bound to lead to something like this.

In short, it was entirely her fault that we were on a bat count in the first place.

As you know, bats are nocturnal animals, coming out at night and roosting by day. But actually it isn't quite as simple as that: most bats don't spend all night feeding, and some have a rest in between feeding bouts, and not necessarily at their usual roost site, either, but at a stop-over. Many have certain intense periods of activity, especially just after dusk, when they are hungry. However, without exception, they disappear during the day, probably to avoid predation by birds, such as Sparrowhawks, which catch them on the wing.

Where they disappear to much depends on the sort of bat in question. Some, such as pipistrelles and the Serotine, go to houses; others, such as Noctules, usually find a hole in a tree. But one way in which everyone can encourage bats to visit is by putting up bat boxes, because almost all types of bats can be drawn to them. Overall, these contraptions are similar to bird boxes, but they have an entrance at the bottom, rather than a hole in the middle – you may have seen them about. Another difference is that bat boxes can also be put up in clusters, something you can't do with bird boxes because birds are territorial – having a neighbour usually drives them mad.

Bats use boxes for all kinds of purposes: for day-roosts, for night-roosts, as meeting places, and as places to breed. Bats usually raise their young in small gatherings made up of adult females and a few teenagers, which are known as maternity-roosts.

In every way, therefore, boxes are beneficial for bats. And this is why bat people spend a great deal of time putting them up: on trees, buildings, telegraph poles, anywhere. In fact, if they could, they would cover Britain's entire landscape with bat boxes, and the bats would undoubtedly benefit.

Our trip today was, as I have mentioned, a count of the contents of some of these aforementioned bat boxes. Not surprisingly, if you are going to put up a bat box, it's best to monitor what bats are using it (this can only be done by individuals with a Bat Licence) and what they are doing. Therefore, many people simply give the bat workers access to their land, and arrange for a number of set visits during the year to see what is going on.

Today's bat boxes had been put up in a roadside strip of wood close to the wonderfully named village of Puddletown, in mid-Dorset (the local river is called the Piddle). To come here, quite naturally, amused Emily and Samuel greatly – and who can blame them? The locals hereabouts have the temerity to sell "Piddle Water," in a shameless attempt to cash in on the joke – but then, presumably it provides some compensation for being the butt of endless jibes by visitors who forget that the locals have almost certainly heard them all before.

For once during this summer, it was a fine and warm day. The clouds had been working so hard to drench the countryside in recent weeks, that nobody would have begrudged them a day off. Even so, when we parked by the appointed verge, the mud lay thickly everywhere. We had brought along two kids only too willing to check its consistency. The wet conditions had certainly made the landscape lush. Huge banks of nettles bordered the road, joined by the cheap lipstick pink of Red Campion and the classier, subtle pinks and whites of Wild Rose – a contrast, perhaps, between the Clare's Accessories and M&S of the flower world. It looked as though negotiating the woodland floor might be quite a battle.

The indefatigable Nick Tomlinson met us once again, friendly as ever. He was taking a ladder off the roof of his car, and contemplating the checking of perhaps the millionth box of his career with his usual gusto. "We have set up twenty-four boxes on this site," he told us. "And there's usually something good here."

He's a tease, that Nick.

Checking bat boxes, I can now tell you, is relatively straightforward at first: you walk up to the tree and lean a ladder against it. But then things become somewhat more difficult. Several rungs up, holding on for dear life with one hand, you then have to open the box with the other, which is very fiddly. In these particular boxes, it meant manoeuvring a catch at the bottom to release the front section, and then pushing the lower half of the front inwards slightly, so that it fell back towards you. As this happens, you hope you'll avoid a mass exodus of bats, such as you often see in films, swarms of animals streaming past you in a vast, onrushing current. And, more propitiously, you pray that there isn't a bees' or hornets' nest lodged inside. If this is the case, you really are in trouble.

And then, if you have managed to survive all this, the really tricky part starts. You have to identify the bats.

I know all this because the Bat People asked me to check a box. And, while it's all good fun watching someone else mount a ladder and fiddle around, it's quite different when you have to do it for yourself. It's certainly a whole lot more exciting.

"Nothing in here," I quavered, once up the ladder, seeing that there were no furry lumps in the darkness above my head. If there had been, I had my jargon at the ready: "pips", "Daubs", "Noctules" and so on.

For the second day in succession, Nick looked worried. "Oh dear, that's number sixteen. Not many left. I expect all the bats will be in the last box we check."

"With you we'd expect nothing less," we chorused.

And, remarkably, that was exactly what happened. Boxes 17 to 22 were filled with nothing more than air and woodlice. But the last two both elicited full-blooded screams of exhilaration from the bat workers. Their eyes filled with tears, their hands were thrust triumphantly into the air. The ones on the ground began a celebratory dance around the ladders, holding out handkerchiefs in Morris-dancer style and slapping them together in high-fives…

They didn't really. "Noctule here," said one, raising his voice not a jot above base level. And the other said, "Aha, a group of Natts." He could have been making verbal comments on a tax return.

I was excited, however. "Natts," I realised, was Bat Worker shorthand for "Natterer's Bats", a new species for us, and not necessarily an easy one to see, either.

"There are eight of them," said the bat worker. "Looks like an all-male summer roost. No sign of any youngsters."

It wasn't possible to see them from the ground. So there was nothing for it but to mount the ladder once again – and this time with the children. Samuel got the nod first. Fearlessly, my son crept up, little by little, towards the top of the ladder. Each rung was an effort for him: a small step for a bat, but a giant leap for Sam-kind. At length we stood shakily at bat-box height, my right hand holding the ladder and my left holding the pocket torch, while Sam was sort of wedged between the ladder and my stomach.

"Can you see them, Sam?" I asked. "Look up there."

He edged up another step.

"Bats," he confirmed at last. And indeed, as he spoke, the light of the torch showed up a cluster of diminutive bodies hanging from the upper part of the box. It took some careful manoeuvring to get a good view, but soon we could see their faces looking down on us in a distinctively unfriendly fashion, as if to say, "What the hell are you doing?" We noticed that these bats weren't completely brown, but had neat white tummies.

"Can I look?" asked Emily, probably about 15 times. I eased Samuel down and then my daughter, who loves a challenge, tried to beat me to the top of the ladder. Together we shone the torch briefly upon the huddled bodies. It looked pretty cosy in there. Whatever did bats do before the advent of tailor-made living quarters?

It was good to see the white tummies of the Natterers' Bats, because this gave them something of an identity. With so many species of bat in Britain, it's good to find clear differences between them, and so far most of the species we had seen, apart from the Daubenton's, had been entirely brown. These little monsters also had long, pixie-like ears. I read later that, unlike Daubenton's and pipistrelles, Natterers' usually feed close to the trees, and they have the relatively unusual habit of plucking a lot of their insect food from the vegetation, rather than from the air, sometimes by hovering in one place. In the winter, apparently, they are quite addicted to tunnels, and gather in such places in large numbers.

"Could I look, please?" asked another voice, far more politely than the last. This time it was my mother.

"I've never seen bats in a box before," she entreated.

I felt like saying: "Are you sure you're up to it, Mother?" But I knew from experience that her mind was made up.

And so my mother, approaching her eightieth year, climbed up a ladder some 4.5 metres (15 feet) above ground to see eight Natterer's Bats, and revelled in it. As I watched her, surrounded by the Bat Group (keeping hold of the ladder), her son, daughter-in-law and small grandchildren, a thought occurred to me.

In 30 years' time, I hoped I might be able to do just the same.

# July

## July 8th - A Shed-load of Hedgehogs

We had been worrying about Hedgehogs all year. They are among Britain's best-known and best-loved animals, yet we were having considerable difficulty finding them. I asked a few people whether they had Hedgehogs visiting their garden, but nobody who did could guarantee them to appear if and when we paid their garden a visit.

The trouble is, our own garden would be ideal for Hedgehogs if it wasn't for one thing: Badgers. As I've mentioned before, we live on the edge of an open space that has an active Badger sett, and that means that the smaller animal cannot survive here. Why? Because Badgers are one of the very few animals that eat Hedgehogs – even Lions in Africa struggle with the spiny creatures and tend to avoid them. But the Badger has strong forepaws and sharp claws that, unlike those of Lions, are small and dexterous enough to rip the Hedgehog apart. It isn't a pleasant thought. And it doesn't make Hedgehogs easy to find when you need one, especially in rural areas.

Our Hedgehog conundrum was solved at the most unlikely of places: a children's soft play centre where my son Samuel was celebrating his fourth birthday. And the reason that it was solved was that somebody at the soft play centre had their own Hedgehog conundrum to solve.

Now don't get me wrong here. This was not my initiative. It was someone else's. It was my son's birthday and I *was* playing with him and his sister and his mates (dads – aren't these places fun? Why take the kids with you?) I was climbing about, going down slides, chasing the kids, wiping away their occasional tears. I am not so obsessed with mammals that I think about subjects like seeing Hedgehogs all the time…

It was during the tea break, when every child was completely occupied and I was not being neglectful in any way, that a fellow parent, Lisa, raised the subject of prickles.

"We've got a Hedgehog problem," she said. "My husband Ian wants to remodel our garden, and he has taken down the shed – except that he hasn't. He can't. Well, not all of it anyway, because we're pretty sure that there's a Hedgehog family underneath."

"Oh really?" I replied, suddenly sensing an opportunity. (However, while sensing this opportunity to see a Hedgehog, I still had my mind fixed firmly on the needs of my children.)

"I've heard that you know about these things," Lisa went on. "We don't want to disturb them, but we also want to get on with the garden. Can you give us some advice?"

"That would be fine," I replied, wondering where I had stashed away my reference book on Hedgehogs. "But I think I'll need to come over and see them first."

And so today, just a few days later, we all made an after-school visit to Ian and Lisa to check on the welfare of their Hedgehogs. It was a gift, really. A Hedgehog outside the Badger zone, just when we needed one, yet just a few minutes away from our own front door.

The garden was large, and full of exciting attractions, not least Laurence and Amelia, the children, who were of a similar age to ours. Within a few moments all four children were playing in earnest. Emily had found the swings, while Samuel had found a large plastic car.

"The Hedgehogs have been under here," said Ian, in his soft Yorkshire accent, pointing to a large blue tarpaulin on the far side of the garden, that was covering the wooden floor of a shed. He was a tall man, with greying hair above a face that was used to smiling. He was exactly the kind of bloke who you might expect to be considerate to Hedgehogs.

"I've had to knock all this down," he went on. "What with the garden being redesigned, we'll need to put up a new shed. But I don't want to drive the Hedgehogs away if they still have babies." (What is it about us men? Within minutes of meeting properly for the first time, we were already talking sheds.)

"Don't worry," I replied, fresh from a hour or two's hard research at my Hedgehog book. "Let's find out how old the babies are, and work out how soon they might leave the nest."

Ian and Lisa had obviously been talking.

"Your children must have had a great time seeing all these different animals over the last few months," commented Ian as we shaped to lift the pallet that he had used as the shed-base. "They must have learnt a lot."

"They have," I responded proudly. "And the great thing is, they still have real enthusiasm for it all."

With some effort we lifted the pallet and immediately spotted a pile of hay about 30 centimetres (1 foot) square, resting against where the cross-beam had lain on the earth. This looked extremely promising.

"Emmie, Sam!" I called. "I think we've got Hedgehogs here."

"It's really a good thing to do," went on Ian. "I'd like to do something similar one day."

Gently he lifted the hay to reveal the tell-tale sight of prickles. By now Laurence and Amelia had joined us, peering over our shoulders. A little more hay was plucked away, and it was now clear that it was an adult Hedgehog, and that it had been awoken from its sleep. It shuffled. Ian and Lisa's children cooed.

"They each have about five thousand spines when they are adult, but only a few hundred when they're born," I told my audience of three. "Emmie, Sam! Come and see the Hedgehog."

"Nee-owwm!" said Samuel, still driving his borrowed toy car, oblivious. Emily was still on the swing.

"Kids. Come and see the Hedgehog. *Now!*"

My children finally dragged themselves over, displaying a distinct lack of enthusiasm.

The rest of the hay was cleared to reveal, not just an adult Hedgehog, but no less than five babies by her side. The disturbance was enough for the mother, who waddled off into the shadows we had created by moving the tarpaulin, leaving her babies in situ. Happily, though, I could see after all my revision, that the youngsters were at least a couple of weeks old, with plenty of soft, white-tipped spines, and that it would be no more than a few days before they would be able to leave the nest, and only another couple of weeks before they were weaned. Now everybody cooed.

"Have a last look before we cover them up, kids," I suggested. "We don't want to disturb them for too long." And within seconds of the animals being covered up, Emily was squealing with delight on the swing once again, and Samuel was practising his three-point turns.

"All well, Ian," I said. "Just leave them for a couple of weeks at most, if you can manage that. They are obviously pretty happy."

"Yes, we can do that. Should we feed them?" he asked.

"I wouldn't bother. There are plenty of beetles and worms about at the moment. But you can always give them cat food, if you really want to."

The conversation shifted to the minutiae of life, while all the four children played in carefree style. And I thought: what better way to see wild mammals? In a garden, making friends, the kids loving every minute of it, near home, minimum effort.

Ian and I watched the children playing.

"They're right enthusiastic, your kids," he said.

He was right. But today, at least, it wasn't quite in the way I had expected. Sometimes I needed to remember that Emily and Samuel weren't little mammal-spotters, they were just kids.

## July 12ᵗʰ – Dining Out on Dormice

What's the oddest mammal found at large in the British Isles?

Our Red-necked Wallabies from Loch Lomond must rank as one of the contenders (G'day, sport… Sorry about the weather, mate…). Bizarrely, there is also a colony of prairie dogs (little burrowing rodents from North America) in Cornwall, along with various other oddities such as porcupines and tropical squirrels around, which occasionally survive in small pockets in scattered places. Some conspiracy theorists would lead us to believe that the country is also awash with big cats, including Mountain Lions. Evidently these are wandering our innocuous woods and fields, doubtless ready to munch up anyone who might doubt their existence.

But what about the truly well-established stuff, here to stay beyond reasonable doubt, and without any question of identity? What's the oddest one of these? Well, there hasn't ever been an officially recognised British title holder, as far as I am aware, but I would personally award it to: the Edible Dormouse.

The Edible Dormouse? A dormouse – edible? Surely it's a misnomer.

Nope. It's a dormouse and it's edible. You can eat it. The Romans ate it quite a bit, and even bred it for the pot.

But nobody eats it now, apart from in Slovenia and a few other parts of Eastern Europe. Up until comparatively recently, people used to hunt the rodents commercially (can you imagine what their itemised tax return must have looked like?) These days it is something of a minority pastime, but to Slovenians, having dormouse-hunters in your midst is still culturally significant, and part of the national identity. To keep the traditions alive, the nation's enthusiasts have formed societies that promote the rodent's hunting and eating. And just in case you are thinking to yourself, "Daft foreigners, the things they get up to", don't forget that we English still practise, uphold and tolerate morris dancing.

But isn't it an extraordinary thought that there is actually an edible rodent that can be found in our country? Rabbits I can understand, and deer are probably delicious, but furry, mouse-related things? Not a nice thought. I suppose if times ever become really hard, and the supermarkets run out of meat, we could resort to catching Edible Dormice and developing a taste for them. We would then have mums saying to their kids, "I've given you dormouse in your sandwiches, love. Your favourite…", and Gordon Ramsay telling hapless restaurateur, "If only you could have served f***ing dormouse, you could have made a f***ing fortune."

But somehow I just can't see it catching on.

It is equally idiosyncratic that the Edible Dormouse occurs in this country at all. The species is not a native, but is found in nearby parts of Continental Europe. It didn't swim over here, of course, but was introduced by the hand of man.

In the early part of the twentieth century, a certain Walter Rothschild had a habit of collecting live animals for his estate at Tring Park, in Hertfordshire. One morning, in 1909, someone discovered that the Edible Dormouse enclosure was no longer occupied. The critters had escaped. By a stroke of good fortune for the Edible Dormice, the nearby landscape – the beech woods of the Chiltern Hills – could have been tailor-made for them, for it is forests of beech to which they are most accustomed. Against the odds, despite small numbers and a built-in tendency not to wander much, they survived and, very gradually, spread. These days, numbers have crept up to about 10,000 individuals, every one of them within a radius of about 35 kilometres (20 miles) from the original release site.

And so it is that anyone wishing to see an Edible Dormouse in Britain needs to make a bee-line for the vicinity of Tring. And that is exactly what we did in our quest to add this little curio to our list of observed mammals. Way back in February we had been invited to a reserve called College Lake for the very reason of seeing them. Now we were taking up the unusual offer, and hoping to keep our good run of mammals going.

The children were getting a little tired of long drives. Sam, especially, was being shirty, and when he dropped his new Spiderman lunchbox out of reach of his car seat, he filled the air with pleading moans so endless and nerve-shredding that a Whitney Houston CD would honestly have been preferable – yes, really.

Determined to put an end to his complaints, I pulled the car over and promptly punctured a tyre. It was not an auspicious start.

"I hope we see them," said Nancy, the Ranger who met us, with a frightening amount of uncertainty in her voice. She was younger than I expected from her name, with a friendly face and slightly diffident manner.

"Why? Are they difficult?"

"Not really," she replied. "But we can't absolutely guarantee them. They are all asleep at the moment, of course. They are nocturnal, you see. And so it's not the most active time of day. And there's no doubt that we usually see them, but who knows? They are still wild animals. We are certainly likely to find one. But I haven't seen one for the last day or two…"

She began to sound like a saleswoman who had had a sudden breakdown of confidence in her goods. Actually, Nancy, bless her, was sounding a bit nervous about the Edible Dormice performing for us.

"Don't worry," I reassured her. "Where do we look? In the trees?"

"Oh no," replied Nancy. "They live in our buildings."

This was a surprise. I had read that Edible Dormice were famous for their agility in the upper canopy of tall trees, which is where they obtained most of their food. They were exceptionally arboreal – in many ways similar to squirrels.

"They occupy our buildings during the day," Nancy went on. "Then, when they wake up they will go and feed in the trees and hedgerows. I guess the buildings are comparatively warm and safe for them when they are asleep. Nothing much can get them in there. Actually, you'll be surprised where you can find them. They usually live in the roof, but sometimes they come down and sit on our shelves and cupboards as well."

She led us through a path through dense woodland, adjacent to a deep railway cutting, from which several trains thundered past theatrically below. We passed boards giving information on the plants and wildlife. We passed piles of logs and brush, and even a small flower meadow that was rampant with oxeye daisy and buttercups. Presently we came to a small wooden outbuilding. It sat snugly under a dense thicket, entirely surrounded by patches of bramble, nettle and dense, tall grass – in typical July profusion – the plants hemming it in so tightly that they could have been residing at a guru's feet. Nancy unlocked the door to reveal what looked suspiciously like a glorified allotment shed, with shovels, saws, bird food, assorted bits of wood, flower seed mixes, several rakes and jars of everything from plant food to wood treatment paint. The whole shed was decorated with spiders' webs of every conceivable design and size. From what Nancy said, it fitted the ideal profile for a dwelling beloved by Edible Dormice.

"Hmm," said Nancy, contemplatively. "They are usually in here. Is anything moving?"

The kids rummaged around. Nothing stirred.

"This should help," said Nancy, producing an apple from her pocket and slicing it into small pieces with a penknife. "Edible Dormice adore apples. If we leave some on the shelf here we might tempt them to wake up and come and take a snack. I suggest you try again in half an hour. I'll show you around the rest of the site. Besides, we might find some of them somewhere else."

Our tour took in several hides overlooking a large, shallow lake that was the product of gravel extraction; an information building fitted with large beams along which, Nancy told us, the Edible Dormice would scamper every night; a room replete with second-hand books for sale (via an honesty box); and several other storage buildings. Finally, we came to the staff room, where Nancy flicked on the kettle and offered us a drink.

"We've even seen the Edible Dormice in here before now," Nancy told us. "They get into the cupboards and chew things. Try that one next to you."

I opened what was obviously a stationery cupboard. It was piled high with papers of various kinds, files, books, pencils, paperclips, envelopes, dividers and magazines. But there was not the slightest sign of an Edible

Dormouse – no more than you would find in any stationery cupboard across the land. But on the top shelf stood a small cardboard box, about 15 centimetres (6 inches) square, that looked as though it had been there for a long time – it was the sort that could be used to hold large numbers of pens or biros. Something made me want to check it. With Nancy's agreement I took a chair, stood on it and peered inside the box.

My hunch was right. Curled up in the box was an Edible Dormouse, fast asleep.

"Gosh, it's much bigger than I expected," said Carolyn, surprised. "I was expecting something mouse-sized. This looks like a squirrel."

And indeed she was right. Edible Dormice, Nancy told us, were often confused with squirrels. This one, indeed, was curled up under a long, bushy tail, which was draped over it like a rug. To complete the lookalike impression, the overall colour of the fur was grey, although admittedly a little smarter and smokier, we thought, than the familiar bland colouration of a Grey Squirrel.

"Look at the ears. They are much larger than a squirrel's," our guide informed us. "The eyes are much bigger, too, which is typical for a nocturnal animal."

To round off the differences, this Edible Dormouse also had a hint of black around the eyes – a sort of highwayman's mask – although the idea of being hijacked by a band of Edible Dormice was not especially frightening.

Emily wasn't at all bothered about identification features. "Ooh, it's so cute," she enthused.

Nancy told us a little more about the lifestyle of the Edible Dormouse: "In the winter they hibernate underground. They don't bother about bedding, just find a crack, next to a tree root perhaps, and make their way down to a hole in the ground that isn't too damp. Several might club together, and they can remain like that for up to six months, from October to March. To survive hibernation, each animal needs to increase their body weight by half, just to carry enough fat reserves. And that's why the Romans used to collect them in the autumn, when they are at their plumpest."

"You'd think the Dormice might change their minds one day and hibernate here," I suggested, laughing. I had noticed that, for the whole time that we had been admiring it, the object of our interest had not stirred one bit. The only movement we could detect was its breathing, which was quite obvious. In fact, we had expected it to break out into a snore any moment. It certainly would have remained safe and undisturbed there – unless, of course, Nancy and the other staff had run out of pens.

And so, happily, we took tea in the company of the Edible Dormouse.

Once we had changed the wheel of our stricken Zafira, we thanked Nancy and made off for the nearby town of Tring, where the original Edible Dormouse breakout had occurred. We drank a toast to this curious little mammal, undoubtedly the only creature we were likely to find this year in the cupboard of an office, and had a celebratory meal.

But we went vegetarian.

## July 17th – Notes from HQ, Part VI

How do you know when you've been truly mammallified? Easy, really. When these previously elusive creatures begin to creep into your daily life. It's when you look out at the garden and see a Fox, when previously you would have seen just trees and lawns. It's when you begin to notice deer footprints all around you. Or even when a bat becomes a little bit more friendly than you might consider ideal.

Well, just that happened this very afternoon. The light was extremely bright outside, with hardly even a dash of evening; hardly the time, you would think, for a bat perambulation. Yet a healthy-sized specimen, which I now knew was likely to be a Serotine, nevertheless decided to get some fresh air, and flaunt itself in broad daylight. It was pushing its luck: Sparrowhawks and other predatory birds, many of which live locally around here, will take flying bats without hesitation.

This bat didn't just fly around the street, or over the trees, either. The Serotine came right down and began to hover expectantly around our French windows, as if it had heard that we were auditioning for a horror film. Around and around it went, as if looking for an imaginary stage door. I have never seen a bat doing this before. Bizarre.

The whole day has been animal magic. We set the four traps overnight in the garden and three were occupied in the morning. Buzz, our resident Yellow-necked Mouse, was in his favourite overnight abode in one corner, burping and urinating as usual – no surprise there. Meanwhile Wood Mice had found their way into the others, enticed into following Buzz's example by their midsummer greed. By now we had seen so many of these mice that even Emily, who usually fizzes with excitement at anything remotely novel, was hardly moved at all. Mammals are running in our family's blood.

And it's mighty satisfying. I took Emily and Samuel for a walk on the common, and almost immediately we succeeded in flushing out a Roe Deer, which sped off with its familiar half-running, half-hopping stride (it is technically known as "stotting"). I didn't even have to tell them what it was, nor did I have to describe the cloven-footed, two-toed tracks that it left. And when a Grey Squirrel scooted past, they nailed the identity of that one easily. The thing is, when we began this mammal jamboree, Samuel couldn't have recognised a deer *or* a squirrel, let alone a Pine Marten. Now he's a mini-expert. And perhaps this project has changed them in other ways? Since they now expect to see animals when they go out into the countryside, surely that makes them appreciate their surroundings more? And although the kids often complain about going shopping, or going to the Post Office and so on, they rarely sound resistant to the idea of spotting mammals. It is not yet, even after seven months, a turn-off.

Incidentally, our local common, like the rest of the countryside, has just begun to get to the tired stage of summer. The leaves of its trees have lost their luxuriance already, and there is even a hint of brown upon a few of them. The berries are coming out in force, however. Another autumn is approaching and we are more than half way through our year of looking for mammals. And the kids are growing up. It's delightful and disconcerting at the same time.

## July 19th – Come on You Reds

I'm not sure what excited the kids most about our prospective visit to Brownsea Island. They knew they were in for a boat trip, and that it would be a day of fun and mucking about, without the parents being distracted by other things, such as cleaning the house or writing a book. They knew there were woods in which to play hide-and-seek, large fields over which to be chased, and fresh mud in which to wallow, out of adult reach. They knew that there would be a café with chocolate biscuits, too, because that's what Mummy and Daddy often talked about. And clearly, in anticipation of crossing the sea to an island, they had thought about a number of other possibilities.

"Are there tropical beaches, with palm trees and bright blue water there?" Emily asked excitedly. This was probably a lot to expect from Poole Harbour, on the Dorset coast.

"Will there be pirates on Bouncy Island?" asked Sam, conspiratorially, with more than a little concern in his big blue eyes.

The children were certainly excited about Granny and Grandpa coming too. Roger and Celia would double the ratio of parents to children, and thus double the attention available to the youth section of the party. Granny and Grandpa were also highly likely to increase the ice cream intake exponentially, and conspire with Emily and Samuel to nudge against the usual parental boundaries of behaviour. Granny and Grandpa would tell them stories in a fresh way, and fuss over them in a different style that they could bask in for a whole day. Granny and Grandpa offered a fresh perspective, and unconditional love, and a buffer against being told off.

Probably the one thing that didn't excite Emily and Samuel anything like so much as all this, was the prospect of seeing the Island's famous Red Squirrels. Nevertheless, these exquisite animals were the main reason for our visit. Brownsea Island is home to about 200 of them, and tourists from all over the south of England come to catch sight of this embattled creature in one of its last stands against the all-conquering Grey Squirrel. For, apart from nearby Furzey Island, also in Poole Harbour, and a substantial population on the Isle of Wight, the nearest Red Squirrels in Britain are found 320 kilometres (200 miles) to the north. They have disappeared from almost everywhere in between.

In common with so much in natural history, the story of the replacement of the Red Squirrel by the Grey in Britain is not as clear-cut as tends to be made out. It isn't a simplistic tale of the good guy, the Red Squirrel and the big bad guy, the Grey, the aggressive invader driving out the pretty native by tooth and fist; there are more forces at play here than you might at first think. For example, did you know that, long before the Grey Squirrel was introduced to Britain, the Red had already suffered several severe population declines? Did you also know that Grey Squirrels were brought over because, back then, people simply liked the look of the newcomers and they made a nice change from those boring old Reds? The term "tree-rat" (or would it be "tree-ratte"?) had not yet been invented at that point.

Anyway, the first drastic decline of the Red Squirrel ever recorded seems to have been in the fifteenth century, when it disappeared completely from Ireland, having been present there for at least the previous 200 years. Nobody knows why this happened, since details are inevitably sketchy, but deforestation has been suggested as a possible explanation. Remarkably, the same thing seems to have happened in Scotland and Wales, with severe declines in the fifteenth and sixteenth century, until by the eighteenth century the Red Squirrel was all but extinct in northern and western Britain – which is hard to believe now. Anyway, the point I am making is that the Red Squirrel has form in the boom-and-bust department.

Despite these earlier losses, the Red Squirrel population always seemed to recover. At the beginning of the last century, indeed, the numbers actually reached their zenith. Red Squirrels were everywhere and, somewhat unfairly, it is this benchmark against which people measure the Red Squirrel's subsequent disappearance today. At the time the animals were indeed so common that a certain Mr Brocklehurst, his land and garden doubtless plagued by the "Red menace", decided that Britain needed a different squirrel. And so, in 1876 he released a few North American Grey Squirrels into a park in Cheshire, and spawned a trend for doing the same elsewhere that carried on for the next half-century.

Some 20 to 30 years after the release of the first Grey Squirrels, the population of Reds once again went into freefall. Of course it would be very easy to draw lazy conclusions from this – i.e. that the rise of one caused the decline of the other – but remember, Red Squirrels had sunk in fortunes before, and the population crash was countrywide, frequently taking place in areas where no Grey Squirrels had yet been introduced. There were probably several causes of this catastrophic reduction, one of the major ones being a serious outbreak of diseases, one of which – the squirrelpox virus – was perhaps introduced with the Grey Squirrels. At the same time, two World Wars greatly increased the rate and amount of deforestation once more, adding to the difficulties of the beleaguered Reds.

Sadly, it seems, this time there was no chance of recovery. In the absence of the native Red Squirrels, the Greys, which were themselves not killed off by the pox, moved in and took their niche, making it impossible for the Reds to make a comeback. So really, it was Grey Squirrels being opportunistic on their own behalf that gave them such a boost in numbers and distribution.

A lot of rubbish has been peddled about what Greys do to Reds. The Greys have been accused of eating the Red's babies, and driving adults out of dreys, but if this does ever happen, it's not on a sufficient enough scale to have much effect. The presence of Grey Squirrels is definitely deleterious to Reds, but in far more subtle ways than that of treetop warfare. On the whole, Greys don't drive out Reds directly. However, they do raid Red Squirrel caches in the spring, which may affect the weight of breeding adult Red Squirrels and cause them to be less productive. Overall, Reds do everything less well in the company of Grey Squirrels. Fewer females breed, fewer breeding females attempt a second litter in the summer, youngsters grow more slowly, and fewer adolescents enter the population. All in all, it seems that Grey Squirrels cause stress to Red Squirrels, without the use of direct violence. They are like employees under an overbearing manager, unable to thrive.

Whatever the complexities of the situation, there is no doubt that the Red Squirrel in Britain is in one almighty pickle. The march of Grey Squirrels has reached Scotland, and it seems likely that, one day, there will be no Red Squirrels at all in any of Britain except in outposts such as islands. Islands like Brownsea, in fact. We knew we were privileged to live close to these animals, remnants of a lost, wild Britain. I only hope that the Grey Squirrel will never find its way there. If it does, a priceless asset will inevitably be lost.

Brownsea is an extraordinary place. It might only be 15 minutes by boat from the bustling port of Poole, and sheltered within a harbour (the second largest natural harbour in the world, after that of Sydney), and thus never more than 1,600 metres (1 mile) from the mainland, but it still retains a distinctiveness of its own that is characteristic of more isolated spots. It really does feel like a foreign country and, indeed, when you arrive at the jetty your first port of call is the National Trust's reception building, which has the feel of a customs house. There they give you a map of the island, similar to the tourist maps you pick up at international airports in major cities, which only adds to the feeling of arrival. The one thing missing is the queue of taxis waiting to whisk you to your hotel.

The Red Squirrels are not the only living oddity there, either. The island supports a population of Sika Deer, which can be elusive; a few Golden Pheasants, which are secretive to a fault (well, they are from China); and, bizarrely, a number of gangs of ornamental birds, including chickens, peacocks and turkeys. These latter birds have the run of the place, and often harass people foolish enough to take a packed lunch to the island's main open area, where these large birds will stand in front of them and wait, in a similarly sinister fashion to the feathered assassins in Hitchcock's famous horror movie, *The Birds*. The island is also planted with more than 60 kinds of trees, so you might find your children climbing all over a medlar or a mulberry tree, adding to the sense of the peculiar.

"You know," said Celia as we made our way to the cafeteria just outside the customs house, "we've lived in Poole all these years and been to Brownsea many times; but we've never actually seen the Red Squirrels." She said it in a low voice, in case it might be the most embarrassing admission in the world.

"They can be a bit tricky," I replied sympathetically. I thought of the many times I had been to Brownsea and been perfectly happy with the sight of a retreating red-brown tail. "Here, I'll buy the coffee. You take a seat."

I hadn't reached the till before Emily ran towards me, shouting. "Squirrel. There's a squirrel under our table!"

And indeed there was. It had been scoffing away at a bird feeder in the cafeteria garden. Then it had been disturbed and made its escape almost beneath the feet of my children and in-laws'. I just caught sight of its tufted ears and flame-red tail as it disappeared over the boundary wall.

"I'm surprised we've seen one here," exclaimed Roger, beaming beneath his white sunhat. "Perhaps they are doing well these days."

He was right. They are doing very well on Brownsea, thank you very much. It's just everywhere else that's the problem.

# August

## August 1st – Whale-ing at Hayling

We first heard about the Northern Bottlenose Whale on the news. It was on "BBC News", "Channel 4 News", "Sky News" and on the news of just about every network you can think of except Al Jazeera. It was in a bad way and it had been stranded on Hayling Island, a double whammy of ill luck if ever there was one, since the Island is in an area of exceptionally dense human population. As usual, a circus had gathered around it already, a toxic cross between journalists, onlookers and well-meaning whale rescuers.

The poor creature had been noticed the previous night on a sandbank near the Langstone Bridge, which connects Hayling Island to the Hampshire mainland. It was clearly alive – just – but being out of the water meant that it was in desperate straits, in grave danger of both dehydration and damage to its internal organs from its own bodyweight. Its plight was public the moment it had first been spotted, which did not take long when you consider that it was 6 metres (20 feet) long and had beached just outside a pub. From then on, it was never going to die in peace.

Cetacean stranding is one of nature's curiosities. How is it that animals that live underwater their entire lives can get themselves into potentially dangerous shallows, let alone land up on a lonely beach out of water, the anathema to their safe environment? It makes little sense. Some strandings can be explained by dead animals that have simply been washed ashore by the tides; others by animals that are too ill to fight against the currents that they would normally ride with ease. But a lot of strandings involve healthy animals, and a proportion of these involve not just one, but many dolphins or whales, and it is very difficult to explain why it happens.

There are theories, of course. Some say that illnesses could be involved, which affect the animals' navigation systems (an inner-ear parasite has been implicated). Others say that young, inexperienced animals, or elderly individuals, simply get lost and confused, just as human drivers of cars so frequently do, and then get exhausted while trying to figure out what to do. Another explanation is that man-made disturbances, including the use of sonar by the military, may cause internal damage by blowing out the part of the animals' brains responsible for navigation. And when one whale or dolphin goes astray, if it is a leader or matriarch, it may cause others in the social group to follow. All of these are perfectly plausible theories, and the chances are that most or all of them have contributed to strandings from time to time.

As for this Northern Bottlenose Whale, there seemed to be no prior illness. It was just lost. Very lost.

Until 2006, it would be fair to say that virtually nobody in Britain had ever even heard of a Northern Bottlenose Whale. However, in January of that year, a young female mistakenly swam up the Thames Estuary and found itself in the heart of London. For a day or two it was a bigger tourist attraction than any other in the city and, by swimming around and generally behaving like a proper whale, it found its way into the city-dwellers' hearts. But, almost invariably for a lost and confused whale, it never made it back to the open sea, despite being cosseted by would-be rescuers, carried back into the estuary on floats, and being given a thorough check-up. In the end, it died of starvation.

The truth is, neither the Northern Bottlenose Whales of London or Hayling Island really had much of a chance. These animals are not like dolphins, many of which hunt fish in the shallows and are used to the vagaries of coastlines; they are true deep-water animals. The Northern Bottlenose Whale subsists mainly on squid that live near the ocean floor. It rarely occurs in waters less than 500 metres (1,600 feet) deep, and it has been recorded hunting at depths of 1,450 metres (4,750 feet) – one of the deepest dives ever recorded for any whale. It is a true leviathan of the depths, able to stay underwater for as long as 70 minutes. This gives you an idea of the environment in which this remarkable animal thrives, and equally a measure of how desperate, confusing and terminal a visit to the shallow Sussex coast would have been.

I felt ambivalent about the whale as far as our project was concerned. Our family pastime was obviously trivial in comparison with this poor whale's almost certain fate. That was perhaps reason enough to give it, and the increasingly labour-intensive operation to "rescue" it, a wide berth. And yet, for all that, I also wanted my children to learn about the environment. A whale, even a sick or starving one, is always an impressive sight, and I was still smarting from our inability to see one in Scotland. Furthermore, if our children could witness the attempts to help the whale, perhaps that would open their eyes to the world of animal husbandry and conservation. Emily, in particular, was already aware that the real world doesn't always correspond to "happily ever after", so perhaps this would help to give her a different angle on the world of nature, too.

We decided to go to see what we could see, slightly afraid of looking like "rubber-neckers" or misery tourists. During the journey to Hayling Island, Carolyn tried to keep up with developments by checking the news websites on her iPhone, so that when we arrived we would know where to go and what to look for. However, in the course of her doing so the news seemed suddenly to go cold. What's more, the crowds of whale-watchers with whom we had expected to mingle just didn't materialise. Hayling, it seemed, was back to normal (except, bizarrely, that the main route through the island was lined with scarecrows for a festival – those Hampshire people are strange).

We arrived at Langstone Bridge. "It's not here," said a kindly lady walking a dog. "It swam into the harbour this morning. It didn't look very well."

Further south we found a man cycling along the seawall. "About two hours ago I saw a boat surrounded by floats moving very slowly out of the harbour," he said, dismissively. "If there was a whale in between the floats I didn't see it."

We drove to the southern tip of the island. We couldn't see a boat with floats, and certainly not a whale. Instead there were windsurfers, yachts and a typical seaside scene of towels, pale, flabby flesh and crying children.

I swore under my breath. As we waited disconsolately on the beach, Carolyn switched on to a local radio station and discovered that, unbeknownst to us, we had been running late all afternoon. The rescue boat had already disgorged its cargo into the Solent, and the whale had been lost to sight.

My wildlife instincts suggested to me that we should stay put. After all, the animal was quite likely to beach again, it probably wouldn't go far, and the tide was dropping, exposing the sandbanks in front of us. However, parental instincts won the day. The kids were cold and tired, and we all needed something to eat. We retreated to a local café.

Bad mistake. Within 45 minutes the Northern Bottlenose had beached once again, right in front of where we had been standing. A little extra patience and we would have seen this magnificent animal of the deep, albeit in a stricken condition.

Within a short time, its suffering was ended by a lethal injection. It was a sad end to a very unhappy episode.

There are a lot of questions to be raised about the value of these costly and highly publicised attempts to "rescue" whales like this. Surely, once the authorities knew that the animal was a Northern Bottlenose Whale, they should have recognised that its chances of survival were virtually nil. Its usual food was hundreds of miles away and, since it had already beached, imminent death was certain. Furthermore, the animal had already been diagnosed with kidney failure when it was floated for the last time, as a result of its organs being crushed beneath its own body weight when it was stuck on land. If the authorities knew it was certain to die, why didn't they just leave it alone, or kill it off as soon as they knew?

The truth is, they acted because of public sentiment. The operation was a bit of a farce. It was a severe case of meddling, which probably caused the animal more suffering than it would have endured on a lonely beach well out of sight. As soon as the animal beached, it became "public property", and the hardest thing for the authorities to have done, both politically and emotionally, would have been in its best interests – that is, nothing.

Indeed, the whole rationale behind some attempted rescues of sea mammals is questionable. Yes, occasionally, if there is a mass stranding, healthy animals can be returned to the sea and survive, but nobody knows how often they survive in the long term. Distressing though it is, perhaps it would be better just to leave some of them to die?.

These matters aside, I was nevertheless incandescent about our failure to show the children the whale. It was another sea mammal missed, and a lost opportunity for an interesting experience. Darkly, I thought to myself, if we can't even see a half-dead whale an hour's drive from our house, what chance did we have of seeing fit, healthy, and elusive creatures that put plenty of energy into staying well out of sight?

## August 25$^{th}$ – Luvvies and Leisler's

A combination of circumstances conspired to point us towards an injection of life for our project in the Bristol area. We had, after a great deal of emailing and miscommunication, finally arranged to go dormouse-box-checking with a lady from the Mammal Society in Cheddar; we also had our eyes on the population of Feral Goats on Brean Down, near Weston-super-Mare, which sounded like dead certs; and we had also received the best ticket in town for anyone with an interest in wildlife and the media.

For some years I had been invited by my great friend Stephen Moss to attend his annual friends-and-family picnic, which this year was at his new house in Mark, on the Somerset Levels. Many of you will not have heard of Stephen, but you most surely will know of his work: he is the man behind such famous TV programmes as *Birding with Bill Oddie*, *The Nature of Britain* and *Springwatch*. For many years he and I have been competing, in the most gentlemanly way, to see who could write the most natural history books – although, admittedly, Stephen is always way out in front. Despite this rivalry, we are good mates and time with him always zips by as we contemplate such lofty subjects as birding, wildlife TV and bringing up children (Stephen has roughly 150 kids, or it always seems that way – actually five). As yet I hadn't be able to attend the annual gathering, but this year the calendar was mercifully free. So we knew, for a few hours at least, that we would be sharing a picnic with some of the brightest sparks in the BBC's acclaimed Natural History Unit, not least Stephen himself.

He will be red-faced to be described as such, but Stephen is an extraordinary man. Not only does he have a large family, with his delightful wife Suzanne, but he also manages to go bird-watching regularly, keep in touch with all manner of friends, hold down a full-time job, manage TV egos, keep up to date with his emails and write several books a year. I have never once heard an editor complain that Stephen delivered his manuscript late; indeed, he usually manages to deliver stuff *before* the deadline (which actually isn't much of a service to other writers). This is a man who is incredibly organised, but still manages to keep a facade of normality, even though he obviously isn't like the rest of us.

To my knowledge, however, Stephen has never shown his family even 10 species of mammals, certainly nowhere near 33 and as for 50 – well, huh! (Perhaps I know now what the real motive for this family project was…)

We arrived at the picnic with several mammal traps and a smidgeon of trepidation. Regarding the former, Stephen had suggested we bring traps along, as there would be other kids present and they might be interested to see some small mammals. As for the latter, it was one of those situations where there would be many strangers to talk to, and Carolyn and I weren't sure how the children might react to the sea of unknown faces. And since there would also be a lot of important wildlife media people present, I wasn't sure how I would react either.

We began our set of conversations a little star-struck. The first person we met had worked on the iconic series *Life on Earth*; the next had just been carousing around the Himalayas filming Snow Leopards; the next person knew David Attenborough so well that he could tell me the colour of the great man's favourite underpants. And so on. The sheer weight of consequential TV people was almost crushing.

Thus, it helped that Mike Dilger was there – not that he isn't a weighty, consequential TV person himself (or so he informs me). It's just that I had known Mike before he really began making a name for himself in programmes like *Nature's Calendar* and *The One Show*. His grinning face set beneath an impressively non-existent head of hair, exuded warmth as he came over to chat. Fame hasn't changed him at all; at the party, floating effortlessly between different groups of people, he was still about as shy as a buffalo on heat (which, in case you are unaware of buffalo biology, is not shy at all).

"How's the family project going?" he enquired, moving to tickle Emily on the chin.

"Not bad," I replied, decidedly relieved to be talking about something I could actually contribute to. "But we're still lacking plenty of the obvious ones. Can't see a shrew to save our lives."

"Have you had a Water Shrew?"

We shook our heads.

"Then I have just the contact for you," he replied. "Phoebe Carter at the Cotswold Water Park. We filmed with her earlier in the year. She was great. She'll find you a Water Shrew, no trouble."

And then it suddenly occurred to me. We were still in need of a healthy number of British mammal species, 17 to be exact. And here, now, in this garden full of wildlife experts, was an absolute treasury of knowledge about the whereabouts of all forms of British wildlife. I had stumbled upon a rule: if you want to learn about anything awkward and wild (apart from Russell Brand, perhaps), speak to a researcher from the BBC Natural History Unit. Unwittingly, by coming to Stephen and Suzanne's picnic, we had stumbled upon a wildlife-focused version of MI6.

Thus the afternoon, for us at least, abruptly turned into a planning forum for our next few weeks of mammal-hunting. Within half an hour, we had information concerning Weasels, Barbastelle bats, Feral Goats and a whole host of other targets. Most of these were distant places for later weeks, but one priceless piece of information suddenly brought a possibility much closer to home. We were talking to a young man called Eddie, a friend of Mike's and one of the various walking and sitting wildlife gazetteers present.

"Do you know anything about the Leisler's Bats in Bristol?" I asked him. I had heard some rumours concerning this tricky species. We had vaguely contemplated the possibility of going bat-watching later on in the day.

"Oh yes," he replied. "Of course. I know exactly where they are, or at least where they were when I last saw them."

And from memory, he drew a map there and then. It was so detailed that it could have been a page from a Bristol street atlas.

Now we didn't just have the next few trips worked out. We had a plan for the evening, too.

The location in Bristol for the Leisler's Bats was one in the category known as an "emergence site". Having been tutored in bat jargon by Nick Tomlinson back home, we had eventually worked out what this was. It was a place where bats, having spent the day at their "roost site" – another term that tripped neatly off our collective tongues – finally "emerge" to spend the early evening feeding. It is, if you like, the equivalent of a door to an office block containing civil servants: when the day is over, they wake up and swarm out into the open air (though really I shouldn't use the word "swarm" – because "swarming" is another technical bat word, and one with acute sexual connotations to boot – more of that later).

The idea, therefore, was to wait where Eddie had directed and, at the appropriate time, about 80 Leisler's Bats should all stream out like – well, like bats out of a roost-site – and fly over us, and we could add their names to the family's tally of mammals seen.

What Eddie did not tell us, however, was that the site, which was on top of a hill and, appropriately enough, next to a graveyard, was also frequented by another misunderstood species that looked more scary than it actually was – the Bristol Youth. When we arrived there was a pack of three of them, dressed exactly as the field guides directed, with hoods over their heads and fags in their mouths. All males, they were laughing and drinking, and probably harmlessly mucking about. But we were in a big city, it was getting dark, the site was a tad enclosed, and all Carolyn and I had to protect us were a pair of kids aged six and four.

Happily, however, I learned something new that night. Leisler's Bats and Bristol Youth are both prone to emergence movements. The graveyard area, it turned out, was the Youths' day-roost, and they soon moved off into the centre of town, presumably to go foraging. We didn't see them again.

However, their place was taken by a man and a woman, with not a hood between them. They came into the open area somewhat furtively, like birds at a feeder, not sure whether it is safe or not to take the plunge. The man carried something in his hand which, with a quick look through my binoculars I could determine was not a knife nor, God forbid, a gun. It was a bat detector.

I introduced myself and the family. "Are you here for the Leisler's Bats?" I asked him.

"Yes," he replied in an unmistakable German accent. "Are you?"

I nodded. His name was Holger and the girl's name was Nadine, and he explained that they were both bat biologists.

"I haff been counting the Leisler's at this emergence during the spring and summer," said Holger. "But I haffen't been for the last month, and I'm not sure what to expect tonight."

I began to wonder whether we might be intruding. Holger and Nadine were obviously here for serious purposes, with counts to make and lofty matters to study. Quite what they made of Emily and Samuel, who were playing on a nearby bench, giggling, or indeed of our ineffectual attempts to stop our children being so noisy, was concealed by their impeccable Middle European politeness.

"I'm a bat," yelled Samuel, and proceeded to lean over until his head touched the bench, pretending to be upside down. We cringed. The bat people smiled politely.

At this moment a bat flew over. It was quite large, and it flew high and fast and directly, as if late for a crucial appointment.

"I sink that is a Leisler's," said Holger. "Pretty sure. It was flying high enough."

I looked over at the children. "I saw it, Daddy," said Emily, and returned to the game.

Holger set his bat detector to the magic frequency of 34 kilohertz, so that if another Leisler's flew past, it would register loud and clear. We all looked towards the tall trees from which the bat had come, and waited.

Nothing happened. In the next 20 minutes no Leisler's Bats appeared, although a few pipistrelles did, and flickered around the streetlight that was now bright and dominant.

Somewhere else, 79 Leisler's Bats must have emerged for the night. Holger looked disappointed. But as far as we were concerned – and I'm almost embarrassed to admit it – one was enough.

We left Bristol hardly gorged, but with a small modicum of satisfaction. The Leisler's Bat isn't a common mammal, except in Ireland, which is its world centre of distribution. The bat people struggle with how the Leisler's actually differs from its close but larger relative, the Noctule, as they seem to frequent similar habitats and eat the same food, the larger and faster insects of the night sky.

It's a conundrum. One day, someone like Holger or Nadine will find out.

## August 26th – Animals on the Edge

Most people associate the Somerset town of Cheddar with one of two things: cheese and the Gorge (and sometimes they will do the latter to the former). However, to mammalogists, Cheddar brings something quite different to mind: Hazel Dormice. The fact is, people have been studying Hazel Dormice in the coppiced woodland around the Gorge for years, and the boxes put up for this purpose have housed many generations of the sleepy rodents, as well as introducing hundreds of people to a very elusive mammal. Despite having their nests checked and counted once a month throughout the summer, the rodents simply cannot resist using the convenient contraptions, and keep coming back, day after day for a seriously deep Hazel Dormouse kip (if this sentence confuses you, remember they are nocturnal).

Having seen Edible Dormice without difficulty in July, our family was now intent upon nailing a dormouse double. It took a bit of arranging, but in the end we had managed to procure the services of Mammal Society employee and dormouse devotee, Alison Tutt, for a morning. She brought along her two children, Lewis and Harriet, making it very much a family box-check.

Now, having been semi-professional mammal-spotters for the best part of eight months, you would have thought that, as a family, we would have turned up for every trip with practised expertise and preparation. Never mind that the whole year had been chaotic from the start, with us forgetting our torches for the February cellar expedition and generally failing to bring along such basic equipment as wet wipes, food and suitable clothing on almost every occasion since. This time, in Cheddar Gorge, in front of a mammal expert and general outdoor aficionado, we probably made ourselves look even more incompetent than usual. Carolyn had forgotten her boots, the kids were wearing wellingtons (Sam's with Spiderman motifs on them), Emily had a dress on that offered no protection against brambles or insects, and we had all put on so many layers in the early morning rain that, in the humidity of the gorge's woodlands, we were all far too hot. So, in addition to carrying my notebook, I also had a rucksack full of coats and jumpers that we didn't need, as well as being overdressed myself. Furthermore, the ground wasn't just soggy, it was also precipitous. Samuel could hardly manage walking at all – so I carried him – and Emily kept falling over. Actually we all kept falling over. There were no paths, only pitfalls.

To make matters worse, the Tutt family had no such problems. Indeed, they looked to have been born to scrambling over chalky slopes in the August wet. They negotiated the tricky ground as surely as Chamois, and looked serenely at home. The two children raced ahead of ours, jumping, investigating and revelling in the outdoors. I thought that we, in our year of mammal-hunting, might have transformed ourselves into outdoorsy types, but the antics of our hosts just made us look like urban outcasts.

Not a lot of this would have mattered much if we could see the blasted Hazel Dormice. But the boxes, on the whole, remained stubbornly empty.

"We didn't see many last month, either" said Alison matter-of-factly. "They are easier to see in the spring." It wasn't very encouraging. By now we had checked 28 of the 50 available boxes.

A Wood Mouse tried to help. It ran away from one of the boxes and looked at first like a dormouse.

"Oh, we've seen loads of Wood Mice," said Emily, a little too dismissively for comfort.

We examined the evacuee's nest. "Ah yes," said Alison. "A Hazel Dormouse's nest would be neater than this. But a lot of people don't realise that Wood Mice can climb trees and use nest-boxes. They can make it right up to the canopy if they want to. But almost all the food they need they find on the ground. Dormice, on the other hand, do all their feeding in the trees."

We edged a little closer to our quarry a few boxes later, when we did find a Dormouse nest.

"It looks as though this nest has been used very recently," said Alison. "It's better woven than a Wood Mouse nest and – here we are – that's the bark of honeysuckle, which is a dead giveaway for a Dormouse nest. They use it to line them. And of course, honeysuckle doesn't grow on the ground. The Dormice are completely arboreal. Or at least, they are until next month, when they go down into little holes in the ground for their long winter sleep. The name comes from the French *dormir*. Let's hope we see one. We're getting closer."

It was precisely 78 per cent of the way through our box-check that we had a breakthrough. Actually, we nearly had a breakout. Having closed off the rear exit of the box with a plastic bag, and then opened the top, Alison was forced to put the shutter down again at great speed and cover the front entrance.

"We've got one," she declared. "I saw a pair of eyes looking out at me and it looked ready to run." She carefully extracted the box from its fixing wire, manoeuvred it so that it was all contained within the bag, and duly poured out a Hazel Dormouse, which ran around the bottom of the plastic bag for all to see.

"Ah, it's sweet," exclaimed Emily.

She was right. There's no getting away from it, Hazel Dormice are very cute indeed. I have heard them described as "overrated" by mammal specialists, but that's probably because these workers resent their lot of catching nothing else but Wood Mice and Bank Voles. Indeed, if there was a committee to design a rodent with wide appeal, the Hazel Dormouse might well be their prototype (mind you, a committee charged with producing the ideal children's programme came up with the *Teletubbies*, so you never know). Firstly, the Hazel Dormouse is small, no bigger than a Wood Mouse; secondly, its fur is a delicious golden-brown colour from head to foot, almost exactly mimicking the hue of a cornflake; thirdly, it has a well-proportioned head, body and tail, the latter being bushy and as long as the body; and then it has oversized, dark doe-eyes, as befit a nocturnal animal, and extremely long whiskers. To complete the picture, it spends a great deal of its life simply curled up and blissfully asleep – or, indeed, torpid.

We admired it for a while, took some photographs, then released it to the safety of the trees. It seemed to escape up into the canopy as fast as a fireman can descend a pole, with an effortlessness typical of a true arboreal specialist. Clearly, it didn't think we were cute at all.

And that was that. The remaining 11 boxes were utterly empty. We had seen one dormouse in the 50 boxes. Phew!

Alison was clearly relieved. I'm sure she was delighted for us and glad for the sake of our project that we had seen the Hazel Dormouse. But I couldn't help thinking that, since we had been successful, she would not have to go through the whole thing again: taking a family of poorly-shod, inappropriately dressed, incompetent mammal-spotters around her relatively simple box-round. But she was too polite to give anything away.

Presently she said: "Right, we had better go. We're going horse-riding this afternoon." And she set off in the car, taking her two nimble, healthy, fast-moving, country-bred kids away to resume their active lives.

We went to Brean Down to look for the Feral Goats there. It was a quick drive from Cheddar, and needed to be, because there is only so much mileage you can do to justify going to see some Goats – especially when there are some on farms just a few miles from where you live. To be honest, the Feral Goat seems a strange animal to have on the British list. But it is and, if you want to see 50 mammals in a year in Britain, you have to take in a few that might not be – shall we say – exciting.

The Wild Goat is not a native of Britain, but it has certainly been on our islands for a long time. Having originated in the Middle East, probably in Turkey or Iran, it was first introduced here in Neolithic times as a domestic animal with a usefully hardy edge. Doubtless many of these individuals escaped almost instantly, establishing themselves in the craggier, more mountainous parts of Britain – at the same time as spectacular animals such as Wolves and Brown Bears were still in the country. Who knows? Some of the Feral Goats in Scotland have ancestry dating back right to those early days. The Feral Goat, therefore, pre-dates such well-established British animals as Rabbits, Brown and Mountain Hares, and Fallow Deer.

It's just that Feral Goats don't look particularly wild. And certainly not on Brean Down, where they share the grassy slopes with Cattle of the same white colour. But we weren't here to question their provenance; we were here to spot them, and then have a cup of coffee.

Brean Down itself is one of the more spectacular features on the somewhat featureless Somerset coast, jutting out 2.5 kilometres ($1^1/2$ miles) between Weston-super-Mare and Burnham-on-Sea (can't these Somerset people settle on simpler names, for goodness' sake?) It is quite spectacular, standing 90 metres (300 feet) tall, and composed of chalky rock with sand near the bottom. It's actually a lost Mendip, being the westernmost of those hills and somewhat disconnected from the rest. It is known to have been settled for 10,000 years, and the bones of such fearsome prehistoric animals as Giant Deer and Woolly Mammoths have been found there. It still houses quite a good collection of wildlife, especially wild flowers, such as the White Rock-rose. Indeed, there is quite a white theme here, what with white chalk, white Cows and white Goats.

The road up to Brean Down is a vast lowland caravan site, complete with shops, blue gas canisters, endless bins and toilets every few hundred metres. Despite the dreary summer, it was pretty full, with families playing ball and pensioners walking hand-in-hand. And it was a shock after the imperious Cheddar Gorge and the delicious loneliness of its not quite mouse-infested woods.

"Let's not stay long," implored Carolyn.

When we arrived in the teashop, the chances of fulfilling that hope seemed remote.

"You want to see the Goats?" asked the waitress, in the same tone that she would doubtless adopt if someone had the temerity to ask for a refill. "Oh, you'll have to climb up to the top to do that."

We had seen the top. There were steps up to it, at least 20,000 of them.

"Please let's not do that," pleaded Carolyn, and Emily, and Samuel. And my heart.

So I had a brainwave and took my telescope from the car boot. I scanned the edges of the cliffs, in the precipitous spots where Feral Goats might live. It took about 30 seconds to find them. They were having a day off from being their usual stunt-goat selves, just feeding idly on some scrub upon a very gentle slope. I could see their horns enough to be sure. They also looked a little more hairy than Domestic Goats. There was darker colouring on some individuals, but their very overall whiteness seemed contrived and artificial. I was sure that if they had been black, like many Scottish goats, they would have commanded more interest.

# September

## September 1ˢᵗ – Notes from HQ, Part VII

Despite the Leisler's Bats, Hazel Dormice and Feral Goats, it had been a disastrous August, at least as far as our expectations were concerned. We had missed what should have been an easy-to-see whale, and we had made several attempts, local and further afield, to see Minks.

But those misses were nothing compared to an extraordinary sequence of crossed lines, unanswered emails and unreliable contacts that began to plague us, in addition to the soggiest August in a lifetime. As far as the latter was concerned, it was a bad month in a meteorologically poor summer (in fact, by some measures it was the wettest summer for 300 years – perhaps not the ideal choice for mammal-watching). We went camping one week in August, and it rained, without fail, every day. Several of those days it rained without stopping. There were rivers in the campsite. We needed flippers to move about. And, while rain by itself does not automatically make seeing mammals more difficult, it does make human beings somewhat more reluctant to see them.

But it wasn't really the rain, it was mishap. Typical of our whole summer of experiences is what happened today. About a month ago I heard, through our local Wildlife Trust magazine, that some Brown Long-eared Bats had taken residence in a nearby education centre, run by the Trust, and were also the stars of a webcam. I rang the staff and, yes, the Brown Long-eared Bats were indeed ensconced in the roof and, yes, it would be perfectly all right for us to take a peep in to see them for a few moments, as well as enjoy them on the screen. The staff member to whom I spoke, Steve Davis, did ask, however, for us to wait a while before viewing, since he was reluctant for us to disturb any females with young.

All perfectly reasonable and fair. We fixed up a visit for September 1st, by which time the young would be independent, and Steve would be back from holiday.

The trouble was, the young were indeed independent when Steve looked today – independent enough to have flown far and wide. They had gone, and so had all the adults. Steve was totally blameless, of course, and he felt unreasonably guilty. He had a good, hard look for the animals all around the building, when he should probably have been doing some other work.

In this case we were thwarted by happenstance. But surprisingly often, our contacts were either reluctant, or just plain unreliable. For example, I had been in contact with a man since June who had promised to show us Harvest Mice, a mammal I had never seen before and was particularly keen to find, especially as it is one of the smallest British rodents, and the only one mainly found in the herb layer – it is so tiny that it feeds among the standing stems of plants. He had assured me that he had an excellent site for these delightful mammals, and would invite us over to Buckinghamshire, when some overnight traps were to be opened. All enthusiasm, he also told us that it was a cast-iron site for Water Shrews, and he was planning to invite some other groups down to see these, too, since he was used to showing people his favourite mammals. During our conversation he also told us that he would look into finding out a place for House Mice, another mammal that we were intending to see somewhere.

As soon as I got off the phone to the man I felt elated. It wasn't just that he had promised to show us several excellent small mammals; he also stood out for his knowledge and willingness to help. Furthermore, since this guy was in the pipeline, it also meant that I didn't go about pursuing any other contacts for Harvest Mice. After all, I didn't want him to go to any unnecessary trouble, when we might be elsewhere, following up another lead for the same animal.

But the guy was a nightmare. He made these promises and kept none of them. He rarely answered emails, and when I pushed him he told me he was busy, but would try the following week. And of course, he never did. The thing is, I didn't mind if he was busy. That's fine. No hard feelings. I just wish I had said to him, "Don't worry. Just don't string us along with promises for bloody Harvest Mice and Water Shrews when you cannot keep them." Of course, had I known in advance, I would have tried somewhere else.

I'm sure that he meant well fundamentally, but less forgivably, there were some who clearly didn't. For example I was particularly getting frustrated with one mammal-group organiser, who was a bit capricious. He always seemed to ensure that we never met up with him and, nearing the zenith of the mammalling year, he promised that he would run small-mammal-trapping sessions, but never went as far as setting a date.

And this was by no means all. We were let down by numerous bat people, Weasel contacts, you name it. Almost every mammal that we hadn't yet seen seemed destined to lead us down a blind alley, either via a telephone line or cyberspace. And even when people replied, they were often far less helpful than I hoped for.

Now I am from a bird-watching background and I found all this incomprehensible. In bird-watching, people are accustomed to sharing information and helping each other: it comes with the territory. If I had decided to try to show my children 300 species of British birds in a year, I know that I would have had no trouble at all mobilising the birding community to help, and would have been awash with offers for this species or that – too many count. Had mammals been birds, if you see what I mean, then I am quite sure that we would have already hit our target by now, and would have been on our way to setting records.

Several people that I spoke to said that they weren't surprised by the cool reaction we had received. Mammal people, they suggested, are often somewhat elitist. They just don't want the general public to know about and appreciate "their" mammals. They want to go on doing their scientific studies and be left in peace, and the idea of kids taking a close look at, say, a Common Shrew is too ghastly to contemplate.

Another factor in the difference between birders and mammal people is that some of them are protectionist for financial reasons. These days, having a few small mammal traps and the requisite experience can earn you good money. Professional ecologists earn consultancy fees, which, while not astronomical, do promise a decent living at least. Perhaps it is not surprising they might be fearful of meddling nature writers and their raucous families.

Anyway, as I said above, I found the general attitude of many mammal scientists quite baffling. But nothing – absolutely nothing – could quite prepare me for the astonishing behaviour of the individual that I relate in the next section…

## September 15th – Barking up the Wrong Tree

On this day we met perhaps our least co-operative mammal of the year, and when we did we couldn't even count him.

It was a measure of our desperation, and the fact that we had been mired on 36 species for over a month at the height of the mammal-watching season, that we had even considered this particular expedition at all. Only half our usual team would be present. Emily was at school and was, therefore, ruled out of the trip, along with Carolyn, who had the job of collecting her. That left Samuel and I to travel to an audience with one of Britain's rarest mammals, the Bechstein's Bat. It wasn't ideal – a bit of a stretching of our one parent and one child rule. But, with so many frustrations building up, we needed some momentum.

I must admit, I was looking forward to seeing this particular species of bat. Not only is it quite intriguing to look at, with the third longest ears of any British species (after – surprise, surprise – the two species of long-eared bats), it is also a mysterious creature, restricted to southern Britain in old-growth woodland. Very little is known about it, and the first breeding colony in Britain was only found in 1964. Its middle-European name also makes it sound rather grand and aristocratic. Having a Bechstein's Bat on our collective family list would give us a certain indefinable gravitas.

Our contact for the Bechstein's certainly treated the bats as if they were members of the aristocracy. He was insistent that the only way we could see the colony would be to tag along to one of his prearranged surveys. When I mentioned that September 15th was a school day and a bit inconvenient, he divulged that it would be the last survey of the year.

He began to sound like one of those troublesome minders acting on behalf of an overindulged starlet.

Nonetheless, I decided that, inconvenience aside, it would be worth a try. The survey was due to start at 10:00am and Sam and I aimed to be there to link up with the last part of the checking and counting. That was the plan. It was explained to us that there could be up to thirty Bechstein's in the wood altogether, which I reckoned would give us an excellent chance of success.

The trip took a good deal longer than expected, and progressed in an atmosphere of mounting frustration. Several times on the journey I stopped to call for directions, but, despite ringing, the mobile number I had been given was never answered, which meant that Sam and I were travelling blind. Eventually, after some detective work, we found a lay-by in which was parked a van with a bat logo on it. But now, with no sign of people anywhere, I was concerned that we would never find the bat surveyors in what was clearly a very large wood. Still the ringing mobile was not answered; it was getting to the stage where it might be easier to fix up an interview with Lord Lucan. As I became more and more distracted, Sam, having finished his own packed lunch, tucked into mine as well. This was not an auspicious beginning.

There was nothing for it but to enter the wood and hope to link up with the box-checkers. But as soon as we entered under the trees, a gloomy pall seemed to descend. This didn't seem to be a "friendly" wood; it was on steeply undulating ground, with heavy, waterlogged soil, and an undergrowth so thick and tall that I'm willing to bet it could have protected Sleeping Beauty for an extra hundred years.

"Don't like it. Want to go home," complained Samuel as we made our way through a passageway of briars.

"We're here to see some lovely bats," I reassured him unconvincingly. "Let's see if we can find the bat people. They'll have ladders."

"Don't want to," he repeated, turning up the volume.

Sam was about to switch to his "above pneumatic drill" decibel level when, at the convergence of three paths, we happened upon a leprechaun dressed in a green tunic sitting on a large, red toadstool. Actually, it was really a young woman from the local Bat Group, but in these circumstances it honestly could have been either. She directed us up a path to where, if all went well, we might finally meet the Bechstein's Bats' self-appointed ambassador to tired, frustrated mammal-watchers with aching backs.

The leader of the survey was in cheery mood. We came upon him descending a ladder, surrounded by a couple of youthful acolytes, both of them professionals. He was younger than I expected, short, round-faced and heavily built. Even so, as we were to discover, his frame still propelled him up ladders and down snakes faster than the counter in the board game. "We've just had 17 Bechstein's up in those boxes over there," he informed me happily, pointing up into the crown of a huge sweet chestnut some 100 metres (325 feet) away, where three boxes were fixed in a bunch like loud-speakers at a stadium.

"That's great," I countered, expectantly. "We've come to see Bechstein's."

"Nothing here, though," he said, looking dismissively up the trunk he had just descended. "Right," he declared to the party. "On to the next one."

At this he abruptly set off down the hill towards the next box-adorned tree, while his army tried to keep up. I looked up towards the Bechstein's Bats' home and wondered why this man hadn't suggested that we might simply mount a ladder and look inside, thus easily completing our family's assignment. Presumably there were more Bechstein's to come, and our obvious haste downhill was necessary to complete this important survey. By the time Sam and I staggered breathlessly to the base of the next trunk, he had already ascended his ladder and was opening up a box. He was extraordinarily quick. We barely had time to feel the anticipation of a possible longed-for addition to our family's list.

But there were no Bechstein's at this cluster of residences at all. Just a bit of poo. The bat professionals entered into a long discussion about droppings, peering at the faeces in their hands with a heady combination of fascination and reverence. Apparently bat droppings are distinctive in the same way that bird pellets are; the poo indicates the diet and the diet can be diagnostic of the bat species.

But under my breath I kept thinking: "I haven't just come all this way to see…"

"Right, next box," declared the bats' minder. And we set off again at military pace.

For the next half-hour or so the check continued in a similar vein, with ladders being ascended and descended with astonishing speed and agility. Under guidance, we checked boxes at a formidable rate, but they were invariably empty of Bechstein's Bats. One box had an enormous, bulging hornet's nest beside it, a pitted, swollen carbuncle like those terrible swellings you sometimes see in medical books. It was enough to put off bats and bat-watchers alike, but ignite a flicker of interest from my evidently flagging son.

Despite the obvious speed and efficiency of the survey, it came as a surprise, even a shock, when it was suddenly announced that an empty box hanging over a stream was our last check of the day.

"But what about the Bechstein's?" I blurted out, showing a little more frustration than I probably should have done.

"That's wildlife!" the bat-man replied, unable to conceal a smile. With that he hoisted his ladder on his shoulder with effortless grace, and began to march back up the hill towards the road.

For a moment I stood there, incredulous. This man knew that Sam and I had taken a great deal of trouble to join his survey. He knew that we had driven here with the sole and specific intention of finding this rare bat. He knew all about our family mammal challenge. Surely he would offer to take Sam and I back the short distance to the Bechstein's tree where we could take a peep in?

But when we finally caught up with him again at the car park, he had nearly finished packing up and the thought had clearly not crossed his mind. Perhaps he hadn't understood.

"Is there any chance you could take us back to look at the Bechstein's?" I enquired.

He shook his head. "Nah. I'm tired of carrying my ladder. And besides, I can't show you them because that would constitute wilful disturbance of the bats at the roost."

I checked his expression to see whether he was joking.

He had just officially taken 17 Bechstein's Bats out of a box, put them in bags, handled them, checked their sexual organs, weighed them, put rings on them and carried them back up a ladder to reshuffle themselves at the roost site. And was he honestly now claiming that it was wilful disturbance to climb a ladder, shine a torch on them, show them to a grateful family for a few seconds and gently shut them away for the season?

Yup, he was.

And was he claiming that, despite his evident facility with handling ladders, he was now too tired to go?

Yup.

I put my foot in it.

"Look, I'll pay you to show them to us. I'll carry the ladder."

Now this was silly, and I knew I was going out on a limb. To him it probably sounded as though I was paying him to break the law. But in my defence I did not understand – or entirely buy – this business about wilful disturbance. Furthermore, we hadn't seen a new mammal for a month, I had been carrying Sam on my shoulders on and off for an hour over heavy terrain, I had had no lunch and now faced a long drive home with nothing to show for it. The prospect was appalling. But my desperation killed the possibility dead. He was now offended.

Our chastened family left with our tails between our legs. There wasn't much conversation on the way home. I felt like giving up entirely. Our family project was supposed to be fun. It was supposed to be informative. We were hoping to blaze a trail of seeing wild mammals in a quiet and legal way without disturbing any of them unduly. I had hoped to be excited and inspired by the enthusiasts we had met. The trip had been a disastrous betrayal of all these hopes.

Not long afterwards, however, I managed to confirm what I instinctively suspected at the time. Other bat workers were quite appalled at our experience when I relayed it to them. Several explained that a Bat Licence actually allows you to disturb these animals for legitimate educational purposes (surely a book is educational), and so it would not have contravened the licence holder's rights to show us the Bechstein's after all. Others privately expressed that they would certainly have made an effort to help us anyway, especially bearing in mind that we had tried to fit into the survey timetable.

I should say that, to the letter of the law, the surveyor was right. But then, if he had co-operated by answering my calls to his mobile phone, Sam and I would have reached him on time to see the Bechstein's Bats legitimately.

Looking back, I suppose I should have picked up the signals earlier. He never really showed much enthusiasm for us to join his survey in the first place, and clearly I never adequately enthused him with the ethos of our family mammal challenge. He doubtless thought it pointless and trivial – and that's a legitimate opinion – but perhaps wasn't convinced enough in his own mind to forbid us from coming at all.

Incredibly, just recently I heard a story that made our unfortunate Bechstein's experience sound as though we had been subject only to the mildest dose of bat worker xenophobia. This story really does call into question the attitude of some of these often dedicated and committed mammal specialists, and how much they genuinely want to promote public interest and goodwill for bats among the general natural history public. To my mind, it underlines a certain confusion in the world of bat politics. Do "Bats need friends", as the old campaign used to enquire, or not?

The story concerns the appearance of a real rarity, a Parti-coloured Bat, a visitor from the Continent. Incidentally, the name refers to the bi-coloured hairs on the animal's back, which are brown close to the skin but have frosted tips, but the species is quite smart-looking as well, with dense, snowy white fur on its tummy. The Parti-coloured happens to be the only European bat to possess two pairs of mammary glands, instead of one, the sort of detail to make the scientists' juices flow.

When a peripatetic individual turned up in Norfolk at about the same time that we were struggling to see the Bechstein's, it was spotted by some bird-watchers as it flew in off the sea. Any migrant bat recorded in these circumstances is likely to be special and, sure enough, once the wanderer was identified as a Parti-coloured, it constituted just the twentieth or so record for Britain in the whole of history. Wow! This set off the British mammal-watchers' grapevine to high alert, and within hours every dedicated spotter in the country must have known about this bat's arrival. So did many others with a less keenly developed interest, as the record also appeared on the famously efficient bird-watchers' information services. It so happened that one of those who was originally summoned by a phone call was our good friend John Dixon. Hugely inconveniently, when he found out about this chance in a lifetime he happened to be at a wedding in Yorkshire.

The Parti-coloured Bat, meanwhile, did not have a clue about the fuss it was causing; it had found its way to a pleasantly dark World War II pillbox and promptly gone to roost. Not surprisingly, after what was probably a journey of several hundred miles, it slept very soundly indeed, so soundly that several ecstatic enthusiasts managed to visit the pillbox and take record photographs without disturbing it at all. If you'll pardon the expression, it didn't bat an eyelid.

John was certainly in a far more distressed state than the object of his desire. After much agony, he decided to leave the wedding. Dutifully remaining until the bride and groom had officially begun their happy journey, he began a very tense three-hour journey of his own towards Kelling, where the bat had been reported. John adores his mammals and cares about them deeply, and he was desperate not to miss the opportunity to witness a wild specimen of this exceptional rarity.

Sadly, however, he was to be disappointed – as were many others. When John got to Kelling, the Parti-coloured Bat had disappeared. To quote another bat enthusiast of my acquaintance – that's wildlife. An unfortunate case of the animals you love so much leaving you woefully unrequited, perhaps?

But no. As it turned out, the bat had been removed deliberately before John managed to get there. In an act of cloak-and-dagger deception, a bat worker in plain clothes (I kid you not) had gone into the pillbox alone, whipped out a bag, removed the slumbering foreign visitor from its comfortable wall, then stuffed bat and bag into his pocket. He then made off through the gathering crowds, disappearing from the scene of his burglary, evidently without causing the slightest stir.

The justification for this bizarre kidnap, was that the bat was removed "for its own protection". But the question here is: protection from what or whom? Only, it seems, from a group of enthusiasts who were prepared to travel hundreds of miles to enjoy the briefest of views. All they would have needed would have been to admire the bat while it was fast asleep, or to watch it when it emerged from the pillbox in the evening to continue its remarkable journey.

Once again, the bat worker concerned was perhaps following the letter of the law, preventing any disturbance to the Parti-coloured Bat that was, technically, illegal. But in this case, it is my opinion, the law is an ass and the result was to the detriment of everybody.

What happened to the bat in the end, nobody knows. I just hope it is still flying about in the wild somewhere and that, one day, it will find its way to John's backyard.

# September 27ᵗʰ – Getting Intimate in the Savernake Forest

Boy, did we need an antidote to bats and everything batty…

Except that they say, if you fall off a bicycle, you should get straight back behind the handlebars. Maybe a bat trip was exactly what we needed. A bat trip on which we might actually feel moderately welcome.

Actually, we had little choice. Months ago I had booked us on a trip to the Savernake Forest with the excellent People's Trust for Endangered Species, with the specific intention of looking for bats. I had paid for it, too, and didn't want to waste our money, even if it was bloody bats again. We also owed it to the National Trust to be there, since they had sent a photographer along to capture images of us enjoying our year of mammal-watching for their magazine.

And then, in positive vein, there was also the prospect of seeing a Barbastelle.

Up until now, despite my best efforts, you probably haven't quite become reconciled to the concept of individuality in bats. A bat is a bat is a bat, you say. They all look the same and they are all boring. But folks, that's only because you haven't been introduced to the Barbastelle. Honestly. I can perfectly understand you thinking, "Oh no, I've got to read about bats again", but really, this bat is different. It isn't brown and tackily membranous, it's big and plump and has long, glossy-black fur, like a dark flying mouse. It has a squashed, pug-like face, also black, and long ears, which – believe it or not – meet together on the forehead, between the eyes. Now, find me another animal in the world whose ears meet together like this, and you are free to overlook the charms of the Barbastelle.

The Barbastelle was also very rare indeed, and I had always wanted to see one. In fact, of all Britain's mammals, let alone bats, the Barbastelle was one I had most wanted to see when we started the project.

We were fortunate indeed that our trip was led by Steve Laurence. He turned out to be friendly, understanding of the children (and of our photographer, Layton), possessed with an encyclopaedic knowledge of his subject and – to ameliorate any sense of intellectual overdrive – a truly wicked sense of humour. He might have been built like a rugby player, but he was gentle to bats and people alike.

We knew we were in for a memorable day when Steve began it talking at length about rabies. In the last few years, a bat worker in Scotland had died after being bitten by a bat, and this stimulated quite a strand of discussion.

"Three people in Europe have died, too, after bites from Serotines," he told us. "That's because those bats bite hard. About six per cent of their population are estimated to be carriers. So we all have to wear gloves and keep up with our rabies jabs."

He followed this with a story. "I had to climb miles up to a roof once to get to a roost of bats. It was a very long way up and took me ages, and when I reached the bats I realised that I didn't have any gloves with me. Well, needless to say, one of the little blighters managed to get hold of my finger and didn't let go, and it drew blood. So I had to go to hospital to get a proper jab…"

"Mind you," he went on. "It matters a great deal where you are bitten. If it's in your finger, you can survive for much longer, but if the bat gets your face, it isn't far to the brain…"

And so on. It wasn't much of a recruitment drive for bat workers, but it certainly helped to break the ice. It only took a few minutes for Steve to wrap our small group around his little finger, bitten or otherwise.

We soon found ourselves in the bat enthusiast's natural habitat: below a tall, deciduous tree with boxes on it, along a forest ride. A young bat worker was sent up a ladder and soon made positive noises about the box's contents, which happened to be 17 Brown Long-eared Bats. These were the first our family had encountered in the year (and our thirty-seventh mammal) and, true to their name, these bats had very long ears indeed. Frankly, they made a rabbit appear seriously poorly endowed. They were the sort of feature that you simply wouldn't mention if you were meeting someone for the first time, for fear of embarrassment or repetition: "Charles, Sir, you do have fine lugholes!" that kind of thing.

The 17 were brought down wrapped collectively in the folds of an old T-shirt (softly, but in a firm grip). They were too sleepy to fly off, so they just stayed hanging there, passively, awaiting their turn to be processed.

"These bats may live for thirty years or more," Steve told us. "Yet they may only be active, in terms of being ready to fly about, for about five per cent of that time." And we could believe it.

He held the first bat out to demonstrate what ordeal awaited the inhabitants of the box. "What we need to do is to determine the age and sex, weigh them and measure their forearms," he informed us. "We used to take the parasites off them, too, because there's a bloke who's been taking bat blood out of ticks and using it for DNA analysis, to see how the different European populations of bats are related. But we don't any more."

"You see these wings, how rounded they are?" Steve went on. "This species of bat only flies at about walking pace, and it stays within the wood and among the trees. It hovers a lot and will sometimes catch its food by landing and wrapping its wings around the victim, in a sort of Dracula's cloak style…"

"…Look at the eyes. These bats see very well and often catch their prey without any echolocation at all."

The processing of the 17 Brown Long-eared Bats took more than an hour and a half in total. And, during that time, Steve never once stumbled in his exposition of bat biology. He answered every question that the participants could throw at him, and had answered most of them before they could even be thrown. I was in awe of his knowledge, something I had become accustomed to with bat people generally. What is it about these animals that engenders such passion and enquiry from certain people?

I'm not sure, but at this stage in their life it was all a little too much for Emily and Samuel. Eventually, they, together with Carolyn, sat at the base of a tree and told stories. Soon I joined them. We all made a tower out of fallen sticks.

Actually, it was just as well that the kids' attention had been drawn away, because the bat conversation was beginning to turn to the subject of sex – one that is never far from any biologist's mind, though mainly in the passive sense, you will understand.

"These male Brown Long-eared Bats are pretty poorly endowed," Steve's voice echoed across the woodland floor. "You can age the males by the colour of the epididymis. It's black in the youngsters, then gets more speckled as more and more sperm is created over the animal's lifetime. See here, this bat is a young one…"

"…The nipples in a bat aren't where we are used to seeing them…"

"…Bats produce a lot of sperm because they try to inseminate as many females as they can. But recent studies are uncovering an unexpected level of fidelity…"

And on and on, enthusiastic post-watershed conversation drifting off into the early autumn breeze. Meanwhile the bats themselves were demonstrating it all in brutally unsubtle fashion. I was reminded of those occasions when teams of junior doctors follow their teachers around a hospital and the patient's intimate physical details are discussed between them: "My gosh, have you observed anything like that before? Best example I've ever seen."

The intimate details of Brown Long-eared Bat breeding biology were briefly interrupted by the arrival of a Noctule that had been processed by the other half of our group. This one was a good deal bigger than the animals we had been dealing with, and it was concomitantly assertive. It gave off shrill calls that were clearly indications of displeasure and, owing to their high pitch and intensity, were actually quite painful to hear. He took one look at Steve and latched on to his gloved finger with teeth sharp enough to pierce the carapace of a hefty beetle.

"Naughty bat," scolded Sam. This was something of an issue for our son, who had been told off recently himself for biting. Why should a bat get away with it?

"See how big this bat is?" said Steve, admiringly. "Lovely rich golden brown, with quite a nice nose? And now, have a go at smelling him…"

We all gathered round. The kids made loud sniffing noises, and recoiled.

"That's ammonia from the urine," Steve laughed. "It might also explain why the fur is so richly coloured."

"Naughty bat," repeated Samuel.

That afternoon, we struck gold with our bats. The lucky dip from a box placed on a pond-side tree revealed, at last, three Barbastelles. They were every bit as weird and different and cuddly as I had anticipated, and everybody crowded around them with a renewed curiosity and pleasure, after three hours of bat processing. These guys were real box-office monsters (the bats, that is).

"See the Barbie dolls," I teased Emily. "Barbie doll" was a nickname for these bats that I had heard from another bat worker. The actual name – "Barbastelle" – literally means "little beard", from the longish fur on the chin.

"That's not Barbie," she replied indignantly. "Daddy, you can be so silly sometimes."

By the late afternoon, we were feeling as tired as the last traces of green left on the leaves of the forest trees. However, for the People's Trust for Endangered Species event itself, the closure of bat-box processing was merely the interval between performances. At nightfall Steve was planning to visit a nearby tunnel to try to catch some more bats. Indeed, he was expecting to do this well into the night, and throughout the night, if necessary. That's because he would be, in effect, visiting a nightclub.

During the autumn I had been hoping for us all to witness an intriguing phenomenon known as "swarming", which coincides with the beginning of the mating season in bats. On calm nights, many hundreds of certain species congregate at the entrances to hibernation sites, such as caves and tunnels, and effectively meet and greet each other and indulge in the beginnings of sexual behaviour. What makes for good viewing is the sheer number of individuals involved, and the fact that they fly in and out of the tunnel entrances repeatedly, making for a spectacular display. The reason for this swarming is that, during the summer, bats exist in genetically isolated colonies. The swarming enables them to broaden their horizons considerably, meeting individuals from elsewhere and mating with strangers. The meetings help to mix-up the gene pool, and probably also enable the bats to exchange information about potential hibernation sites.

The serious business of breeding carries on through the autumn and winter, in the hibernation sites. Males often wake up and copulate with sleepy females between bouts of profound slumber. The babies, one to each female each season, are born in June, regardless of when copulation took place, owing to a physiological delay in fertilisation.

Only a few species of bats carry out swarming behaviour, including the Brown Long-eared, Daubenton's and Natterer's Bat. Had we joined Steve for the night trip, I also knew we would have had an excellent chance of seeing two further species, the Brandt's Bat (Bratz bat, according to Emily) and the Whiskered Bat – two species that are so similar that they are best told apart (typically) by the shape of the male's penis. But we were all just too tired. Attending would have broken our rule of combining fun with observing the mammals.

And besides, I knew that the conversation would be even *more* post-watershed than it had been earlier in the day.

## September 28th – The Killer Among the Rocks

It was late September, and we were getting distinctly edgy about our lack of shrews. This was really a ridiculous predicament to be in – almost a disgrace. Shrews are among Britain's most abundant mammals, with populations of 41,700,00 (Common Shrew), 8,600,000 (Pygmy Shrew) and 1,900,000 (Water Shrew) at the start of each breeding season. And although we had heard their mega-high-pitched calls in the long grass from time to time, we hadn't yet managed to see a single one. We had therefore missed about 50 million shrews, which you might conclude was more than a little careless.

However, the picture wasn't quite as simple as that. Shrews are incredibly secretive. They live, in the case of Common and Pygmy Shrews, in dense patches of grass and other vegetation, so they are permanently hidden by cover, and, indeed, they routinely feed in small underground tunnels. They are also extremely light and diminutive, making even mice look gross, bloated and overweight; the Pygmy Shrew, which may weigh as little as 2.5 grams ($1^1/2$ drams) and as much as 6 grams ($3^1/2$ drams), making it one of the smallest mammals in the world.

They are intriguing to look at. You might lump every small mammal into a mouse category, but this would only be a very superficial impression. They have bodies that look squashed vertically, and decidedly horizontally elongated. The legs are extremely short, adding to the cylindrical look, and their tails comparatively short. But it's their heads and faces that really mark them out. The ears are almost hidden by thick, glossy fur, and their eyes are greatly reduced. Their head is dominated by a long snout, fitted with outsized whiskers. The snout is always moving around, in a somewhat mechanical fashion, making it look like one end of a worm, or a feeler, or a Dalek's eyestalk. This feature makes shrews seem peculiar, even other-worldly.

But should you get it into your head that these midgets must be gentle creatures that wouldn't hurt a fly, then think again. Instead, they are voracious predators, sinking their teeth into everything that moves within the labyrinthine undergrowth of the field layer. They wouldn't just hurt a fly, they would lacerate its exoskeleton, and cause the theatrical explosion of its internal juices, resulting in an agonising death – think *Texas Chainsaw Massacre* multiplied by *Psycho*, to a factor of 10. Nothing is safe as far as a shrew is concerned – not flies, nor earthworms, nor spiders, nor beetles, nor grasshoppers. Daddy-long-legs, would first be daddy-no-legs and then no-legs-no-daddy, all in a matter of seconds. Shrews are vicious, bloodthirsty and voracious. They cannot go for more than about an hour without eating, 24 hours a day, every day of the year. They are killing machines.

As such, they are really quite irresistible.

Not only do small invertebrates wake up in the night, sweating with shrew-fear, but shrews get severely het up about each other, too. They are fervently territorial, and simply cannot stand each other's company whenever they meet (hostilities are temporarily suspended for breeding purposes). If a shrew comes face-to-face with another shrew, neither will back down and, like two BMW drivers heading towards each other on a single track road, the inevitable intransigence causes a fight to ensue.

Fantastic. That is my kind of creature. A bit of spite and spunk.

However, as I mentioned above, shrews are very difficult to see and, to make life still more awkward, even harder to catch. Although curious by nature, it seems that they are suspicious of traditional mammal traps, and they are so light on their feet that it is certain that they sometimes enter chambers, help themselves to the food on offer (which is usually maggots, or fly larvae known to fishermen as "casters"), and then creep out again without tripping the catch. There is also the fuzzy legal problem of catching them in the first place. You cannot set out to trap shrews intentionally without a licence, and on your average mammal-trapping session you can only obtain them as "collateral damage", if you will – i.e. catching them unintentionally, when your real target is other small mammals. Quite frankly, it's batty. But shrews are delicate, and if traps are set without adequate food and bedding, those traps can easily prove to be a shrew's final resting place. And, believe it or not, if a shrew dies on your watch, you have to report it to Natural England.

Our other shrew problem I have mentioned before. We had trusted our local mammal group to run plenty of trips where shrews were likely to be caught, but none had yet been forthcoming. So, although we had expected to be able to show the children lots of shrews with effortless ease, we were now in the absurd position of scratching around for these abundant mammals. We might as well have been trying to buy apples in an orchard, but unable to find the owner to complete the transaction.

Well, in the last week I had scratched a little harder and finally found someone to run a shrew trip for us. One was called Sally, a woman who ran a bat hospital from her bedroom, the other was a lady called Jan, who, like most other small-mammal enthusiasts hereabouts, was also a member of the splendid Dorset Bat Group. We felt guilty enlisting these blameless people to find us shrews, but if I am being entirely honest, we were getting a bit frazzled at the lack of the long-snouted mass murderers, and I was prepared to start leaning harder on people's goodwill. Shameful, isn't it?

Sally and Jan had been contacted by the Dorset Wildlife Trust during the summer to survey the small mammals off the foreshore off Kimmeridge Bay, close to Swanage, on Dorset's Jurassic Coast. This is one of the finest patches of coastline anywhere in Southern England, with the chalky rock doorway of Durdle Dor, the two Old Harry Rocks (which are a sort of poor man's Needles), the stratified mini-cliffs at Dancing Ledge, and the gentle sandy beaches of Studland Bay. Kimmeridge, for its part, was Britain's first marine nature reserve, renowned for its seahorses and exceptional underwater fauna. It is a sheltered spot, with a long, gentle drop from the land to the rocky beach, neatly curvaceous and protected both west and east.

Excitingly for us, part of the reason for the Nature Reserve's request had been a couple of reports of Pygmy Shrews among the rocks close to the high water mark. Presumably cursing our family's preoccupation with awkward mammals, Jan had driven down the previous night to set the traps in likely places. Now, at an outrageously early hour, we were to rendezvous with Sally and Jan to see what the nightly activities of small mammals had ushered into the traps.

We stood yawning on the slipway. The sea was calm enough to skim a stone across the Channel. The sun was out and there was a warm, end-of-summer feel to the day. Hundreds of swallows skimmed overhead and struck purposefully southward. The grassy sward on the gently rising land surrounding the bay had barely lost the exclamatory green of summer. We could see the reflections of the rocks on the beach, crammed together like commuters in a tube train, still and uncomplaining, barely shimmering on the water's surface. Right out to sea, a boat made such steady progress that it might have been swimming on its back.

The peace of the place was infectious. But we would have appreciated it a lot more if we hadn't had to meet at the crack of dawn.

Early morning, it must be said, is not the ideal time for anyone in our family, apart perhaps from Emily, who is bright and sparky whenever she is awake. The rendezvous time was 7:30am, so Carolyn and I had left the house on empty stomachs and brought drinks and breakfast with us to quell any storms of youthful tantrums – or adult tantrums, come to that – that hunger might have engendered. The kids were still munching breakfast bars when Sally (who is partly nocturnal, since she spends half her life looking after bats) turned up. Shortly afterwards, Jan – a lady in her fifties with a mild and thorough manner that concealed a keen, dry sense of humour, did so too, looking a little ruffled. She was wearing a worried expression.

"I only put out seven traps. I hope we've got something," she said.

Immediately my heart sank. Seven didn't sound very many, especially considering the prickly reputation earned by Pygmy Shrews, who enter traps with the same suspicion a millionaire reserves for a visit to his wallet. I suppose I had hoped that there might be around 500 of them, spread along a kilometre or more of beach, to give us an even chance.

Unfortunately, and predictably, there was nothing in the traps except a Wood Mouse. Not knowing Jan very well, we all made every effort we could to suggest that, if this individual was not actually the first Wood Mouse we had seen this year (it was at least the twentieth), then it was, by a long distance, the very best, and well worth the effort. I'm not sure we fooled anyone, especially when the children yawned and began to ask to go home mid-way through Jan's examination of its genitalia. Still, I can record that the Wood Mouse was a female.

Our day was partly saved when a man from the Kimmeridge Centre, named Steve, pitched up and began to show us what a remarkable place Kimmeridge Bay really was. He demonstrated this in somewhat unconventional style, by kicking over a shoreline rock with his boot. Normally, if you do this in a garden or woodland, you might reveal a couple of earthworms, an earwig and a beetle, say, which soon scurry away out of sight. But here there were enough invertebrates for a Bushtucker Trial on "I'm a Celebrity, Get me out of Here". It was simply teeming with them, hundreds under every rock, sand-hoppers, spiders and who knows what else? There were creepy-crawlies covering ever square millimetre of exposed beach, not just under the rocks but under the seaweed, too. It was a quite astonishing sight, enough to make any insectivorous shrew's eyes pop out of its head – small though their eyes are.

"There are a number of very rare creatures on this beach," said Steve. "We have identified several sand-hoppers found in very few other areas of Britain. It's a biodiversity hotspot."

Except, I thought to myself, for mammals.

"Hang on, what's this?" exclaimed Steve, suddenly. His sub-surface examinations had disturbed something, which was moving through the rocks at a run.

"It's a shrew!" yelled Sally.

I spotted it almost under my feet.

"Quick, Carolyn, get the children here."

The ground was tricky at best, and the rocks sharp and slippery, the seaweed gooey as treacle. My exhortation was enough to set off a sort of dance, whereby four adults and two children jumped one way, then another, in an effort to spot the shrew. At the same time there were shouts of "here!" every few moments, as the shrew, our choreographer, moved us rapidly from one side of the beach to the other and back again. It could have been described as a hot-shrew shuffle.

Eventually, we all saw it as it disappeared down an abandoned drainpipe.

"Common Shrew," said Sally. "It was too big for a Pygmy, and too much contrast between the back and the tummy."

It's amazing what an incredibly bad view of the back end of a small mammal will do. Essentially, it transformed the trip to Kimmeridge from a mildly interesting trip to the beach, into a triumph. Well OK, it wasn't a very big triumph, but this year I had learned that every sighting of a new mammal was something to savour. I had also grown fond of shrews, these little assassins, just in the course of researching them and trying to work out how best to see them. I hoped that we might see plenty more before the year was out.

So early had we started the day that we all made it to church later that morning. And during the service, I could have prayed – but didn't – for all those invertebrates swarming about under the rocks, every one living in a terrifying world, each a target for the jaws of the killer among the rocks.

# October

## October 4th – Fens and Peaks

A sudden flurry of successful spottings had begun to raise the possibility that, despite our poor summer, we might actually reach our goal of seeing 50 mammals in a year in Britain. I began to make strategies and plans, and even to harbour the green shoots of genuine optimism. Perhaps, after all the frustrations of failed contacts and missed sightings of summer, we would now slide effortlessly and imperiously towards our total, completing the whole thing before the leaves had fallen off the trees?

At the same time the world's financial markets began to crash. For a while we began to worry about the cost of what we were doing. To drive anywhere had suddenly become frighteningly expensive. Were we being irresponsible? Should we be cavorting round the country trying to find furry mammals when more serious things were going on in the world? Did we have our heads in the sand?

We had a think, and then concluded that we didn't. Part of the ethos of our year-long journey was that in life, you need challenge, fun and diversion, regardless of circumstance. In a way this project was a statement against the need to be overwhelmed by such prosaic things as money. To see mammals is a free activity, and of itself, so is adventure and the joy of being in the countryside. We needed to carry on, if we could.

Besides, Carolyn had developed a taste for staying in Premier Inns.

To be honest, I think she had probably got rather sick of looking for mammals ("Oh no, are we going to see another bat? I'm tired of looking at bats," she would say). I could not blame her. She doesn't see herself as a natural wildlife-spotter, and after months dedicatedly following her husband's absurd plan around the country, it had all begun to get her down. Heroically, from my perspective, she was keeping to the plot, long after most wives would probably have told me to stick a Pine Marten down my throat.

However, she had not lost her great passion for travelling. This is a woman who has travelled the world from Pakistan (a year, no less) to Australia, from Rwanda to Rio, Peru to Bolivia, and lapped it all up along the way. She was invited to join the Mujaheddin to fight the Russians near the Khyber Pass, and she survived an earthquake near La Paz. This is a woman with serious airmiles and a love of colourful people and rich experiences. Her interest in the world and its possibilities was part of what originally led me to fall in love with her. Knowing her as I do, I guess seeing four species of very slightly different mouse was bound to struggle for her attention.

But this love for going to new places, which kept her sane when hunting mammals, was also an opportunity for us. Having spent much of our time this year in the southern counties of England, we now shifted focus a little to contemplate going greater distances up north. To our advantage, there were quite a few easy targets scattered about to add to our total of 39 species, found in places such as the Fens and Derbyshire's Peak District. On this day, we broke out to see them.

Actually, one trip that I was particularly hoping to take this weekend had fallen through. A man called Martin Kitchen, who ran holidays and day-trips in Northumberland under the name of "Northern Experience Wildlife Tours", had invited us to join him on a boat trip off the coast from Seahouses, in search of sea mammals. In recent weeks he had recorded several species of dolphin, and even Minke Whales, in the Druridge Bay area, and we were eager to join him, since our encounters with whales and dolphins up to now had been thin, to say the least. He had offered us the whole trip free, in support of our project, and had even offered to get several of his colleagues stationed down the coast to relay to us any land-based sightings. Yet despite all this kindness, a ferocious weather front had lashed the north of Britain and rendered it pointless getting out of bed, let alone taking to the seas. Once again we were thwarted in our attempts to see any cetaceans.

Instead, therefore, we had decided to go for a couple of deer species that, up until now, we had held in reserve as "likely to see". One of these was the exotically named Chinese Water Deer, an animal that inhabits the wetlands of the Orient and is one of the less likely animals you might expect to thrive in Britain. It was introduced into Woburn Park in 1896 and at the time no one would have treated it as anything but a curiosity alongside the other strange animals that lived there at the time, such as Grey Squirrels. But by 1945 it was noted in the wild for the first time, and self-sustaining populations have been living in the south and east of England ever since, increasing to 2,100 animals by 2004.

The other deer we were after would probably be much more familiar to most readers. It is called the Muntjac or, to give it its full title, the Reeves's Muntjac, to distinguish it from the world's other nine muntjac deer, which rejoice in such names as Bornean Yellow Muntjac and Gong Shan Muntjac. This animal was also a member of the ever-increasing immigrant camp at Woburn Park – a sort of animal's Sangatte – no doubt they would have beamed pictures of the attempted escapees on the evening news if they had had it at the time. In 1901 the Muntjac was deliberately introduced into the nearby woodlands which, to be honest, were a much better match for its habitat than anything available to the Chinese Water Deer. The spread of this animal, also from China, has been much more complete than for its compatriot, and there are now between 50,000 and 100,000 Muntjacs at large in Britain.

Chinese creatures in Britain? Whatever next, a Panda?

Well actually, yes. Way back in the Lower Pleistocene, a couple of million years ago, there was indeed just such an animal wandering around our green and fertile land, known as the English Panda. Nobody really knows much about what it looked like, but I bet it wasn't half as friendly as its modern relative.

I had asked around various contacts and they had all came back with the same advice when trying to find a Chinese Water Deer: "You need to go to Woodwalton Fen."

Thus, last night we packed up the car for a weekend of mammal-watching. Staying overnight near Peterborough, we hoped to catch up with Chinese Water Deer in the morning, to give us enough time to drive west for a quick peek in the Peak District for Mountain Hares, before zipping down to Chester to a very important appointment on Sunday morning. If everything went well, I had planned that we might reach the mid-forties of mammals by the time we arrived back home. Then, of course, it should be plain sailing to our family's target.

To be honest, it wasn't really the ideal way to undertake a task bound up with appreciation. However, in the course of challenges like this, one always hopes for a particular commodity that invariably seems to evaporate as quickly as a politician's promise: convenience. Of course we would rather have had time to take each mammal in turn, get great sightings of it, be able to study it at our leisure, and then to be ready for the next sighting after a nice breather. But when you put together the entropic mix of busy schedules, children, the unpredictability of wildlife and the need for sheer effort towards any goal, a mad dash such as we were contemplating was simply inevitable at some point.

This weekend was such a time.

Our morning at the Fen was bracing. Well, all right, it was absolutely freezing. It didn't help that, by the time we were making our first tentative steps from the car park across the bridge that led to the main drag, the sun was only just rising above the flat countryside. Our breath billowed out in front of us as we walked, as if we were a family of four steam engines that had somehow become displaced on to a grassy path. Within minutes most of the feeling in our 40 fingers had gone. And to make matters worse, the dew was so thick that it seemed as though the countryside had a cold. The wet literally leapt from the grass to drench our trousers with every step that we took.

The complaints didn't take long to come. Our children had already been subjected to an early start before the light was even shining through the window. They hadn't had any breakfast, and not much of our usual tender care. Now they had been thrust out into a chilly October morning for what had been billed – and fervently hoped for – as a gentle pre-breakfast amble to see some deer. It was hardly surprising that they were a touch crotchety. It was a minor miracle, perhaps, that they were actually walking forwards at all, and not sitting down, as they sometimes do when they go on junior strike.

Mind you, the scenery was novel and the light was nothing less than spectacular. The sunrise was all-consuming and overbearing. First it made the sky look like an upset paintbox, all purples, pinks and deep, threatening blues. Then, once the sun got high enough, its rays seemed to shoot through our small party, enveloping and soaking and licking us as they burnt up along the east-west path, so much so that we felt like part of the sunrise itself. At the same time the low light made everything look bright and different: the moisture on the top of the molehills shining, the odd yellow, path-side leaf suddenly lighting up; the rising dew making a visible spray.

We had been instructed to take the straight, 1,600 metre- (1 mile-) long path through the reedbeds to a raised bank, from which, we had been promised, we should be able to see the Chinese Water Deer grazing in the fields. But long before we reached the bank, I noticed a shape on the path about 200 metres (650 feet) ahead. Then there was another. And another. I asked Samuel for the telescope.

He frowned. "I'm carrying the telescope!" he exclaimed, and clenched his arms tightly around it. Since he could barely lift the Zeiss with its tripod in the first place, this was quite an effort.

"Daddy needs the telescope," said Daddy firmly, as the shapes began to disappear into the foliage surrounding the path.

"I'm carrying the telescope," he repeated, defiantly. When Samuel is cross, his expression bypasses piqued, annoyed and angry, and goes straight from neutral to fourth-gear furious.

"Is Samuel going to be very helpful and give Daddy the telescope? Daddy wants to look at some deer." I explained, with just a smidgeon of desperation in my voice. I hadn't come to Woodwalton Fen to be thwarted by an outbreak of childish possessiveness.

I'm sure, in the distance, the shapes were laughing.

Eventually I prised the telescope off its temporary owner, probably, and quite shamefully, by telling Samuel that he wouldn't get a nice breakfast unless he *gave Daddy the telescope* (which was a lie). But I was so frazzled that I cannot remember what bribe or threat I might have used.

Astonishingly, the shapes had indeed stayed to watch the "Fen of the Tiny Tearaways", and I was able to focus quite clearly on them once I had set everything up. It was immediately obvious that they were deer, and straight away I noticed that they had decidedly smart, dark coats. They did, however, completely lack the usual lithe, long-limbed appearance of all the deer we had seen this year, in favour of a short, compact, stocky build and diminutive stature. Significantly, they also held a most unusual posture, in which they seemed to be bending down, with the shoulders lower than the back, as if they were downcast or depressed. I recognised this from individuals I had seen before. They were Muntjacs.

Although the kids had clearly seen the animals, both with the naked eye and through the telescope, we decided to progress along the track to see if we could get a better look. After all, the Muntjac is a distinctive animal. Besides the features I have mentioned, it also has a black stripe on the face, and a curious lobe (a scent gland) behind the eyes, that is used for marking posts and other prominences to delineate territories. Males have a rudimentary pair of straight antlers.

I suppose I never really expected to see any of this, so it came as a surprise that, after walking 100 or so metres at kid's pace and not without conversation, a Muntjac decided to cross the path again. This time we could see it well – a deer the size of a medium-sized dog. When it realised its mistake and saw us, it made off at pace, making a strangled bark and holding its short, white tail-tuft aloft, vertically erect. This is no doubt a very serious signal to other Muntjacs that danger is nigh, but to us the tail looked just a little silly. The kids giggled.

But three or four Muntjacs in 10 minutes constituted a good start to the day. We had harboured worries about seeing this species at all, not because it is rare or restricted, but simply because it can be a little secretive, especially during the day. We had tried other places for it, notably near Tring on our trip for the Edible Dormice in July, but had failed to see one at all – which was a little galling, because John Dixon had advised that "they pop out of every wood and copse there." Our encounter here had been, therefore, doubly fulfilling.

We continued to the bank. It did overlook farmland with marshy patches, as we'd been promised. And, equally as we had been promised, there were Chinese Water Deer, at least two, grazing there, although rather distantly. However, the sages of the area had not informed us that, at the top of the bank, it would be so exposed that even the relatively gentle north-westerly wind gave a chill factor of at least 75 degrees below freezing. The moment any of us popped our heads over the bank, the cold almost took them off. And much as I heroically lined up the telescope on the deer – playing the part of the indomitable saviour and protector of my family – I couldn't get the kids to appreciate these animals properly. They saw them all right, but I don't suppose that, shivering and complaining, they could distinguish them with very much certainty from Woolly Mammoths.

"Can you see the slightly creamy colouration, without the white patch on the bottom?"

Blank looks. Children shivering.

"Small size, large ears?"

Children close to tears.

"The male doesn't have antlers, only tusks, but I can't see that from this distance…"

Rebellion. Children and wife already half-way back to the car.

Our trip to the Peak District was in aid of trying to find Mountain Hares, but nobody I spoke to in advance of the visit seemed to be very optimistic.

"If you want to see Mountain Hares, by far the best time is in February," said one contact. "They are white, then, and easy to see."

"I'm going next week."

"Oh."

"And I'm hoping to show them to a couple of children, aged six and four."

Irritated sigh. Phone clicks.

"The thing is, they don't live near the road," said the second contact. "You'll need to walk for a couple of miles, at least, and hope that you flush one from the heather. You only find them on the bleakest moorland. October isn't a very good time. Why don't you try again in February?"

What these contacts didn't understand was that, as far as this current year was concerned, February had actually finished. Had I known in February that we should have been looking for Mountain Hares in the Pennines, we would have gone then. But I didn't.

The other problem that we had was that the Mountain Hares of the Peaks were the only ones in reasonable reach of where we lived, a few hours drive at most. We knew that, up in the Central Highlands of Scotland these animals were reasonably common, but the idea of going all the way up there was horrendous. My mammal-spotting book had been quite optimistic about the chances of finding them down in this southern part of their range, where they had been introduced, but that's not what the experts had warned.

The truth is, the Mountain Hare is very much the hardy relative of the common and widespread Brown Hare. In the Peak District it only occurs at least 130 metres (425 feet) above sea level. The fact that we have it here at all is a reminder of our Ice Age past, when the same animal would have shared its habitat with Reindeer and Muskoxen and Neanderthals. Now, up in Scotland, all those have gone, although the skiers have replaced the last-named, and it can, at times, be hard to tell the difference. One of the more splendid quirks of the Mountain Hare is that, between late October and February, it moults and changes colour from greyish-brown to white, becoming quite unmistakable and very hard to miss. Naturally, the idea of this was originally to hide it amongst the snowdrifts, into which it could burrow when necessary, in order to survive. Unfortunately, however, there usually aren't very many big snowdrifts in this part of the world nowadays, rendering its winter coat about as useful as tweed jackets, short-back-and-sides haircuts and those little bugs on springs that used to adorn teenage hats – as with these, its fashionable days are long behind it.

It's tough up there. Not only do the Mountain Hares live in the Arctic Circle and other cold places, but they also do it without a formal permanent burrow– which is about as hard as you get, and a whole lot more impressively macho than the posturing of daft football supporters who watch snow-bound matches completely bare-chested. Furthermore, the Mountain Hares manage it all while nibbling away at heather and grass for most of the year, and don't even rely on being intoxicated. Really, one day someone should go up to a burly Newcastle United supporter and tell him he is no tougher than a little Derbyshire bunny.

We had been told to try the area around the Derwent and Ladybower Reservoirs, in the centre of the Peak District National Park. The man in the shop by the car park, who peddled incredibly detailed maps to make sure that hikers wouldn't get lost, took a look at our family and frowned alarmingly. He sounded slightly relieved when I informed him that all we were after was Mountain Hares, and our chances of getting stuck on the top of a High Peak were therefore limited. He suggested an area slightly to the east of us.

"You will only find them up on the open moorland," he warned us. "You will probably need to walk at least three miles."

It felt invigorating to be among the hills. Above us we could see dull brown bracken-covered slopes, dotted with rugged sheep that vacantly chewed the vegetation in the manner of gum-masticating chavs; rocky paths criss-crossing the moors (byways hewn by thousands of middle-class feet); and tall conifer forests adhering in patches to the hillsides. We weren't used to seeing these upland sights, and it seemed that they couldn't help but lure us into their bosom. And perhaps we were energized, too, because of the company we were in. Nobody hereabouts was any kind of slouch: some were park workers, professional outdoorsmen and women; some were hikers, with 200-quid boots, cagoules and special fibreglass sticks to help them keep their balance; while others were bikers, with their trademark mud-bespattered bottoms. These glanced at us haughtily as they zipped past, or, having touched down from the heights, lovingly placed their extreme wheels on the back of their stylish day-motors, and raced off.

The truth is that we were hopelessly out of our league. The two children wore wellington boots, attire that is frowned upon whenever you leave the lowlands, coats that were doubtfully waterproof, and hats that were doubtlessly not. Emily insisted on wearing a pink scarf that could have been bought at Clare's Accessories, I don't remember. Carolyn's boots had been borrowed from her most stylish sister, but were hardly mountain-worthy. At least my boots and jacket were sufficiently respectable to ensure that, should I be sent ahead to find the rescue services, I would at least exude some outdoor gravitas when I started pleading.

Thus we were all set for our Mountain Hare excursion. It was afternoon, there was rain in the air, the tops of the moor were already in mist and there was a keen wind coming from the west. We headed indomitably uphill, past Derwent Reservoir's mightily impressive weir (over 30 metres/100 feet high) and on to the hiking trails. We probably made a climb of about 90 metres (300 feet), past gates with weighted balances to help them shut, past small streams of tumbling water, and up a zigzagging path with slippery rocks in the middle and slithery mud on either side. We held the children's hands all the while. Our route took us through an open conifer wood, where the strengthening wind made both treetops and kids moan, the latter trying to shelter their faces from the elements. We made it out on to a more open area and staggered on until, by a corner marshalled by sheep as bored as sales assistants in a mobile-phone shop, we took scant shelter by a lone rowan tree.

"You'd better find out how far we have to go," suggested Carolyn, staring at me in a pleading posture and looking deliciously windblown and outdoorsy. The kids cuddled close to her, which seemed a good idea.

I have always rather enjoyed those moments when I have to be just a little tougher and possess more stamina than the rest of the family. It makes me feel good: presumably, it's the realisation that I have some manly virtues that are hidden under normal circumstances – namely, a bit more strength than a wife and two children under the age of seven…

I stormed up the hillside until my progress was halted suddenly by an old knee-twinge. A few more turns took me to a gate and, behind it, an enticing tract of open moorland, which I presumed was the habitat of Mountain Hares.

But it was just a little too far. We had already spent an hour and a half getting to this point. The rain was becoming more enthusiastic, and the October day, which had begun in such bright and mesmerising fashion at Woodwalton Fen, was whimpering to an end in the damp, dull anti-climax of moderate-altitude mizzle. I decided that we should turn back.

"Who's for hot chocolate down at the shop?" I asked my relieved family.

We raced back downhill and, returned to our natural habitat, sitting on a wall with hot drinks in our hands, we realised that the upland walk had given us a lift.

"Next year, I think we should take a holiday in the Lake District, and do lots of walking like this," suggested Carolyn.

With that we set off towards Chester.

## October 5th – The Angel of the North

It's funny whom you get to know when you are investigating the possibility of seeing Harvest Mice. Having completely failed to connect with our unreliable contact down south, I had begun to cast my net much wider to see whether anyone else might be trapping these creatures regularly. I didn't take long to find out that, as far as *Micromys minutus* was concerned, rodentophile opinion was unanimous. All roads led to Chester Zoo, and a lady called Penny Rudd.

I had spoken to her on the phone a couple of times, and it soon became clear that Penny was almost evangelistic in her appreciation for these small creatures. She ran regular trapping sessions in the grounds of the zoo for the local mammal group, and for visitors, and she routinely invited TV crews in to film the Harvest Mice in the zoo's breeding programme. I suspected that she lived, breathed and slept Harvest Mice until the conversation got on to other rodents and shrews. I told her about the gaps in our list.

"Oh, we catch lots of Pygmy Shrews," she enthused.

How about House Mice?

"You shouldn't have a problem seeing them here. They lurk in some of the less tidy corners of the zoo."

That did it for me. I knew from that moment on that we would simply have to come up to Chester.

We had agreed to meet Penny early in the morning for a small-mammal-trapping session. But as soon as I opened the curtains of our motel room, my heart sank. The clouds were thick and heavy, and it was thundering down with rain. Evidently it had been doing just that since 11 o'clock the previous evening, and now this part of Cheshire was completely soaked. This wasn't just normal rain, either. It was the tail-end of a hurricane thrashing about in its death throes, and threatened to make the morning a washout. Unless, of course, we intended to trap fish.

However, no cancellation call came from Penny, and we made the appointment in the zoo car park. "It's going to be a bit wet. You'll need your wellies," said Penny, ominously.

She was a middle-aged lady with an impressive head of long, blonde hair, which was trained either side of her face, beneath a pink bobble-hat. Immediately she struck me as possessing a rare combination of warmth and almost frightening competence. There was a slight whiff of the Carol Thatcher type about her – that same "can-do" attitude, despite any circumstances that might be slung her way. I'm sure that, had Penny ever entered "I'm a Celebrity, Get Me Out of Here", she would have trounced the rest of the weedy cast with no problem at all. And, with a sludgy field to cross, followed a seriously waterlogged bottomland, she was exactly the sort of person we needed right now.

In order to get to the trapping site, we had to dodge cows, wade through mud and basically jump over some puddles that began to compete with Derwent Reservoir in terms of sheer surface area. As we finally stood next to the first ribbon that indicated a mammal trap, breathing heavily and trying to brush thick mud off our coats, I couldn't help but cast my eye around for Ant and Dec.

"We have fourteen traps out," said Penny. "My colleague Sarah put them out last night. Let's just hope that none of them are under water."

The trapping site could have been made for small mammals. It was lush (well all right, just about everywhere today was lush), with rank vegetation of all kinds, including rushes and reeds and bullrush and sedge, dense from top to bottom and providing all the ground-level runs and labyrinthine passages that a shrew, vole or mouse could possibly wish for, with the concomitant microfauna of insects and other invertebrates. The Kestrel that constantly hovered over us was proof, too, that this sodden field, despite its ragged appearance and easily written-off ordinariness, was a paradise for small forms of life. I hoped that my children, immersed in such places at their tender age, would learn to appreciate the value of untended mini-wildernesses.

Despite the rain, and subsequent low expectations, the mammal-trapping turned out to be extraordinarily successful – by a mile our best of the year. By the time we had reached the fourteenth and final trap, our running total was: one Wood Mouse, two Bank Voles, one Field Vole and three – no less than three – Common Shrews. We were particularly pleased with the latter, since our Kimmeridge shrew had been giving us the run-around and we had not seen it properly. These shrews were great: all long snouts and hyperactivity. They kept on devouring the casters that had been put out for them, even when running around in the old aquarium that Penny had brought along for viewing purposes. As I have mentioned before, shrews are singularly unusual creatures, and it really felt as though we were inspecting little aliens in front of our eyes.

Now it would have been churlish to express disappointment at such a bonanza of small mammals, but we had to remind ourselves that we had actually not yet seen anything new for our list. Of course it didn't matter very much, but I can remember musing on how pleasing it would be if the very last trap might somehow produce something novel, in Natterer's Bat style.

Amazingly, it did. Out popped what turned out to be one of the star mammals of the whole year – a Water Shrew.

It's quite possible that you've never heard of a Water Shrew, let alone seen one and, if so, you're in majority company. But this is a little gem of a creature, so much so that, when it emerged from the trap, we all gave a collective gasp. Up until now, all the rodents and shrews we had seen were individual in their way, but by necessity clothed in cryptic colouration. We were quite unprepared for the crisp and contrasting hues of the Water Shrew; if the rest of its neighbours were dressed casually, this was a shrew in a dinner jacket. It was a rich slate black on top and gleaming white below, with a sharp line of contrast between the two. The only break from this pattern was the white tips to the back of its ears and behind the eyes. It was also a stage up in size from the Common Shrew.

"Look at the feet," suggested Penny. "The Water Shrew has a network of hairs on its feet that help it to swim. There are also hairs on the underside of the tail to keep it buoyant."

The Water Shrew held the kids spellbound for about as long as any mammal so far this the year.

"It's great," said Emily, the indefatigable enthusiast.

The shy and cryptic Water Shrew is like the bloodthirsty counterpart to the vegetarian Water Vole, the two frequently sharing the same habitat. It can swim just as well, too, including underwater, where it pursues small fish, newts, insects and their larvae, crustaceans and various other invertebrates. It was once frequently called the Otter Shrew. It will even take frogs much larger than itself, which it apparently immobilises by injecting them with venomous saliva when it bites. Penny made sure she kept her fingers well away from it, because a bite from a Water Shrew can cause swelling that will last several days. Apparently, this character wastes no time in sinking its teeth into small-mammal enthusiasts. And given the difference in size between the trappers and the trapped, who could blame it?

Five happy mammal-hunters unfazed by rain and damp, we released it at a base of a reedbed,

Penny hadn't finished with us yet. On the premise of showing us the Harvest Mice that were part of the zoo's behind-the-scenes captive-breeding programme, plus searching for the odd miscreant House Mouse here or there, she led us free-of-charge into the zoo, the institution that was both her livelihood and her passion. From the moment we entered the gates we knew that this was Penny's natural habitat, not from her behaviour, but from that, believe it or not, of the animals themselves.

Take the chimps, for instance. The whole troop seemed to perk up when she arrived and, far from being indifferent as they would have been for us, several came over specifically to show off. This, of course, was great value to the kids, who stuck their tongues out and generally mucked about with their close cousins. Penny knew every single individual by name, and would usually make some comment, such as, "Oh Desmond, you are such a silly chimp", as Desmond showed us his ample bottom or pursed his lips. Under Penny's tutelage, we discovered what the various gestures meant, and also understood the hierarchies, the jealousies and the factions. Not surprisingly, the dominant male, Dylan, just lay down on his platform and gazed imperiously about him. Once, for a moment, he deigned to look at us, and that was it.

The orang-utans were even more affected by Penny's appearance, and this led to a truly magic moment. One of the female Sumatran Orang-utans, by the name of Emma, was on the far side of her enclosure when we arrived, just sitting around. When Penny arrived, however, she perked up immediately and started climbing down the tree in which she had parked herself. Before we knew it Emma was perched on the narrow platform next to the public-viewing window, adjacent to where we stood. In her arms she cradled a baby, by the name of Indah, who was just a few months old.

"She's come to show me how her baby is getting on," said Penny. "She's very proud of her." And clearly she was, too. Emma and Penny just looked lovingly at each other and, although it was through glass, they might as well have embraced.

"You see, I raised her," Penny explained. "She spent her early months under my care. We know each other very well. Don't we, Emma, my darling?"

"You raised her? You're her surrogate mother, then?"

"That's right," she replied, and smiled. Emma, if anything, came even closer to the window. But now, my spellbound children were getting something going with Indah. They were looking at each other through the glass and making faces. Soon Indah put his hand on the glass, pressing it so that his palm was flat; both children did the same, in a slow, deliberate game of high fives. Then Indah, taking the initiative, moved his hand to one side and then made a circular movement with it. On the other side of the glass, Emily and Samuel did the same.

"It looks like they are making friends," laughed Carolyn.

We didn't make friends with the animal in the opposite enclosure, however. It didn't even raise an eye for Penny. Admittedly, it was a Reticulated Python, the longest snake in the world. But the magic of our visit hadn't worn off. I'll swear to you that every single python I have seen in every zoo I have been to before today has invariably been engaged in exactly the same activity: doing nothing and basically mimicking a stuffed specimen. But this python, which was over 7.5 metres (25 feet) long, was so active it could have been auditioning for *The Jungle Book*. It uncoiled itself (a process that took some considerable time), and deigned to climb up a tree trunk, slide along the top of it and make landfall in another tree trunk on the other side. OK, admittedly a monkey can do this in two seconds flat, but for a reticulated python it was about a month's worth of activity.

Everything seemed to show for us. The rhinoceroses were taking a mudbath, the jaguars were prowling, the lions had a nearly new-born cub and the elephants – much to the children's delight – were depositing vast dollops of poo. Penny, the zoo registrar (responsible for the comings and goings of animals and transfers between zoos), knew all of the animals' names, and all of the characters.

One of the best exhibits was the bat enclosure. As you will be aware, our family was pretty familiar with bats by now, but some of these boys were a whole series of sizes up, even from a Noctule. Some were Rodrigues Fruit Bats, from an island in the Indian Ocean where I had once seen them wild; they flew about in the upper reaches of the dimly-lit building, wings as broad as a daily newspaper. Other bats swooped past much closer; in fact, they came past so close that we could feel the draught of their wings.

I have been to dozens of zoos in my time, some inspirational, some tired, some deeply depressing, some almost criminal. But this zoo was profoundly impressive in every way, right down to all the staff that we met. It was clear that Penny's pride was entirely justified and widely shared.

Now, you are certainly going to think that we are completely mad when I tell you that, in this unique place stocked with some of the most exciting animals in the world – in glossy close-up – and accompanied by an inspirational mine of knowledge and enthusiasm, we nonetheless had an appointment to keep with mice. Two sorts actually: some captive Harvest Mice and, hopefully, a few rogue House Mice. Yes, we were still on a mission.

For the Harvest Mice Penny took us behind the scenes, into a privileged world where the public isn't allowed. We entered a labyrinthine building, left by a special exit close to the perimeter fence, climbed over a few pipes and other masonry and finally came to what looked like a Portakabin. Nobody looking in from the outside would have known what dwelt there; no-one could have guessed it was the headquarters of the Harvest Mouse's attempt to take over the world – or at least, Cheshire.

The Portakabin was packed with dozens and dozens of cages; they were stacked on shelves that ran up to the roof. Each was no more than 45 centimetres (18 inches) in length, but they were all filled with straw, and every single one of them contained significant numbers of Harvest Mice. The cages were carefully labelled to assure the correct breeding procedures were being followed. Release this number of mice into the world, I thought, and you will soon establish a viable population with no problem at all. I half expected to see a map on the wall marking the extent of gains made so far, and those projected.

"Cheshire is about as far north as the Harvest Mouse naturally occurs," said Penny. "It's one of the world's tiniest rodents, and anywhere further up the winters would be too much for it. Would you like to have a proper look at one?"

Mike, the man who was in charge of the captive breeding programme, took down a cage and fiddled with the hay inside. Now, I knew already that the Harvest Mouse was diminutive; I had told the children that it was a pint-sized mouse. We all knew that, whatever words you might use to describe a Harvest Mice, the word "big" would not be among them. But, as Mike took one of the creatures in his hand, none of us could help ourselves.

"It's tiny," said Carolyn.

"Aw, it's so small and cute," said Emily.

"I'm stunned just how minute it is," I said, trying to exude more gravitas than the rest of my family.

It's true. The appeal of these mice certainly lies in their undersized dimensions, but also in their orange-brown fur, large eyes and long tails. And these are not the only features of interest, either. Uniquely, the Harvest Mouse also builds a free-standing nest in which to live that is about the size of a tennis ball (workers sometimes even provide old, punctured tennis balls for the mice to use), it is woven out of shredded grass stems and is placed 30 to 60 centimetres (1 to 2 feet) above the ground, strongly tethered to standing grass stems. This home among stems is typical of the species. In the summer it has the unusual habit of finding its food (seeds, berries, insects) up among the upper tiers of herbs and forbs, climbing acrobatically about like a four-footed Tarzan. Other mice and voles are just too heavy to make a living up here.

It was while we were chatting to Mike that the subject of House Mice came up. You will understand that it happened quite naturally in the course of free-flowing rodent-speak.

"Oh, why don't you try over the road in the haybarns?" he suggested.

So we did. Penny picked out one key from her impressive collection and we crossed the road to a fenced-off barn. "Just look in and around the hay," she said.

The children climbed the bales, jumped around and ran this way and that. It's not normally recommended as a method for finding mammals, but it worked this time. Within minutes a House Mouse duly appeared on the ground, a tad annoyed by the disturbance. It stood upright and washed itself. Apart from being larger than the Harvest Mice, it was clear to see that this was quite a different animal indeed. It had much less friendly features, with smaller eyes and a sharper face than any other mice we had seen. It was also greyer and carried an obvious air of mischief.

In some ways it seemed strange to see a House Mouse in a zoo, in amongst a collection of animals, yet not part of that collection; the unloved orbiting the cherished. Yet also, it seemed entirely appropriate. The House Mouse is the most widespread land animal in the world, apart from man. It occurs on every continent, everywhere. It even lives among the scientists in Antarctica.

We didn't stay long. We were all moused-out. We had seen six species of wild rodent during the morning. And besides, Penny declared that she needed to get home.

"I've got some animals to feed," she said.

"Animals? What animals?"

"I've got three cats, three dogs, three Wallabies, twenty Harvest Mice, four chinchillas, fourteen hens, twenty-eight tortoises, various cockatoos and cockatiels, four horses and two sheep – but I've probably missed some out."

So Penny, having worked at the zoo, went home every day to an almost unimaginable menagerie of her own. What enthusiasm, what passion! It confirmed to us everything we needed to know about this remarkable woman.

## October 8th – The Surrey Bat Group

It was only because things had been going well that I even considered trying for a Nathusius' Pipistrelle. To all intents and purposes, it was a long shot. The year was getting late and the weather, so important in determining the flying times of bats, becoming more fickle by each autumn day. Furthermore, the kids' school term – which happened to be Sam's first – was also in full swing, with various clubs running, parties to attend and youthful friends to entertain, squeezing our family timetable until it could hardly breathe. Throw in the small detail that the best Nathusius' Pipistrelle site we knew was a two-hour drive away, and you will realise that the logistics of seeing this bat were, to say the least, complicated.

Actually, it was much worse than that. The location we had uncovered was a National Trust site that closed at sunset. When I first discovered this place, which I did by emailing a couple of bat-group representatives, I was told that I would have to (a) find a member of the Surrey Bat Group, who would be able to accompany us and identify the Nathusius' Pipistrelle and (b) sweet-talk the National Trust staff in order to enable us to enter the site at dusk and leave after dark.

So, all I needed was a gap in the timetable to get father, mother and two children to the site after school, on an October evening when bats might be flying about, to meet a person from a bat group who might be free on the right evening, at the same time as a National Trust employee might be willing to allow us into the site.

Easy, really.

Now of course, logistics are simple compared to the complications of the mammal-spotting itself, because sadly, we did not have any agreement from, nor any chance of influencing the object of our interest itself, the Nathusius' Pipistrelle. Far from it, in fact. The first time I spoke to our bat-group contact, Derek, he seemed to veer on the side of putting us off, if only ever so gently.

"You want to see a Nathusius' Pipistrelle," he had said, in the style of somebody talking back to someone elderly, or ill, or just a little dotty.

"Yes, that's right."

"Well, they are quite unpredictable. I mean, if we go there, we tend to see mainly normal pipistrelles: Sopranos and Commons… As you might expect." The doubt came loud and clear.

"OK. So how often do you see Nathusius' Pipistrelle?"

He carried on in measured fashion. "Well, not that often. Let's say that, if we do find a Nathusius', we are pleasantly surprised." He paused, still teetering between a naturally affable temperament and telling us we were nuts. "That said, it is a good place to see them. But I'm a little worried that you might not…"

"OK, Derek. See you Tuesday. Thanks."

It so happened that my first Nathusius' date was ruined by the weather. The second was ruined by the fact that the National Trust Caretaker, Andrew – with unforgivable negligence to the needs of a mad mammal-spotting family – had deigned, disgracefully, to go on holiday (holidays – what is the world coming to?) However, on my third attempt, something very odd happened: the family was free, Derek was free, Andrew had returned from his holiday and, glory of glories, the weather was clear and relatively mild, inching towards the 10°C (50°F) that, the experts had agreed, would unleash an orgy of foraging bats into the Surrey skies.

To add to the wonder, the traffic was in our favour and we met with Derek on the dot of 6:30pm. There was a Noctule flying merrily over the car park, and I'm sure that, in the distance, I just made out the unmistakable shape of my fairy godmother washing her wand in the nearby lake, ready to awaken the Nathusius' into fly-past mode. What could possibly go wrong?

Derek turned out to be great value. I'm sure I'm not doing him a disservice to suggest that he was the quintessence of what you might expect a bat expert to look like. He was brushing with retirement age, sported glasses and had the most diverting long and profuse grey beard, giving him a sort of Middle Earth benevolence. In one hand he held a bat detector that had clearly done the hard hours; in the other he carried a gnarled walking stick of similar antiquity.

Now I'm not about to string out the account of our evening, just to say that it was everything I had hoped it to be, an absolute bat-fest (and an Oktober-fest to boot). The Noctule was just the start. It flew high over the lake that dominated the landscape and was soon joined by another, the two of them throwing out a volley of ultrasonics so that the bat detectors danced to the tune of something resembling club music. Meanwhile, Daubenton's Bats were soon out in force – at least six of them at once – sweeping low over the surface of the acre-broad lake and giving off a crackle that resembled very loud white noise. We were able to catch many of them in the light of our CB2 spotlight, and not just us adults, either. Usually, if either Emily or Samuel operated the big spotlight they were about as accurate as an England penalty in a World Cup Quarter-final, but tonight they managed to illuminate several of these fast-flying hunters.

And then there were the pipistrelles. These bats hugged the edge of the lake, close to the denser woodland vegetation that fringed the water, and they flew higher up than the Daubenton's Bats. Their erratic appearance worried us at first; during our visit they would appear in force for a few minutes and then disappear for long enough for us to panic, before swishing past once again. The first individual was a Soprano Pipistrelle, the cryptic species that most loves watery habitats (it eats midges) and emits ultrasonic sounds that fart through the bat detector at a peak intensity corresponding to 55 kilohertz. Later on we noted at least one Common Pipistrelle at 45 kilohertz, but we took disparagingly little notice of it. What we needed what a pipistrelle to belt out its peak energy call at 39 kilohertz, noticeably lower than the other two species. That would confirm it as the third species, Nathusius' Pipistrelle.

It didn't appear until it was almost dark. By then I could hardly see the dial of my detector, but Derek yelled out its name and, straining our eyes, we just managed to see it flicker past on its second or third run. After a while, the torch beam lit it up enough to see that it was a diminutive bat, but not much else. We certainly couldn't see, as our mammal book helpfully informed us, that the baculum on the dorsal side was concavely curved. Actually, we had no idea what the baculum was and, besides, can you ever remember the difference between convex and concave? I certainly never can.

So why, might you ask, if all we were going to "admire" of the Nathusius' Pipistrelle, when we found it, was a tiny difference in the frequency of the most intense calls, and these on a bat detector, and with no visual distinction to pick up whatsoever, did we bother to travel for two hours each way to see this bat at all? What on earth was the animal's appeal, apart from being another species on the road to 50?

I can definitely answer this. It's all a question of the generally mysterious nature of bats. Even today, very little is known about these remarkable animals: where they travel, how far they fly, what exactly they eat and how they get it. Some very basic information is lacking even for common species. What appealed to me about the Nathusius' Pipistrelle is how it reflects our lack of knowledge of bats, and how things might be happening under our nose without us having a clue about them. Have you ever previously heard of a Nathusius' Pipistrelle? Probably not. After all, this particular bat was unknown in this country until 1940, when one turned up in the Shetlands. Even by 2006, there were still fewer than 200 records of an animal that occurs in Continental Europe in such places as Germany and Estonia, and so it was nothing but a casual rarity. However, just recently it has been discovered breeding in Britain for the first time, and it now seems to turn up far more often than it ever did before. Clearly something is changing, but what and why? In Europe, recent studies suggest that the Nathusius' Pipistrelle migrates south-west in autumn like many birds do, wintering in France and Northern Spain, and returning again in early spring. Some have obviously begun to cross the North Sea as well and, finding conditions to their liking here, have stayed to breed. Perhaps they overwinter here, too? Nobody knows. It's a frequent picture. Now that they are just beginning to be better understood, bats are surprising us. Almost every year sees unexpected records and curious changes.

So you see, although we had a tentative brush with the Nathusius' Pipistrelle, which was very peripheral indeed, it seemed to me that the fleeting nature of the meeting was somehow appropriate. We had met with a hidden representative of a stealthy takeover of our country, as if we were somehow part of a great conspiracy that few people knew about. And it was curiously thrilling.

We obviously thanked Derek for his part in showing us the "Nat Pip", as it is often called. But in a way I regretted meeting him. It was nothing to do with his help and kindness, of course. But it was all about a conversation we had on the way back through the gloom to the car park. He was telling me all about the astonishing creatures he had seen abroad.

"I've been very lucky," he said. "I've seen a lot of good things: Maned Wolf in Argentina, Polar Bear, Giant Anteater, Blue Whale off California, Jaguar…"

"Goodness me," I replied. "How many species of mammals have you seen."

"I would guess about three hundred and fifty," he said contemplatively.

My heart sank. All of a sudden our quest to see 50 often unspectacular mammals in this country seemed a little dull and paltry.

Perhaps next year?

## October 18th – Out and About in the Water Park

Today, we went to see a piece of Britain's living history returned, and saw some of its prehistory, too. In between we found an alien and a psychopath, which wasn't a bad haul for a day in the Cotswolds. Who needs Jaguars and Brown Bears?

Originally, the day had been arranged for the purposes of seeing a Water Shrew. Mike Dilger had given me the contact details of a young woman called Phoebe Carter, who happens to be one of Britain's top experts on this animal and has actually written a book entitled, unambiguously, *The Water Shrew*. However, the trip to Chester had somewhat stolen the thunder of this particular quest. Nevertheless, Phoebe suggested that we still come, since there was a possibility of finding Pygmy Shrews, and the Park also had an ongoing Mink-trapping programme.

"And besides," Phoebe had said, "I can try to show you the Beavers – or at least, their signs."

"Beavers?" I had asked, astonished.

"Yes, we have some Beavers in the park. They are part of a study to see whether they can be reintroduced into Britain; they've been here for three years. We should see some logs and sticks that have been gnawed, if not the animals themselves."

It was too good an opportunity to miss.

We met Phoebe at the Cotswold Water Park's main car park. She was in her late twenties, at a guess, and pretty in the most wholesome sense, slim and tall, with long blonde hair and blue eyes. Somehow, if you'll forgive me for saying so, she just didn't look like a Water Shrew expert.

She drove a somewhat ramshackle vehicle piled high with equipment, a sort of laboratory on wheels. To the children's delight, on the back seat were two soft and friendly dogs, one brown and one black-and-white, both with floppy ears. They were called Marley and Tilly.

Phoebe introduced herself and said she had bad news.

"I'm really sorry," she said. "I didn't set any mammal traps out last night. I was worried that it was too cold, and that if we caught anything it might not survive. So I didn't put them out until early this morning. We probably won't catch much."

We were fine with that – a minor setback.

"And I doubt whether you'll see a Mink, either," Phoebe went on. "I have been catching them regularly in a site to the east of here, but when I tried to get to it yesterday, I couldn't reach the river because I was attacked by a herd of heifers."

It was a little disappointing, but I sympathised with Phoebe over the heifers, having once ended up in a ditch myself when trying to escape a hundred curious animals. It's one of those things that sounds funny until it happens to you, such as being locked in a public toilet overnight, or slipping on a banana skin. (I actually know a genuine victim of the latter – she broke her arm and has never lived it down.)

Phoebe explained that our first task should be to check another Mink trap in a different area. "It's a long shot," she warned.

It might have been a long shot, but it was a long drive, too. We seemed to make dozens of turns, and drive down a series of narrow lanes, before finally pulling up at what looked like an assemblage of farm buildings, neatly put together with Cotswold stone. If it was a farm, it was almost as big as a small village. As if to make the point, it had its own resplendent red post box.

I had half expected Phoebe to make us put on blindfolds for this part of this foray into the secret depths of the Cotswold Water Park, but she merely led us through a gate, over a track piled high with cattle dung and mud, and finally into a deliciously slushy field. It contained a herd of Phoebe's new nemesis, cattle, and she looked a shade pale at the prospect of walking past these beasts again.

She needn't have worried. The herd was very much preoccupied. One member was a bull, and at the moment that we approached him he was performing what bulls are paid to do. And doing it with cross-eyed relish, too. We tried to hide Emily's eyes, but to no avail.

This led to one of those questions that so make parents cringe: "What are the Cows doing, Mummy?"

Carolyn was smart. "What do you think they are doing?" she batted back.

Emily thought for a little while. And then a little light went on in her head. Where she got the idea from I have no idea.

"I know," she beamed. "They're doing the conga." Of course, she didn't understand the smirks and laughter. Bless her cotton socks.

The Mink trap was a floating wooden platform tethered to the bank. It was in essence a flat raft, perhaps 60 centimetres (2 foot) square, but along the middle was a raised roof that formed a tunnel inside. When the animal entered the tunnel, it tripped a wire door and was captured. There was no bait, nothing. Success relied entirely on the intruder's curiosity.

Phoebe's warnings earlier proved unfounded. As she pulled the platform in we could all see that the door had tripped. There was an animal inside, very dark brown and furry. It was an American Mink.

Now, I have to admit that I didn't ever expect to describe it this way, but the Mink was stunning. I had seen a few before swimming in the water, where they tend to look like large Water Voles, with their rounded heads just above the surface, and really, they aren't that impressive. I had never seen the complete animal before, and never at such close quarters. It was simply beautiful: sleek, athletic, with a pleasing round face and small ears, plus a long, bushy tail that was almost as long as the rest of the animal itself. The light glinted off its rich brown fur, fur that was so perfectly neat that it could have been combed just minutes before.

And why shouldn't I have thought of it in that admiring way? The Mink is such a reviled creature that you expect it to be unsightly, or at least not pleasing on the eye. But of course, the animal itself is gloriously adapted to its freshwater environment, streamlined and graceful and admirable. Yes, it shouldn't be here. Yes, it eats too many Water Voles and other animals, and is often an environmental disaster. But that doesn't detract from its impact as a creature, unique and autonomous from human opinion. It was, I am almost ashamed to admit, one of the most attractive animals we had seen all year.

It was also one of the smelliest. Mink are, of course, well known for their musky scent, which gives an indication of their presence nearby, even when the animals themselves cannot be seen. Emily turned up her nose at it, but I found it quite pleasing. It seemed a little like Stinging Nettles after rain, if you can imagine that. Oh crikey. I'm beginning to sound like one of those TV wine nerds. What next? The smell of the Water Shrew is a little like a combination of marmalade mixed with tarragon, with just a hint of old socks which have been used to clean a Welsh dresser made of Malaysian ebony?

The small-mammal-trapping turned out to be just as dire as Phoebe had suggested it would. We took the cars down another maze of small roads (I'm sure Phoebe was just trying to make the area seem less navigable than it really was) and ended up next to what was clearly a newly built estate beside a lake with many arms and channels. Each smart dwelling here had a water frontage, gates front and back, and expensive cars in the driveways. Perhaps we had driven all the way to Dubai?

"What's with all these new-builds?" we asked Phoebe.

"They're all holiday homes," she replied. "People come here from London and the Home Counties to get away from it all. It's within easy reach and there's plenty to do: water sports, walking, cycling, horse riding – the Cotswolds have always been a big tourist area. It's quite trendy to buy property here in the Water Park. Or at least it was until a month or two ago, before the credit crisis."

Much as I liked the Water Park (after all, we had seen a Mink here), it seemed a curious place to buy a holiday home. This was hardly the heart of the famed Cotswolds area, with its pretty villages and gentle, undulating scenery, leafy hills and lazy rivers. This was a flat land with a lot of lakes, not so different from many flat, watery places closer to the major conurbations. Still, the filthy rich seemed to have taken a shine to it. And they seem to know about trends and fashions. If I was them I wouldn't be writing a book about a year in Britain, I'd be in Africa or South America. Somewhere with that perfect combination of large mammals and four-star hotels and a children's listening service.

Word about the trendy reputation of the area hadn't reached the small mammals. For the first time this year we did a check of more than 10 traps and didn't catch a thing. Not even a Wood Mouse.

However, Phoebe didn't let us down. A quick drive to a different area, an insalubrious ditch next to a busy road, revealed two more traps and one contained a Water Shrew. It was a heady moment to unite subject and author.

Don't tell Phoebe Carter, but this Water Shrew wasn't quite as smart as the Cheshire one from last week. Not as stupendously black-and-white, but still pretty good. And no view of this little psychopath should ever be taken lightly; it really is a cracker. Once again the kids had a good look as it ran around a tank, and once again the pint-sized monster was hyperactive and weird.

I had always associated Beavers with Canadian lakes, which is what most people probably do. So I was surprised to hear from Phoebe that they were once British. Apparently, there are two species in the world, the American and Eurasian, and the latter is still found in the wild in parts of Eastern Europe and Russia. It used to occur all over mainland Europe, and in Britain, too, and there are even a few places named after it. The last record in England was in about 900 AD, and in Wales in 1188; the Beaver survived in Scotland until the sixteenth century, well after the discovery of its relative in the lands of the New World.

Of course, 500 years is a long time to go missing. But in recent years it seems that we British have begun to hanker after our distant past, at least in wildlife terms. We don't miss the plague, the bloodlust of kings or widespread infestations of lice, but we find the concept of Beavers, Wolves and Wild Boars in our lands somewhat romantic. Perhaps we feel guilty that we have rendered these animals extinct in our country, together with Lynxes and Brown Bears? And so we should – after all, our forebears have left so little of our country untouched and unaltered, much to the detriment of our mammalian fauna. We have one of the lowest diversities of large mammals in Europe, so the reintroduction of any such animal is to be broadly welcomed.

Perhaps, too, we are reacting to the fact that, terrorism, wars and financial crises notwithstanding, our lives here are just a little too safe? Perhaps we long for the frisson of excitement that the presence of large animals, especially Wild Boars and Lynxes, in the countryside could add to a country walk? If so, I am broadly in favour of that. (Talking of which, the presence of an enormous Woolly Mammoth skull in the Cotswold Water Park Information Centre was a reminder that, for much of the human history of these islands, mammal-hunting was definitely not a walk in the park).

The concept of reintroductions, though, is an interesting, and often highly controversial salve to our conscience. In the last few decades we have very successfully returned Red Kites and Sea Eagles to the wild in this country, to widespread approval. However, the idea of having Beavers at large in the country is an interesting exercise in how far this can go without widespread opposition.

Beavers are not the sort of animals that can disappear into the countryside without having any effect; they are more assertive than that. They alter habitat to their own ends, damming rivers to create more habitat for themselves (and other wildlife), and gnawing bark and even felling trees. Fishery interests in Scotland, where the main wild Beaver introduction is about to take place in 2009, are worried about what they will do about the habitat of salmon. They believe that the return of salmon upriver to their breeding grounds will be hampered by Beaver dams and that the smolts (young salmon) will not be able to swim past the dams downriver to the sea They are also worried about potential damage to forestry and watercourses.

The trouble is, the people who oppose these schemes always seem to be the same loud voices. Farmers declare that Sea Eagles take live lambs – sorry, they are just completely and utterly wrong. Similarly, sensible scientific research shows that Beaver dams have no effect on salmon spawning, so the fishery people are wrong too. Cormorants have been proven to have very little effect on river or sea fishing (enclosed fisheries are another matter). After all this discredited opposition, it seems to me that it becomes harder and harder to take what some farmers and fisherman say seriously. And that's not good for anyone, because these people's opinions still need to be heard. I suspect they are just angry after years of being ignored and patronised by successive governments.

Our Beaver safari, meanwhile, was to take place in two stages. Firstly, in daylight, Phoebe would lead us to the site where the Beavers lived, and show us some of their field-signs. Then, later on, we would return to the same lake by ourselves at dusk and see whether we could spot the animals as they left the lodge.

For the third time that day Phoebe took us on a mystery tour into the depths of the Water Park. Eventually we stopped in a lay-by along a narrow road. The remote setting lent a frisson of excitement to the endeavour, as if we were about to do something highly illegal.

"It's only a short walk from here to the Beaver hide," said Phoebe. "But first I have something to show you."

And from out of the boot of her car she produced a Beaver pelt. She laid it on the bonnet and allowed the kids to stroke it. The fur was soft brown, and rich and fulsome, as you might expect, since Beavers are hunted throughout their range for their skins. But what none of us expected was the sheer size; it seemed almost to cover the bonnet, and measured 90 centimetres (3 feet) from the head to the beginning of the tail. The pelt clearly came from a pretty formidable beast, although a harmless one, of course, since Beavers are vegetarians (that's not to imply, by the way, that vegetarians are necessarily harmless – look at Madonna). Moreover, the tail was weird: long, laterally flattened and covered with scales, as if it had been borrowed from a lizard or some other reptile. This tail is used as a paddle, to store fat in the winter and to slap on the water as a warning sign.

Remarkably, by the way, Beavers are rodents – the largest in the Northern Hemisphere. That makes them relatives of mice and voles, although it is easier to see the resemblance to squirrels, especially in the Beaver's sharp and ample front teeth.

"The skin comes from a Polish animal," said Phoebe.

The kids were impressed. "Is that what we are going to see?" asked Samuel. We nodded our heads.

It turned out to be quite a walk to the hide. For Phoebe, who was obviously quite fit, it was a doddle, but for our youngsters it was a drag, and we had to coax them for much of it, pointing out signs along the way – a water tower, puddles, tractors beside another set of new-builds, more puddles, men with hats, puddles, mud – "Oh look, there's a really big puddle." Samuel kept getting left behind, and it vexed him. If a Beaver had been around in the daylight, it would have heard us long before we arrived.

At last, however, we came to the lake where the Beavers were being housed. We paid a brief visit to the hide to get our bearings for later on, and then Phoebe led us into a strip of woodland adjoining the water where, she told us, we were sure to find signs of the animals' work. She was as good as her word. Right next to the waterside there were signs everywhere. And I'm not talking about subtle stuff – not incised cones, like those left by squirrels, or neatly shelled nuts worked on by mice. These were proper, distinctive, impossible-to-miss signs. There were dozens of sticks lying about that had been gnawed down "to the bone", and large scabs of bark missing from trees, in a distinctive ring shape. And, just in case we had overlooked these indications, there was also a fallen tree, cut down in that classic Beaver way, gnawed right around so that it tapered in above and below, like the "waist" of an egg timer. The rodents had also been crawling up the fallen tree and left their mark there. There was also a well-worn "path" through the grass down to the water's edge.

"Autumn's a good time to see Beaver activity," said Phoebe. "The animals are beginning to horde food for the winter, and they could be doing some work on the lodge."

"What do the Beavers eat?" Carolyn asked.

"In summer they eat all sorts of vegetation, including grass and leaves and twigs. But in winter it's mainly just bark, and they need about two kilograms a day. They have cut this tree down so that they can get at the bark. It doesn't sound very appetising, does it?"

We shook our heads. "Ugh," said Emily.

The children collected up special "beavered" sticks to take home. Within moments, Samuel had recognised their potential as weapons.

"What are the Beavers actually doing here in the Water Park?" I asked, fending off his attacks.

"The idea is to study their effect on the habitat here and to see how they get on. They are confined to this fifteen-hectare lake and the surrounding strip at the moment, so we can closely monitor everything they do. It's such a long time since they've been in Britain that nobody knows how they might settle, at least in the long term. At present we aren't going to introduce them to the rest of the site, but it could happen eventually. The signs are good so far. There seems to be more wildlife about now on this lake than before we introduced them, which is very positive."

Originally, six Beavers had been introduced to the Lower Mill Estate in 2005, comprising two families and, therefore, two potential colonies (Beavers live in extended families). The six were named Tony and Cherie, Gordon and Sarah and John and Pauline. And that turned out to be asking for trouble. Inevitably, strife broke out between the clans and one family had to be relocated away from the Water Park. Which goes to show that there are always going to be tensions between neighbours of similar ilk. The analogy with powerful politicians was further enhanced by the fact that the Beavers were housed on a very exclusive estate, with nearby buildings valued in the millions.

Our return to the Beaver lake at dusk had to be handled with great care. The kids were worn out, and they had been be bribed up to the hilt in order to get them to walk back at all. Phoebe had also warned us to keep very quiet on the walk up to the hide, otherwise we would probably miss seeing the Beavers altogether. This necessitated more bribes. In fact, we had been to M&S and got them food so utterly delicious that the ruse worked brilliantly. I doubt whether Emily and Samuel had managed to keep so perfectly quiet throughout the whole year.

It worked, too. The hide was about 300 metres (1,000 feet) opposite the Beaver lodge. When I noticed that a Grey Heron that had been standing on the lodge suddenly flew off, giving an irritable alarm call, its broad wings flapping hard, I suspected that it had been flushed out by a Beaver. Within moments there was a low, flat head and back moving slowly left to right, leaving a wake behind it. In the near darkness it was hard to see, but the kids just about made it out through the telescope. It wasn't much – but it was a British Beaver!

Shoo

As a postscript to our visit, we learned later that official permission had been granted to begin a reintroduction scheme in Argyllshire, Scotland. It will be the first ever formal reintroduction of a wild mammal into Britain. About 20 Norwegian Beavers will be released, after quarantine, in the spring of 2009, and will be closely monitored in a much more wild setting than the homes of the Cotswold Water Park animals.

Let's hope they do well: establish themselves, delight visitors and even keep the fisherman sweet.

And then, what next? Lynxes, please.

## October 25th – A Highland Fling

Please don't ever get the impression that this mammal-hunting family might in any way be prone to answering unsolicited emails. But it so happens that, one day in mid-October, despite our better judgment, we happened to do just that. Thing is, the email came not from a car insurance company, nor from some nice people wanting to lend us money in return for paying them three times as much, nor from a pharmaceutical company offering to make my member as long as the M1. No, it came from the Bird-watching and Wildlife Club, based in a hotel up in the Cairngorms, in Grantown-on-Spey. It offered tons of wildlife sightings up in Scotland, including the magical possibility of seeing two new species for our project, the Mountain Hare and the Bottlenose Dolphin. Who could resist such an offer?

Actually, we did resist the offer. By now we couldn't afford a break in the Highlands. But happily for us Toby Virgo, who ran the club, saw enough in our family's project to offer us free accommodation and food over the October half-term, for three nights. Sometimes even mammal-spotters get perks.

He was even more generous to offer us accommodation for five. As it happened, we were to be joined in our adventure by my 18-year-old niece Stephanie, who lives in Sydney, Australia (lucky girl), and was on a gap year. It seems highly doubtful that her original plans included standing in the freezing cold looking for animals, but I can tell you, she was about to get a gutful of it anyway.

The only memorable part of our journey up to Scotland was in our overnight accommodation, when Samuel, who had been infuriated by something that escapes me now but was only a matter of momentary conflict, decided that it was time to disown us.

"I want a better family," he said, with a frown as wide as the Forth Road Bridge.

The drive was long and cramped. Near Glasgow we got stuck in one of those phantom traffic jams, the cause of which you never work out and is thus so more frustrating than any others – at least you want to see the crushed metal that has held you up for a hour.

Gradually, the roads became less crowded and the hills got higher. Indeed, close to our destination we could even see some snow on the ridgetops, causing much youthful anticipation, and not just for Emily and Samuel. As I mentioned before, our kids had never really experienced snow – not to step on, and model with their fingers, not to revel in. It turned out that, at least since her early childhood, neither had Steph. Let's face it, Australia is to snow what Milton Keynes is to growing papayas, so despite having her early years dotted with references to Santa on his sledge, pulled by Reindeer from Lapland, Steph had come to live in a country where almost all the sledging is on a cricket field, and where the only fauna available for pulling such vehicles would have to hop. So Steph just keep looking up, goggle-eyed, at the cream-coloured hilltops and saying, "Awesome!" every few miles.

Grantown-on-Spey immediately struck me as a wealthy, clean-cut town. The grand Georgian buildings in the town-centre square were made of solid granite, with large windows and big, opulent entrances; some dated from the 1760s, when the town was originally laid out. There were black slate roofs and towering chimneys everywhere. The shops weren't normal shops: they sold fashion accessories and kitchen units and pottery items.

The hotels, of which there were dozens, looked imposing and expensive. Some buildings had balconies from which Christmas lights already hung. It looked as though Grantown was still decked out for a royal visit, as it had been in 1860, when Queen Victoria came to town.

When we first saw the Grant Arms Hotel (the name Grantown derives from the surname Grant, not "Grand Town"), we knew we had fallen on our feet. It was right on the tree-lined square, and it seemed to be a whole block long. Inside the rooms were large and warm, and inviting. And not for this hotel a dreary old door that you open in the normal way; the Grant Arms had a revolving door, which for some reason caught the children's imagination in a way that nothing else did. Throughout every meal the kids kept on badgering us to come with them to "see the outside"; this was a euphemism for the quick fix of a go on the revolving door. The Grant Arms was christened the "Whirly Door Hotel".

Apart from this notable feature, there was something else unique in the hotel, too. Just behind reception was a flat screen showing a picture of some deer on a hillside, together with running text, Sky-News style, informing us of local wildlife sightings. "There have been Hen Harriers in the Findhorn Valley recently," it said. "Red Squirrels still at Aragach. Look out for Ptarmigan on the top of Cairngorm..." and so on. It looked as though we had come to the right place.

Later on, I went to see Toby to seek his advice on finding the Mountain Hares and Bottlenose Dolphins. I was directed to a door just off reception. As I opened it, the atmosphere completely changed; it was like going through the wardrobe and finding Narnia. There was an instant sense of peace and calm, projected by piped bird song (it was a bit out of season for Cuckoos and Blackcaps, but never mind), and the long corridor leading to the Club Room was bedecked by impressive photographs of Highland wildlife, together with detailed maps. The room itself was as quiet as a library and, indeed, housed books and leaflets and yet more maps. Somebody hereabouts clearly had a thing about finding their way around.

In such a place I didn't expect to encounter someone with a Midlands accent.

"Welcome," said Toby Virgo. He was a clean-cut young man with a round face and a shot of very dark hair, and he looked like a healthy advertisement for the Highland lifestyle – he was a refugee from the south, who had previously worked at a Highland estate helping people to hunt deer. He explained that he was the Director of Operations for the Club, and would do his best to help us find the mammals that we needed.

"Well, a Mountain Hare would be a good start," I said.

Within minutes I had directions to find this elusive mammal. And Bottlenose Dolphins. And even a site where, if I sacrificed a pig and burnt a four-leaved clover, I might even be able to spot a Wildcat.

We were the only family at dinner. The rest of the guests would pile in later. We almost had the impressive dining room to ourselves. It was very quiet, serene almost. The places were laid impeccably, and the glasses and cutlery looked expensive. Several smiling staff were at our service, while those few guests that had come for an early meal – mostly elderly couples – murmured respectfully.

And we had two children under seven. Oh dear.

Our entrance was hard to miss. We had been given a big round table near to the centre of the dining room, and the children just ran straight to it, weaving through other tables and just missing several staff carrying drinks. Once there, Emily and Samuel bickered over who sat next to Steph, who was their next big thing. They fiddled with their cutlery and Samuel pretended his knife was a gun. They denounced the offer of anything but lemonade. Parental blood pressure was rising fast.

And then Jacob came to the table. He was a Polish waiter with a sense of humour as dry as ginger ale. He was dressed immaculately, had very short, dark hair, glasses and a glint in the eye. He looked at Samuel and stood up very straight.

"You going to shoot me?"

My son blushed and went quiet. Emily smiled. Jacob took our drinks orders with a straight face.

"You like whisky, young man?" he asked, and Sam tried to hide behind me, grinning.

"And for the girl, a gin and tonic?" said Jacob. There was something about his humour, his manner and his accent that held our kids spellbound. When he left the room, the usual pandemonium broke out; each time he came to our table he had a hypnotic effect on our children.

"You – are you being good?" he would say, pointing. And they would be, whichever one caught his piercing gaze.

The meal passed more peacefully than we expected.

## October 26ᵗʰ – Hares and Races

Toby Virgo had told us that finding the Mountain Hares should be a doddle. Well all right, he didn't say it outright. He actually said that you never know with wildlife, and although Mountain Hares were fairly widespread and common, he couldn't absolutely guarantee that one would cross our path to order. Nevertheless, there was a particular spot where they were more likely to be co-operative than anywhere else.

What was he expecting us to do? Sue him?

"Go down the single-track road along the Findhorn Valley," he instructed us. "As you reach the end there is a small car park near the entrance to the private estate. Park here, walk into the heather pretty much anywhere, and you ought to flush one out."

And so we followed his instructions to the letter. The only trouble was, the weather didn't co-operate. When we turned off the A9, the leaden clouds duly delivered rain. Nothing much at first, just showers. But half way down the hill this rain had turned to hail – great big stones that bounced on the road in front of us and made exciting clatters against the car windows. Three-quarters of the way down, sleet was obscuring our view of the looming, scree-covered hillsides and the dull ink-grey Findhorn River below. And once we reached the car park, we were in the midst of a full-blown blizzard.

Steph was excited. "This is just awesome," she declared contentedly.

It was, to be honest. The Findhorn Valley is something of a wind-tunnel. It's a U-shaped valley, with shapely sides, but little tall vegetation. The wind batters everything. It played with our car as if testing it out for a potential shove towards the valley bottom. The flakes of snow zipped past horizontally, covering the valley sides in a flimsy white veil, but leaving the immediate vicinity untouched. Indeed, all the elements were having a party. The Findhorn was supposed to be a meandering river, with middle-aged twists and turns and a relatively gentle flow. But not today. It was infused with several days of heavy and persistent rainfall, a kind of riverine Viagra that made its flow heave against its own banks, trying to regain its youthful, turbulent daring, chucking waves over the lips of the banks and roaring with new found energy.

"Is this where the Mountain Hares are supposed to be?" asked Carolyn. I'm not saying she sounded sceptical or anything; just that she sounded like a barrister cross-examining a witness.

"Yes, Toby says that we should just walk around here for a little while and try to flush one from the heather."

"But we're in a blizzard. It's minus two degrees outside. The children are cold."

Steph tried to play mediator. "This is awesome," she said. The blizzard turned itself up a notch.

"I suggest we go somewhere else," said Carolyn. "And get a cup of coffee."

"No, let's stay here for a bit," I replied. "I'm sure the weather will clear soon. It has been showery, so it should improve quickly. Look, we've come all this way, after all, haven't we? I don't think the Hares are especially difficult to see in decent conditions."

I didn't believe myself. But the weather did – how gullible can you get? The blizzard ceased. Incredibly, the sun came out. Thirty seconds before it seemed to be having a day off. That didn't mean that conditions were pleasant. We emerged from the car and were almost knocked over by the icy blast. We could barely keep the car doors open. It became difficult to prepare for the Mountain Hare-hunt, since we knew that at least five layers of clothing were necessary, even for a 10-minute spin. And getting a four-year-old into five layers is not easy, I can tell you.

For her part, Emily decided to stay in the car. We tried to tempt her out by the prospect of seeing some Red Deer that were up on the hillside, but to no avail. It was the first time in the whole mammal-watching year that she had decisively put her foot down in this way, so we decided to respect it; her tolerance – and that of both children – had been admirable ever since January, and she had earned the choice. But it did put a severe limit on the time that we would have in the outside. Ten minutes would probably be it under these extreme conditions.

All we could do, really, was to climb the slope straight in front of us and hope that a Mountain Hare would come out of hiding. We spread out and put our feet to the soil, springy from sphagnum moss and heather, Carolyn and Steph taking the flanks, and Sam and I in the middle. The wind tore at us and it threatened snow again. "This really needs to be quick," I thought to myself.

It was. Steph flushed the animal first and shouted above the wind. We all looked up and saw it cut across our path, streak down the hill as far as the road, and and run along the thoroughfare until, like a Formula 1 car, it took the bend at full speed and disappeared.

"It was so fast!" exclaimed Steph.

"Did you see it?" I asked Sam.

"Yes, a rabbit," he replied. Leaving aside taxonomic considerations, and the fact that the Mountain Hare was sporting the beginnings of its winter coat, with a few white blotches here and there, that was good enough confirmation for me.

Emily was, of course, most disappointed to have missed the Hare. We tried to console her by letting her find the Red Deer through the telescope, but they were distant and still. I had rather hoped that she might hear a stag roaring and see the does running, but perhaps the cold and wind had dampened any ardour up on the slopes. For Emily, after having ploughed her way through sightings of 46 species of British mammal, it was something of a let-down. And although she asked whether we could find the Mountain Hare again, we declined, suspecting that, at its rate of progress, it would probably be on the shores of the Irish Sea by now. Besides, conditions had barely improved.

On the way back to civilisation, just for the record, we spotted the Findhorn Valley's herd of Feral Goats. They were black, rather than white, and they looked more "wild" than those in Somerset. But they were Goats. We didn't stop.

If you ever ask an expert cetacean watcher, "What's the best land-based site in Britain to see dolphins?" you are bound to get the same response every time. Without hesitation they will say "Chanonry Point", a place on the Moray Firth that has assumed star status among Britain's wildlife-watch-points. It's not just because it's reliable – about 50 dolphins reside year-round in the Firth's rich waters. The main reason is that, when they do show, the dolphins usually perform like their theme-park cousins, giving an astonishing bravura extravaganza of leaping and frolicking –

all in front of delighted onlookers who may, by a quirk of topography, be just a few metres away. Chanonry Point, on the northern shore of the Firth, is situated opposite Fort George, another point that juts out from the south side, and between the two peninsulas the low-tide race brings a concentration of fish that, in turn, brings the dolphins swimming.

When originally contemplating this trip to Scotland I had assumed that the dolphin displays were as reliable as they were spectacular. However, despite the fact that the Bottlenose Dolphins are resident in these waters, their appearances at Chanonry Point at low tide are very much more regular in the summer, when they are said to appear on 90 per cent of days. In October, however, when we were making our visit, the percentage drops sharply – Toby said that only about half the visits are successful – making it far more of a gamble. In short, for our afternoon visit, we would need a bit of luck to see these wonderful creatures.

Actually, we didn't help ourselves by lengthening our own odds considerably. Our visit to Chanonry did coincide with a low tide, but Toby had advised us that an hour after the lowest water was actually the most likely time, and by a cruel twist of fate, that took us into the gloom of late evening – the nights were now closing in fast. To be honest, we needed the dolphins to work to our timetable. Otherwise, this important part of our Scottish jaunt would provide us with sea mammal disappointment yet again. After missing everything except Common Porpoise on our first trip to Scotland, then missing out on the Northumberland boat trip and failing to see any sea mammals from the Dorset coast, we were beginning to acquire a defeatist dose of year-long sea mammal bankruptcy. We didn't have a credit crunch (at least not yet); we were experiencing a cetacean crunch.

Chanonry Point itself was pleasant enough, with a links golf course, a few holiday cottages and a lighthouse. Sam's lighthouse-mad phase was over now, though, and the point was battered by the same keen wind that we had suffered in the Findhorn Valley. So, not surprisingly, our dolphin-watch at Chanonry was a struggle. For about an hour we sheltered behind the lighthouse compound's perimeter wall, and occasionally ventured on to the shingle by the water's edge. But it wasn't working. As time went on, the choppy waters became more and more murky, in league with the sky. A Grey Seal stuck its head up, then another and another, leading us to suspect that there was an ideal concentration of fish for a hungry dolphin.

But the darkness, together with an approaching storm with angry clouds and driving rain, defeated us.

If we couldn't see Bottlenose Dolphins at Chanonry Point, the best place for them in Britain, what did that say about our sea-mammal-watching efforts overall? What was it about us and whales and dolphins? Were we destined to draw a blank with them this year? If so, that seemed almost a reckless dereliction of a mammal-watching family's duty.

## October 27th - Reined In

Bearing in mind our failure with the dolphins as darkness fell last night, today's strategy was never going to be anything but obvious. Go straight back to Chanonry Point, and all coasts east, and simply try again, spending all day if necessary gazing at the sea. After all, the resident Bottlenose Dolphins were clearly around somewhere, the sea was reasonably calm, and with enough time on the Moray Firth we were more or less guaranteed to see them. No argument.

So we went to the Cairngorm Range, up into the mountains. Yes, I know this sounds batty, but we were undone by the snow. Snow sounded more exciting than dolphins. It was crisp and new, and promised fun, while the dolphins felt like drudgery – dull waves and hours of likely frustration. Overnight the tops of the mountains had changed: they were no longer dusted white, they were *seriously* white. Above a certain altitude we knew that we could reach a freshly coated wonderland. We would throw snowballs and make a snowman, and all five of us would be young, just for the day.

And if you think you might have detected that our commitment to our mammal cause was weakening, you would be right. In fact, I hardly dare admit it, but yesterday, in between Mountain Hares and Chanonry Point, we went to Loch Ness and turned into tourists for a few hours. We went into the Loch Ness Centre where they admitted there really wasn't a monster, and we went shopping and did normal things. And it was fun, whereas Chanonry Point was an utter drag.

You've guessed it. We were all feeling fed up with spotting mammals. Not that we wanted to fail to get to 50. It's just that we had been on the case for 10 months, and we had nearly reached our target. In such a position, it was doubly exasperating when we failed to spot the ones we were looking for.

So we drove along the road towards the Cairngorm Centre, where we intended to take the funicular railway, and dive into that marvellous snow. In fact, by now there was snow all around us; not much – a few centimetres – but a glorious contrast to the dark forests on the foothills, and a thrilling indication of what lay above.

And then a strange thing happened. A very strange thing indeed. As we drove along, past the National Park headquarters, there was a sign saying "Funicular Railway closed." The road up to it was closed by a red gate and two men in Day-Glo jackets stood importantly next to it. When we asked them what was wrong, they said, "It's snowing."

Hang on a minute. This was a ski resort. And they were telling us that it was shut because of snow?

"The road up to the car park is too dangerous," said the men in doom-laden voices. "And the temperature is forecast to fall further."

It didn't sound very convincing. The atmosphere didn't feel particularly cold – indeed, the snow right where we were was beginning to melt. We had no choice, however. What was the point of making a fuss? Even so, it would make a good headline: "Few Centimetres of Snow Shut Ski Resort".

We were gutted to be confined to the foothills. But at least there was still the possibility of the Reindeer safari. We retraced our steps a couple of hundred metres and bought our tickets for this well-publicised tourist attraction. The procedure, we were told, was for all of us to take our cars along to a rendezvous point, and then walk from there for half an hour to see the herd of Reindeer that lived just above the tree line. The next departure would be at 11 o'clock.

The Reindeer of the Cairngorms constitute one of only two herds in Britain, the other being on the Glenlivet Estate 50 kilometres (30 miles) away. These are not truly wild animals: they were introduced in 1952, by a Swede who was either eccentric or homesick (and probably both), and felt that these iconic and useful animals should be part of the British landscape. Ever since, they have been managed by the appropriately named Reindeer Company Limited. The management involves keeping some animals at the Reindeer Centre, where we were now parked, and about 50 more in relatively free-ranging comfort on the harsh slopes of the Cairngorm Range. The latter animals would be the subject of our visit. We were to walk up to where the herd had decided to graze, and would be able to hand-feed some of them. It sounded like fun.

Not long afterwards the Reindeer people told us that the hill trip to the herd would be delayed.

And then, after another 15 minutes, they told us that the trip was unfortunately cancelled.

"Oh, why is that?" I asked them.

"The road up the hill is closed," the Reindeer person replied.

But surely they knew that? The Day-Glo men and their shut gate were no more than a few hundred metres away. Knowing that their rendezvous point was a little way up the same road, had they seriously not read the sign and liaised with the park authorities? We were incredulous.

And very grumpy. The funicular railway was shut; the free-ranging Reindeer were out of reach; and we had wasted a precious 45 minutes. Not even the building of a very small snowman, or the choice of about 20 different flavours of hot chocolate in the Glenmore shop made us feel any better. Except for Steph, bless her, who, with her in-built 18-year-old way of looking at life, managed to put a positive spin on everything. Without her we would have simply fumed.

And then we thought: why don't we try walking up the road to see whether we can find the Reindeer herd ourselves? We even considered making the Reindeer count towards our 50 species, but with the not-very-wild Beavers from the Cotswolds logged, that seemed to be a little cheeky. Nevertheless, out of curiosity and fun we walked, carrying a flimsy, tray-like sledge that Carolyn had insisted we brought with us, in case the snow was thick enough. Two parents, an 18-year-old and two children under seven, warm-togged but not mountaineering-togged, in trainers and wellington boots, began to walk the gentle road that, just a few hours before, had been deemed to be too dangerous, in conditions that were forecast to worsen but had actually ameliorated. I think that our little party, and other parties like ours, just made the National Park authorities look silly.

"They just did it so they wouldn't have to pay wages for a day," said a woman in a shop to us later, mischievously.

It was a good walk, too. The tarmac made it easy, and the snow was a constant, but happy distraction. Sam decided that our sledge was not actually a sledge, but a spade, and he made it his job to clear the snow from the road. He would stop, bend down, lift a big pile up in the sledge, and place it down, red-faced with grim determination, a couple of centimetres one way or another. Had we not chivvied him along, he would probably still be doing it now.

By this time the sky, which had been resolutely low and threatening, began to clear intermittently. It never showed the tops of the hills (perhaps the Park Authorities hadn't allowed it to), but it lifted enough for us to enjoy the view at times – the dark but open forest of native Scots Pine, the road winding uphill and the open moorland above the tree line. The further we went, the closer we got to the latter, and the possibility of seeing the Reindeer in the snow-covered landscape.

But we never made it. At a point in mid-afternoon the weather did close in. By now, with cold hands, wet bottoms from ineffectual sledging, and covered by the residue of well-aimed snowballs, we were in no fit state to play around with mountain weather. We retreated down the hill, our final defeat probably no more than a few hundred metres from where the Arctic animals were grazing.

We felt robbed.

As a final attempt to save the day, we sprinted to the Moray Firth once again. This time we could only reach the south side, at Fort George, opposite Chanonry Point, and with less of a reputation. Once again the light was fading, and again the waters of the firth did not look promising. It was also so cold and windy that, apart from Emily and me, everybody stayed inside the car.

The two of us deserved reward, and in a way we got it. While we stood there on the shore of the firth, shaking, a flock of Whooper Swans flew overhead, making loud trumpeting calls. They flew in the effortless, but regal way that swans always do, all 15 of them in a neat V-shaped skein, progressing imperiously against the wind. Their plumage, already spectacularly white against the thunderously blackening sky, was for a moment rendered spinetinglingly brilliant, almost golden, by a sudden shock of unadulterated sunset, just as they went over our heads.

It was a gift; the last appearance of the sun on our second Scottish adventure. But no dolphins showed.

We had never really considered trying for Wildcats up here in the Cairngorms. We knew that, by reputation, they are almost impossible to see. But with the dolphins failing, and nothing much more to lose, it seemed worth a go, even though even Toby had admitted that our chances were exceedingly slim. It would definitely be our last chance of the year.

"They have been filmed on the moor beyond Abernethy Forest. Try there," he suggested. "But I've never seen one. Good luck."

The only taker I had for this trip was Emily, the most zealous enthusiast and adventurer of the family. When we left, Carolyn and Samuel were both in bed, looking as luxuriously settled as cats on hearths, a far cry from Wildcats somewhere out in the freezing night. The two of us packed the car with enough gloves and jumpers and scarves to survive if we broke down, and set off into the night, taking the spotlight in the hope of seeing the most elusive animal in Britain.

The snow began as soon as we set off. Before long it was falling in earnest. Not surprisingly, there wasn't much traffic on the road; nobody else was taking a chance. Within minutes we were driving though the forest Toby had mentioned, excitingly isolated, our whole focus within the beam of our headlights. The surrounding blackness, with the snow falling, was whitening, if you see what I mean, giving an extra pale dimension to the interior between the trees. The silhouettes of jagged branches and trunks were softening with the settling flakes. The snow provided a screen in front of our windscreen wipers through which the world outside, in the Highland forest, seemed quite unreal.

We didn't just pass through forest, however. I could have coped with that all night. The most dangerous thing in the forest would probably be what we dearly wished we could see. But it was the settlements that we passed, all alone, that started to make the shivers go down my spine. We could see isolated buildings, their lights extinguished, and they were strangely alarming. One was completely blackened, with boards and broken up windows. It looked frighteningly bleak and full of menace. Perhaps it was because it looked just like a building in a horror film. But it made me squeeze the accelerator instinctively. We passed a moor of impossible loneliness, too. How could anything live out there? It reminded me of the moor where Sherlock Holmes looked for the Hound of the Baskervilles, the mist always rising, and hidden dangers lurking in the darkness.

A muted voice spoke over the anxious soundtrack of my mind. "Daddy," said Emily. "I'm a little bit scared. Can we go home?"

"Yes, darling," I replied. "That's a good idea. But don't worry. There's nothing to be afraid of."

And we turned around and sped back towards Grantown, the snow falling with still more determination than it had earlier in the drive. It must have fallen on the Wildcats that had chose to go hunting that night, too, but we never saw them.

Reassured, Emily soon fell asleep. It was a stylish way to drift off, in a Scottish forest in the snow, late at night.

As for me, I never quite relaxed until I saw the friendly lights of Grantown-on-Spey in the near distance – and not before time, either.

## October 28th – At Last!

The morning of October 28th marked the endgame in a long search. It came after several months of frustration. The object of the search had been elusive and slippery. Several times we had come close to a proper experience with it, but never quite enough to be completely satisfied.

It was Steph who alerted us to its presence. She knocked on the door of our room in an excited state – indeed, she was ecstatic.

"It's been snowing," she whooped. "Look out of your window. It's lying everywhere! Thick!"

Grantown-on-Spey had indeed been transformed into a wonderland. Around 5–10 centimetres (2–4 inches) of snow covered everything. The main street was white but for two slushy tracks made by the day's traffic. Cars and lorries were progressing at barely walking pace. Pedestrians were moving gingerly, dressed to the eyeballs, with woolly hats and thick gloves, unsure of their feet. On the grass outside the hotel, some bright spark had already built a snowman, albeit a somewhat pitiful, unadorned one. Our car was covered so completely, it looked as though somebody had put a dust jacket over it; such a shame we had 650 miles to travel today.

Yes, we were going home, but not before we were due some serious snow immersion. We took our weedy blue sledge down to the golf course, where we knew there would be hills and bumps. Our hunch was right. Before us were acres of virgin snow, on gentle, child-friendly slopes. We ran, we sledged, we fell over, we got cold and wet. It was light-headed delight for all ages. Our sides hurt with scrapes and laughter.

I have to admit it. Forget the Mountain Hares, the Bottlenose Dolphins and the Wildcats. In our hearts we realised it was the snow we had come for, even if we hadn't known this when we left home. It made our Scottish jaunt special, unforgettable, a memory-fest in a year of memories, a jewel among unexpected gifts.

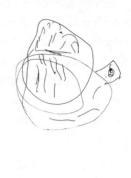

hegog

# November

## November 12th – Pest Control

Not surprisingly, news of our family's eccentric way of life (for one year only) had filtered through to most of our friends and some of the members of our church – not that the two were mutually exclusive, of course.

People became accustomed to asking us questions like, "Have you seen any dolphins yet?" or, "How are the mice getting along?" and starting conversations that way. At times we suspected that, despite their apparent interest, deep down they probably thought we were quite mad. But, on the other hand, there are times, as it turns out, that even slightly barmy people can turn out to be pretty useful.

I thought I knew David, one of the blokes at church, quite well until he became strangely furtive. Within a few weeks he changed from a friendly, talkative mate with whom you could share the worries of the world, to someone who seemed to avoid me and shift his gaze elsewhere. I wondered whether I had offended him, or if our kids might have had a row. Or something. It was worrying.

Eventually, however, David approached me directly one Sunday after the morning service.

"Dominic," he said, looking around to check whether anyone could hear us. "I've got a bit of a problem, and I need your help."

My heart sank. Money problems? Alcohol? Women? I took a deep breath.

"Come and sit down and we'll talk about it," I said in my best counsel-ese, putting my arm around his shoulder.

"I've a problem at home," he began as we sat away from the crowd. It looked as though David was about to burst into tears. A couple of older ladies cast glances towards us, then looked away quickly.

"A home problem?" Oh no. Did David know what a hopeless counsellor I was? My track record wasn't good. I mean, it really wasn't good at all. Even if he wasn't suicidal now, he soon would be.

But the poor man was desperate. I had to listen. Remember, Dominic, I told myself, just listen. Don't appear shocked. Don't judge.

David finally found the strength to come clean. He put his head in his hands and took a deep breath. "Dominic, I think we've got mice," he said.

"Mice?"

I must have sounded shocked, because David replied. "Oh, all right. I'm sure we've got mice. I admit it. Definitely. I've seen them."

"You've got mice," I stated back to him. It's good to state the problem back to the client. "Is that all?"

"Well, yes. Unless they are rats. They're in the living room. And in the kitchen. And under the stairs. I've heard that you've got some traps. That you are – you know – interested in rodents. Can you help me?"

And I did. Within a couple of days I made a visit to David's house. While his two sons looked on in fascination, I set up a couple of Longworths in the study and under the stairs. The following day David's observations were confirmed: two traps, two fat and defecating Wood Mice. We released them in a local park. The rodents weren't pleased at all, running off with all the enthusiasm of a WAG being asked to read a mathematics textbook.

The next day, there were two more, fatter than the last. Any more of this and the traps would be too small for the intruders.

"David," I said. "You've got a problem. Call pest control." He did and, as far as I know, his house is now clear of the unwelcome strangers.

These days David is always cheery and comes over readily to have a chat. But I'm worried about John. He's been acting strangely of late. A little furtive. Not like him. Can't make eye-contact...

## November 20th – Notes from HQ, Part VIII

It was late October, after a terrific month of mammal-watching, when we saw our forty-seventh mammal of the year. Now, three weeks later, with the year beginning to run out of months, we were still a magic three animals short of our year-long target, having allowed ourselves a brief moratorium on mammal trips (Well, OK, in a stressful moment, Carolyn had declared "I never want to go mammal-watching again!") However, without any more progress, stress was now just beginning to creep up on us. The various options remaining loomed large: Pygmy Shrews, Moles and Weasels anywhere about; Bottlenose Dolphins off any coast; Black Rats in some dock somewhere; Wild Boar in a few scattered places. Incredibly, I even began to have dreams about them. In one instance the whole family were all wading through a stream (I don't know why) and, under a rock, we managed to disturb a Pygmy Shrew, which everyone saw perfectly. As I slept I felt the relief and delight coursing through my body. Then, upon awaking, I realised that the jinx of this animal had not been broken, and had an increasing chance of not being broken, and my mental health nosedived. This project was getting more and more under my skin, and by proxy, my family's too.

Of course, what we all should have been thinking was that 47 was a pretty excellent total, and left it at that. After all, we parents were all mammalled out by now and looking forward to a more normal life. We should have borne in mind that, at the start of the year, all we truly wanted was a few family adventures, so that we would spend time together and grow a year older together. We should have been proud and thrilled to have seen such superb animals as Pine Marten, Otter, Water Shrew, Mountain Hare and Barbastelle. Yet, somehow, because we had set ourselves the task of seeing 50, we felt that 47 wasn't good enough.

With a little reflection, I think that part of the "unfinished" feeling was that we had missed some animals that we really should have seen during the summer, and particularly wanted to see. How could a family spend a year watching mammals in Britain without spotting a dolphin, for instance, when our islands are one of best places for sea mammals in Europe? The antics of one particular mammal-group organiser had also effectively robbed us of Pygmy Shrews so far, and others had let us down with Harvest Mice, and I hated the resentful feelings that came with that; moreover, the doleful weather throughout the summer had undoubtedly contributed to a failure to see these animals. Actually, later on I heard from other mammal-watchers that it had been an exceptionally poor year for Harvest Mice, so perhaps I am being hard on everyone, but really, with a whole summer available, we should have seen one by now.

In theory, we were still in with a chance of all of these. For example, remarkably, neither Pygmy Shrew nor Harvest Mouse hibernate, but somehow survive all through the winter months, although in the latter case there can sometimes be 90 per cent mortality in the cold season. However, the problem here is that the mammal-trapping season unofficially ends in October; after that, there is a real danger that any animals trapped could die overnight. So, in attempting to see such creatures late in the year, one needs to be very careful.

I did, however, go to Alana Ecology once more and beg for a few more traps. This was because, when we had been out with Penny Rudd near Chester Zoo, she introduced us to some traps that I had not seen in operation before. Known as "Trip-traps," these were made of clear perspex and were much more sensitive than the traditional Longworths. Penny had told us that they were effective for catching shrews and, by extension, Harvest Mice too. So I bought seven and put them out on carefully-selected mild nights, including a few placed in the grounds of a nearby riverside hotel. But never once did I catch any shrews, although there were a lot more fat and contented Wood Mice around in East Dorset than there had been a few weeks before. And, you'll be pleased to know, no animals died; far from it, all were distinctly portly and perky after their overnight stay.

We did make one dedicated trip for Pygmy Shrew, to Kimmeridge Bay once again. On such a sensitive site, having obtained the required permission, I was advised only to put the traps out during the day. And although it was wonderful to clamber over those rocks, and watch a bunch of hard-nosed kayakers put out into the calm waters, not even a Wood Mouse made an appearance, let alone a Pygmy Shrew.

And I doubt whether I am giving away a fact too early, but we never did see a Pygmy Shrew at all in 2008. Actually, I tell a lie. I myself did see a Pygmy Shrew, very close to home, although it was a dead one.

And talking of dead animals…

MOLE

# December

## December 10th-15th – Mountains out of Molehills

In our state of negativity, one particular beast that seemed to offer more solace than most was the Mole. After all, we knew they were everywhere. The children had seen molehills aplenty within a few hundred metres of where we lived and so, in a sense, already appreciated these animals. Mind you, they had also watched the dreaded "Fimbles" when they were younger, so they might have expected Moles to roll along their tunnels and have a ready store of books to read. They needed educating.

I began to ask around. I enquired among those that I took out on bird-watching courses.

"Oh yes," they would reply. "We have plenty of Moles."

But then came the stock question and answer. "Do you ever see them?"

"No."

That was the problem. Moles, as we all know, live underground. They do occasionally surface, but that, according to the Mole experts I rang, usually happens in May and June, when the young Moles disperse to a patch of earth that they can call their own. I wish I had known this vital piece of information back then, especially in Scotland, where a Mole had clearly been working hard in the garden of Stag Cottage. In view of its shallow runs and lopsided digging, it was obviously something of an amateur. But, aside from a few cursory looks, we hadn't tried very hard to see it at the time. Regrets, we had plenty.

I began to ask around pest-control experts. Yes, I literally cold-called to see whether, in the course of their work, they might perhaps trap a live Mole that my children could see. They all replied in the same way.

"No, we always trap them to kill them. They enter the tunnel contraption and a spring trips and bashes down on their heads. Do your children want to see a squashed, mashed Mole?"

Well, hardly.

I asked everyone I knew. Friends, acquaintances, the man who fixed the boiler. I stopped short of asking people I met on the street, but only just. I'll swear that people began to avoid me, too, just because I kept bringing up the subject of Moles.

Eventually, however, I took action and had a bit of luck. The action bit involved ordering a couple of humane Mole traps from our friends at Alana Ecology. The good fortune stemmed from finding someone locally who had a Mole problem in their garden. The couple who fitted the bill were called Cliff and Ann, and they were the most delightful, amenable people you could possibly meet. As it turned out, they needed to be.

The Mole trap was essentially a plastic pipe, not round but square in cross-section. It was about 20 centimetres (9 inches) long, and simple but brilliant. The ends of the pipe were each fitted with a door that opened upwards as you pushed it from the outside; the idea was that as the Mole entered the trap fully, the door would shut behind it by gravity, and the Mole's strong but hefty claws would not be subtle enough to gain purchase below the door to lift it open and escape. Thus, if they entered they would be trapped and not squished. Perfect: catch your Mole alive, show your children, take early retirement.

As far as the practical application of the trap was concerned, things also seemed simple at the start. The pipe was to be fitted along the Mole's tunnel, the "run" that it would use at regular intervals to get around its territory. Once you found the run, you could simply replace a section of it with the trap, and, if you did the job well enough, the Mole would barely detect that the outside of its tunnel was plastic and not earth – but by then, of course, it would be too late. What could possibly go wrong?

So, on the afternoon of December 10<sup>th</sup>, I took two Mole traps over to Cliff and Ann. The idea was that I would set them by myself, and then the kids would come over when the Mole was trapped. Now retired, my friends lived in a bungalow not far from us, but it was a bungalow with a difference, being right in the country and having its own field attached. In the field was a Horse, to fuel Ann's passion for horse riding. We were also accompanied by a cat and a dog. I got the impression that this was a couple who loved animals.

But not Moles. The idea was that I should catch their Mole and relocate it. They didn't like Moles. In fairness, very few gardeners do.

We walked down the field towards a large ditch, accompanied, somewhat alarmingly, by the Horse. It was a big Horse, too, and as curious as a paparazzo. We soon came to a small cluster of molehills.

"These are the most recent," said Cliff.

My first problem was that there weren't many of them. The second was that some were half way down the ditch, and pretty inaccessible. We kneeled down by the most convenient ones. My instruction leaflet said: "Place the trap in a run between one hill and another. Use a mole stick to find out where the run goes. Simply place the mole stick in the earth. If it goes in easily and then resists, you have located the run."

My third problem was that I didn't have a mole stick. But fortunately I had remembered to bring a special "beavered" stick from the Cotswold Water Park. I placed it in the soil between two molehills, as instructed. It went in easily, then resisted. A good start.

The next task was to find another part of the same run about 20 centimetres (9 inches) away. Then Cliff and I could dig out the soil and place the trap. I duly placed the Beaver stick into a likely looking patch of soil close to the hill; excellent, it did exactly the same – sunk in, then resisted.

"Cliff, do you have a trowel?" I asked. "I think we're in business."

"No, but I'll get a spade," he replied, and went off. After a little while he came back, whistling merrily. By now the horse had disappeared to find some fresh grass, but the dog stayed put. Ann had gone off to do something far more useful than put a Mole trap in.

Cliff volunteered and began to dig. Since we had located two points on the Mole's run, he placed the blade at right angles to the direction of the run, so that when he dug, the hole in the soil would become apparent.

The trouble was, it didn't. He dug at both ends of our supposed section of run. Nothing. No Mole tunnels.

"That's odd. Maybe the stick isn't working," I suggested. I selected a random patch of turf. The stick went in easily, then resisted. I tried another, nowhere near the molehills. It did exactly the same. It was clear that the soil hereabouts was so soggy that any stick could be poked in without resistance at the surface. In other words, we hadn't found a Mole run, we had simply found soggy soil.

"Well, the Mole run must be somewhere between the two hills," mused Cliff, stroking his chin. "Why don't we just dig down until we find an entrance tunnel, and work back from there?"

The plan was agreed and executed. Cliff, since it was his garden, took on the task of digging. As he did so, I began to notice that we had already turned over quite a considerable amount of soil. More of this and we were going to do more damage than the Mole had ever done.

Fifteen centimetres (6 inches) down Cliff thought he had found something. But it just turned out to be a false trail. By the time we had gouged out a hole 30 centimetres (1 foot) deep and 15 centimetres (6 inches) across, we still hadn't located any tunnels.

"These Moles must be digging very deep," said Cliff.

"My instructions say that the runs should just be a few centimetres below the surface," I said. "But it is odd. Shall we try digging between two different molehills, away from these?"

We did, and again, after much shifting of earth, found nothing. By now I suspect that the Mole itself was laughing enough to choke on its earthworms. Cliff was sweating with the effort, and I with embarrassment.

"We could always try the hills over by the shed," suggested Cliff after a while, puffing. "They aren't as recent, but they might not be so deep."

"If you don't mind…"

He shook his head, and we left our excavations, the soil piled high above the two ugly holes. In the second site I took over the digging. But the result was pretty similar. The soil gave easily and the tunnels failed to give themselves away. To add to the frustration, I almost sliced a cable.

By now the afternoon had worn on, and Cliff and Ann's neighbour had come over for a chat. Unsurprisingly, the subject of Moles came up.

"We just can't find the tunnels, they're too deep," lamented Cliff.

"Oh, I've got Moles all over my garden," said the neighbour. "You can see the runs easily in my flowerbed and near the pond. In fact, you can feel them with your feet."

And so I said to a lady I had never met before in my life, "Oh, so could we put a Mole trap in your garden?"

And she said yes. Shortly after this, Carolyn arrived with the children.

"We're just about to put a Mole trap in this lady's garden," I told her. "Are you coming along too?"

"Which lady's garden?"

"Cliff and Ann's next-door neighbour. Cliff and Ann's Moles have been digging too deep…"

"What?"

The whole family trooped into the garden. It was a glorious piece of God's earth, backing on to a river, with something of a swamp behind. It was flanked on two sides by woodland, and within it there was a neatly tended vegetable patch, a pond and, somewhat incongruously, a 6 metre- (20 foot-) long boat, high and dry – waiting for the sailing season, or a miracle, I'm not sure which.

Truth be told, the Mole runs were quite obvious. There weren't any hills, but there were distinct ridges of earth in places, and the lady was right, you could feel the give when you put your feet on some of them. It so happened that the best and most obvious runs went through the vegetable patch. I made as though to begin digging.

"You can't dig there!" exclaimed Carolyn, horrified.

"But look at these Mole runs, they are really obvious."

"Dom, they're in a vegetable patch. There are plants placed at precise distances from one another, there's netting over it."

I had to admit, she was right. By now Cliff had rejoined us, with another man I didn't recognise. It turned out that he was the husband of Cliff and Ann's neighbour.

"We're putting down a Mole trap," I explained, in case he was wondering what a middle-aged man with a spade, a fraught wife and two children under seven were doing in his garden.

"How do you do?" he enquired undaunted. I wondered if it was he who was responsible for the ark in his garden.

"I really think you should try somewhere else," quailed Carolyn. "I really do."

I shifted my attention to the grass near the pond. I began digging. Cliff talked to his neighbour. Emily asked where the people's dog was. Sam just stood there shivering.

In such awkward circumstances, I found a tunnel at last, the Mole's run. I more or less discovered the other and placed the trap in between them.

"Oh, by the way," I said to Cliff. "The instructions said that the trap needed to be checked regularly. Please could you call me?"

I gave both men a book to thank them for their efforts, and we left under something of a cloud.

A day later I received a telephone message from Cliff. "No Mole," it said simply.

Two days later Ann rang. "No Mole. I'm sorry," she said.

Three days after the trap was set, Cliff rang to say, "I have removed the trap from our neighbour's garden. I'll try to set it up in our garden instead. But if we don't see you, do have a happy Christmas."

And that was that. They never caught one.

It turned out to be just as well that Cliff and Ann couldn't catch a Mole. I soon learned from another pest-control expert that Moles usually die in humane traps, despite the name. Either they remain trapped and quickly die of starvation (they need to eat at least every four hours), or they die from the stress of being captured. So in the end I am glad we weren't responsible for killing one of these intriguing animals.

Just at the end of this saga, I received an unexpected phone call from another couple, another set of my bird-watching students to whom I had enquired about Moles in their garden.

"Dominic, we've got a Mole all right, but it's dead," said a man called Julian. "It's in the shed. Would you like to come round for it?"

You bet we did. The very next morning a delegation came round to a house near Wimborne, Dorset, for the explicit purpose of seeing a dead Mole.

"Our neighbour's cat got it," said Julian, presenting the Mole on a piece of paper towel. Apart from a slight bleeding from the nose, it was in perfect condition. Actually, I was tempted to check for a heartbeat.

The kids were impressed, and I immediately felt glad that we had taken all this trouble with Moles, even if our forty-eighth mammal of the year was not very, shall we say, alive. It was a chunky individual, very recently in great shape. We could all appreciate its funny nose, big whiskers, rather absurd apology for a tail and the enormous, paddle-like forelimbs that can dig it out of sight in about a minute. Even more salient was the Mole's feather-soft fur, which the kids enjoyed stroking.

Sarah, Julian's partner, offered us a cup of coffee and biscuits. And although a dead Mole was not quite what we had hoped for a few days ago, we ate and drank with a high degree of satisfaction.

## December 21st – Last Gasp Wales

In the dying embers of the year, I could just about reconcile myself to missing Harvest Mouse and Pygmy Shrew, and perhaps Weasel too, despite spending the whole of 2008 wanting and trying to see them. It wasn't easy, but with friends and family around me – and the pills, of course – I was preparing to move on in life. But the idea that we might miss dolphins, and Bottlenose Dolphins in particular – that was almost unbearable. It's not just that these sea mammals are pretty common, and that to miss them altogether for a whole year would look somewhat incompetent and careless; it was the fact that they are truly iconic mammals, and I desperately wanted our progeny to see them. The kids had model dolphins in their bedrooms; they had read books about dolphins; and dolphins were always appearing in the media. These were special creatures that every child should see, if they could.

Except that we couldn't. Or at least, we hadn't, not so far. We had tried many times, but always without success, as you will have read.

However, as far as dolphins were concerned, we still did have a genuine chance of catching up with them. Our failure at Chanonry Point had been annoying, but not terminal. There were several places along Britain's shoreline where Bottlenose Dolphins were regular, even in the middle of winter. One such was Portland Bill, only an hour or so to drive from our house. But it had been an exceptionally poor autumn for them, with very few records. Another was the Isle of Man: large pods had been reported in the last week in Douglas Harbour. But that was quite a trip, especially just before Christmas. What, though, about Newquay, a town overlooking Cardigan Bay in West Wales? I knew that the dolphins there were numerous, and pretty reliable.

But would they show towards the end of December? I phoned an organisation called the Cardigan Bay Marine Wildlife Centre and spoke to a lady there by the name of Sarah. I explained our project.

"So, have you see any dolphins recently?" I asked.

"I haven't, but then I haven't looked; I've been on leave the last few days," she replied. "Wait a moment, I'll ask a couple of my colleagues."

I heard a muffled question and some answers. It sounded as though it was a "no" all round. My heart sank as Sarah came back to the phone.

"My colleagues haven't seen any, either," she replied. "Oh, now, hang on – there's one. A dolphin. It's in the harbour. I've just seen one jump out of the water! You phoned at exactly the right time."

And that was it. Sold to the family from Dorset. We'd be going to Newquay.

Miraculously, Carolyn managed to organise Christmas far enough in advance for us to make a trip to Wales on one of the shortest days of the year. She had agreed that we would spend one night, and two if necessary, in Newquay, in order to see those wretched dolphins. I'm sure that it was a big sacrifice for her, but she took it in her stride – to her eternal credit and my admiration and adoration. What a woman, I tell you. What a woman!

We arrived in Newquay at dusk, after a five-hour drive. I think, during the journey, Emily mentioned *High School Musical* at least 50 times – and that isn't counting when she was playing *HSM* Top Trumps with Mum. Sam spent much of the trip giving away the identity of everyone's presents.

"Mummy," he would say. "I'm not going to tell you what you're getting for Christmas, but it's a *Mamma Mia!* DVD."

"Please don't tell me, Sam."

"Daddy, would you like to know what you're getting?"

"No thanks, Sam."

"You're getting a football shirt."

And so on. Therefore, despite the latest recruitment drive by MI5, we won't be putting his name down yet.

We had striven hard to get to Newquay before darkness fell. I just wanted the chance to watch the sea, somewhere. I had that feeling that, if we could just cast our eyes over the water, even if briefly, there would be some dolphins in the harbour waiting for us. And if there were, such a bonus would take all the pressure off having to see them tomorrow. I just had that feeling. It was in my bones.

Funny about instincts, isn't it? There wasn't a sausage.

wood mose

That night we made our first and only genuine attempt in the whole year, somewhat incidentally, to see a Polecat. The reason for this was that we had been frightened off previously by the Polecat's reputation for being almost impossible to see. Do you know anyone who has seen one in the wild? Exactly.

Polecats are carnivores in the mould of Stoats and Mink, and look similar to the latter, apart from having white on the lower muzzle and between the eyes and ears, and having, in the winter at least, thick yellowish fur on the tummy. Unlike Mink, they are true natives, but share that animal's broad diet, which includes mammals, birds and amphibians. Polecats are well known for their habit of killing large numbers of frogs, a favourite food item in marshes, and large numbers of rats around farms. Indeed, in the wintertime, lowland farms next to light woodland, are probably the best places to look for them. And roads. The official mammal-watcher's advice when looking for these animals is simply to drive around on country roads at night.

The Polecat has been making a reputation for itself in recent years by launching out of its heartland in Wales and spreading into the English rural landscape; but Wales is still the easiest place to see it. However, Polecats are not very active in mid-winter and, to be honest, we didn't try very hard, only driving for about half an hour. We got what we deserved – nothing.

# December 22nd – We're Going on a Boar-hunt

What is the last thing you want to be faced with when you're very, very keen indeed (OK, desperate) to spot a dolphin out at sea? What weather conditions are absolute killers for cetacean-watching? Storms? Maybe, but it depends on the location. Fog? Absolutely.

When we looked out from our hotel room this morning, there was thick fog. Can you believe it? Our hearts sank. We had driven five hours to one of the best places to see dolphins in Britain, and now it was foggy. Foggy! It wasn't foggy anywhere else in the United Kingdom. Just here, in dolphin-land.

Still, we had all day. It would clear, wouldn't it?

The landlord at the pub where we were staying wasn't very optimistic. "It looks set in," he said gloomily, and I was angry with him for saying it, as if it were his fault. This was the same landlord who had said that the dolphins would probably come in on the high tide, which was five long hours away, worryingly close to the fading of the light. I profoundly hoped he was wrong on every single count.

At breakfast, I looked out of the window more than a touch gloomily, which was silly, because we couldn't even see the sea, fog or no fog. The kids were no help. They were only thinking about the coming season.

"Daddy," said Samuel. "What are you getting for Christmas? Did you know it was a football shirt?"

"Eat your breakfast, Sam," I replied.

Wearily, we made our way to our room to consider our prospects. On the landing, which had a big window overlooking the bay, it was obvious that the fog had lifted a little. Although some distance away, it was now easy enough to make out the waves in the nearest patch of water. And a movement, too, on the surface. Perhaps it was a gull.

My binoculars were to hand. No, it wasn't a gull. It was a fin. And not just a fin, but a dolphin's fin.

At last, 357 days after we had first looked for Bottlenose Dolphins, at Portland Bill on the first of January, the critters had finally shown themselves.

We had planned carefully for this moment. Although my heart was thumping, I set up the telescope inside our bedroom at child's height to overlook that blessed patch of sea. I focused carefully as Emily, first, and then Samuel looked over my shoulder. And there they were, three of them, surfacing regularly and intermittently. After a few nervous moments, Emily said: "I see them." And she did a little dance of triumph. We all did. And Samuel looked hard in the right place, so I assume he saw them, too.

Over the next few minutes the Bottlenose Dolphins showed themselves quite a few times. And just because we were in Newquay, we weren't just assuming they were the species we expected. We saw them well enough to pick out the grey colouration, obvious beak and rather tall, centrally placed dorsal fin. They broke the surface of the water regularly, in synchronised swimming style, three at a time. Even at some distance we could still detect an air of playfulness about them.

There are few more remarkable mammals in Britain than the Bottlenose Dolphin. It has a truly global distribution, so you can see it both in Cardigan Bay and in the Pacific Ocean off Australia. There are two discrete types, separated only by behaviour, one inhabiting shallow, coastal areas, such as the ones we were looking at, and others ranging over the deep oceans way offshore. This animal is so intelligent that it has sophisticated communication skills that extend to conversing, in a limited fashion, with people. It can recognise other members of its species and thereby build up an impressive list of social contacts (it probably uses Facebook when people aren't looking.) It is thought to be promiscuous and yet, almost uniquely among animals, it is known to operate a "babysitting" service, in which "friends" look after the young when the mother has to go on a dive for food. It often uses co-operative methods for catching fish, such as forming a team and herding its prey into the shallows, where it is easier to catch. At the same time it is renowned for its *joie de vivre*, spending its time riding the bow-waves of boats, swimming around objects of curiosity and routinely throwing itself high into the air, practising aerobatics for no other reason that they are fun.

Now that's a special animal.

The effect of seeing the dolphins early in the day was twofold. Firstly, we managed to relax and enjoy this coastal town for a short while: we had a walk on the beach, enjoying the fresh breeze, the rivulets of water left behind by the tide, the still-orange tinge of the bracken-covered hillsides. We tried kicking the seaweed on the strand-line in case a Pygmy Shrew (now knocked-out cold) might be hiding underneath, and looked out to the placid sea to see if we could spot the Bottlenose Dolphins again. And secondly, at the same time, it allowed us to make an appointment with a man called David Slater in the Forest of Dean. Tonight, for one night only, we were going on a Boar-hunt.

Many people will probably know that the Wild Boar was originally native to Britain, but was wiped out in historical times, probably by the turn of the fourteenth century, although records continue into the seventeenth century of animals that might have been Wild Boar. Whenever it actually happened, however, the result was the same: extinction. However, in the 1980s, it became faddish to farm Wild Boar for the first time in, perhaps, thousands of years. The animals tasted good and were "different" from good old Domestic Pigs, although the latter are descended from the former. Not surprisingly, of the various farms set up in this country, some were secure and some were insecure, in both the practical and economic sense, with the result that, inevitably, by accident or mishap some Wild Boar found themselves free again in their ancestral homeland. Thus, in a few places, such as the East Sussex/Kent border, west Dorset and Herefordshire, small populations of increasingly wild animals grew. The Boars were back in town – or at least, in woodlands.

Our family had tried to look for Wild Boar in our home county one November evening, but with a conspicuous lack of success. We hadn't got a sniff of them, despite lurking for hours in suitably dark, wooded places as the night drew in (OK, we were in the car). To be honest, it seemed from our research that a lack of success was the default setting for Boar-hunters. These animals were just incredibly hard to see.

However, as with previous researches, all roads led to one location if we wished to maximise our chances, and to one individual: David Slater. It so happened that I had been in email contact with him for several weeks, and I had already been impressed by his willingness to help us look for some of his favourite animals. And amazingly, despite the fact that it was almost Christmas and that he was about to fly out to Spain on holiday, he seemed perfectly happy to give up his time – even on December 22nd – to fulfil our mission.

We met David in his home town late in the afternoon. He was a middle-aged man with a somewhat rustic look, quite well-built and sporting a head of curly hair.

"I've been baiting the Boar for the last couple of nights," he told us as he got into the front seat. "And I've brought along some for tonight, too. If we're lucky, the piggies will come just as it gets dark. There's a house right in the middle of the Forest where they have been active in the last few days."

It sounded promising. We made a short drive and soon came to the entrance to a forestry track, guarded by a locked gate.

"The lady who owns the house has promised to meet us here at four o'clock to unlock it. I'll give her a call now," said David.

There was no answer. David looked crestfallen. "That's odd," he said. "She should be home by now. Never mind. I'll call again in a minute."

He did, and nobody answered. Time passed. We began to eat the food that we had brought for the evening. It started to get dark. Emily listened to music, Samuel had brought along some teddy bears that he kept throwing on to the roof of the car. I played with the night-vision scope that I had brought along. David was glued to his phone, becoming increasingly agitated. After half an hour, David tried the Forestry Commission. It was their track, after all. They were running a skeleton staff so near to Christmas, and nobody was available. Finally, David tried a friend of his who had a key, but also lived half an hour away. He got through, but the dusk was now gone.

After an hour it was dark. We were supposed to be going on a Boar-hunt. But here was a locked gate. Uh-oh! A locked gate. We can't get over it, we can't get under it. Oh no, we can't get through it, either.

"How many Wild Boar are there in the Forest of Dean," I asked David, trying to pass the time.

"Well, the Forestry Commission says about thirty, but I think there are about ten," he replied. "It's very hard to tell. People keep very quiet about the real numbers. And something's changed. The Boar used to be quite easy to see. We could even find them during the day. But now they have gone completely nocturnal and very shy. So I think poachers are shooting them."

"I've heard that they do a lot of damage. Wasn't a football pitch ruined by Boar in the Forest recently?"

David gave a rueful grin. "That's typical of the media," he replied. "Yes, a Boar came on to the ground, but it only affected a small corner of the pitch, nothing to stop them playing or anything. The incident was just blown up by the papers; it was nothing. It's always the same. Wild Boar get a bad press, for no real reason. They've got a reputation for being dangerous, too, but it's mainly curiosity. I can tell you, they are big, hairy animals, bigger than a large dog, and much more muscular. And if you encounter them, they will sometimes not run away, but come straight towards you, grunting. It's very intimidating. I can remember the first time I saw one – my heart was beating and I was sweating. But it's mostly just bluster."

After that description, the idea of seeing a Wild Boar became more and more irresistible. But it took another half-hour before David's friend turned up, unlocked the gate and wished us good luck. We entered the forest.

"Don't feel under any pressure, or anything," said Carolyn. "But we have been trying for fifty mammal species all year, we have forty-nine and the Wild Boar would allow us to reach our target."

We crept along the forest track, scrutinising the field of view of our headlight beams with intense concentration. It became quite eerie, just us in our car amid the ancient, tall forest. The occasional moth and falling leaf gave us heart flutters. That's not to say that they looked anything like a Wild Boar, of course; it was just the movement that alerted us.

We came to the house. "Just manoeuvre down this track," whispered David, "and see if the headlights pick one up. I put the bait out here last night."

Nothing stirred.

"OK, I'll put some more bait out. If we then just stay put for half an hour in the dark, we'll see if anything happens."

We parked up and David poured a bag of corn on to the ground. Then, bizarrely, he poured some diesel on it, apparently to make it smelly enough to attract the boars. We waited. First, we ate what sandwiches we could, in relative silence. Then we began to chat quietly. It wasn't long, hardly surprisingly, that the kids' patience began to crumble. In desperation, I started to make up a story, in our usual family method, incorporating the kids' favourite characters. So in the darkness in the middle of the Forest of Dean, manoeuvring the night-vision scope this way and that, I interwove some absurd story about Gabriella and Sharpay (from *HSM*), a fairy, a Tyrannosaurus rex and a Brachiosaurus, while David and Carolyn listened on with bemusement in the early evening air. You would have thought this sacrifice of my credibility would have earned concessions from a Wild Boar, but it didn't. Again, nothing stirred.

"Let's try the Forestry bait site," suggested David. So we drove on for a short while along the dirt road, hoping for a Boar in the headlights. We came to a crossroads.

"It's around here. Let's be very slow and careful. Just manoeuvre so that we can look over the ridge."

Again, we parked up and waited for ages. But the forest was very quiet that night. An owl hooted in grand style, adding to the ghostly atmosphere.

"Oh come on, let's get out and I'll show you the bait site," suggested David after more fruitless minutes. "At least there will be some signs."

We exited into the night. With the CB2 to keep us company, the expedition felt thrilling, but in a safe sort of way. We strolled down a slope, heavy with moss and fallen leaves, the latter mulching into the soil and making the going gooey. In the torchlight, the odd drop of condensation lit up the grass, while to the side the bracken looked worn down to the skeleton. Tree trunks illuminated by the light appeared ordered and regimented, as if they had chosen the hours of darkness to practise their drills, only to stand at ease once again in the morning. I looked upwards, seeing little. The cloud cover had kept the night relatively warm, but at the same time it made the dark profound and heavy and clinging. The kids' hands held Carolyn's and mine tightly.

Very soon we came to an area where the ground vegetation had been removed, and a patch of thick, clotted mud covered the ground, as black as tar pitch. All around it there were depressions as wide as apples.

"Those depressions are the tracks of Wild Boar," David told us. "You can just make out the two halves of the cloven feet. They are much broader and rounder than deer tracks, and the two halves join up to the rear. And this mud is the wallow. The animals usually come here at dusk."

The torch illuminated a glistening patch of wet on a tree, just 30 centimetres (1 foot) or so up the trunk. "Ah," David said. "That's where the Boar have been marking with urine. It's still wet, so it means that they were here earlier tonight."

We returned to the car. A little further on, David showed us a grass verge where the Boar had been feeding. It looked as though someone had taken a spade and turned over the soil, making what was previously a flat sward look like a choppy sea, with earth for the bulk of the waves and grass for the crests. I would have to admit, it looked quite devastating. If a whole football pitch had been affected, it would indeed have been unplayable.

"The Wild Boar are good for the ecology of the area," said David. "Turning over and aerating the soil like that. It doesn't take long to recover."

Suddenly, Carolyn interrupted: "What's that?"

Everyone looked. "Did you see a Boar?" I asked.

"No, there in the wood. I can see a light. Looks like a torch, just over there under the trees. There! No, it's gone now. It seems to me that either somebody turned out a torch, or they hid behind the trees."

"Are there any houses near here?" I asked David.

"No, we're in the middle of the forest. It's probably poachers," he replied. "I don't think we'd better stay here. I've heard that they aren't particularly pleasant people."

So we drove off away from the mysterious light, disinclined to make new friends here in the forest. And of course, it was the Christmas holidays, a good time to come poaching, and expect a deserted forest. For us, it was definitely a good time to stay in the car and put distance between us and strangers.

"That will flush the Wild Boar for miles," warned David. "The piggies can forage about twenty kilometres a night. They won't be anywhere near here, now."

We took the track back to the bait point near the house. Again, there was nothing. Now the children were beginning to fall asleep. We tried a different part of the forest, but the short journey was just too much for them. Memories of the Wildcat in Scotland came flooding back, but this time there was to be no wild animal sighting, not even for Carolyn and I.

"Sorry about that," said David as we drove up to his front door. But we were only grateful for his efforts. Few in the whole year had tried harder on our behalf.

"Enjoy your holiday in Spain," we called out, as we began our journey home through the December night, past festive lights and, somewhere in the depths of the woods, poachers with torches and guns.

## December 29th - Rats!

Seeing the Wild Boar would have been a great way to get to 50 species. Exactly the way I would have envisioned, a search out in the wilds with a dose of novelty and adventure. The dolphins would also have been

worthy contenders for the mammal that made us reach 50, since they
have charisma and mass appeal. Even a Weasel running across the road,
although brief, would at least have had the merit of being a hard-to-see
native species in the depths of the wild. But I hardly need tell you that
life's not like that. Our fiftieth was really a bit of a fudge. It was a beautiful
animal, but not very wild. It wasn't in a dark wood, or on a mountainside;
it was in a barn in Basingstoke. And it was a rat.

The fact is, we had run out of options. So we chose to end our year by
going to a facility where a man taught people about pest control, and kept
a barn full of House Mice, Common (Brown) Rats and Black Rats for that
purpose. It would be unglamorous and functional in terms of mammal-
hunting. And probably, had we been faced with more options, we would
never have counted the Black Rats that we expected to see. But it wasn't
a zoo, and one crucial fact that lent weight to the trip was this: all three
of these species do live in buildings. So they were living in more typical
conditions than, say, a Roe Deer or a Rabbit would be.

And you'll be surprised – really surprised – just how much fun and
fascination can be had in a barn full of rodents.

The owner of the facility was a man by the name of Steve Havers.
He was tall, intellectual-sounding and, in some ways, had the air of
the benevolent schoolmaster. His wife, Maggie, was just as kindly,
and they took to the children like professional grandparents, which
they were.

"Steve really does love rodents," Maggie had confided on the phone.
"If you start him talking, he'll never stop."

We were led into a barn-like building, long and with a roof that sloped to
the ground in a semi-circle, like a giant cloche. It had been kitted out with
classroom facilities, a kitchen and a bedroom, although the atmosphere
was more like a laboratory. It was spacious and oddly welcoming.

Steve beckoned us into the classroom. It had the usual row of seats, but in
one corner there was a table loaded with specimens: skulls, fir cones, exciting
bottles of chemicals and a number of strange bits of masonry. There were
pictures on the wall of rats and mice. It was a shrine to rodents.

Steve held up a pipe, then a piece of guttering, and finally some
air-conditioning panels, all of which had been chewed by rats and were
in a serious state of disrepair. His manner was like a conjurer, and his
admiration for the perpetrators complete.

"Amazing animals, aren't they?" he said happily. "Look here, they've actually gnawed into this container of rat poison. And see this brick? It comes from a hospital in Central London; the indentation is caused by a hundred years of rats running along it. Of course, they chew through cables and mattresses and paper – all kinds of unlikely things. And they have had a go at this bar of soap, too. Thought it was worth eating."

The specimens weren't all from rodents, though. Among his collection of skulls, Steve had a Roe Deer and a Badger, too.

"I must show you the kitchen," said Steve. At first this seemed a peculiar invitation, bearing in mind that we had come to see the Black Rats. But then it clicked. This wasn't a real kitchen; it was a dummy kitchen, without any appliances that actually worked.

"The idea is for my groups to have a look round the pretend kitchen and to find signs of pest activity," said Steve. "I have placed a few clues around, like gnawed edges and droppings. It helps them when they face a real kitchen on their own, and have to find any signs of trouble."

The kids looked in, spellbound. Next door was the hotel room, in which the same principle applied. For a hotel it was pretty old-fashioned, with heavy curtains and sheets on the bed – and presumably, that's what the rodents liked. I cannot imagine what lurked under the beds and, even though it was all pretend, I had shared enough rooms with rats in my time for it to send a shiver down my spine.

"Steve, I think you should show them the rats," said Maggie, firmly. I knew this was wife-speak for "come on", and within seconds her husband had opened a large door to the main part of the building. This was more like an empty superstore, kept in permanent semi-darkness and cooled by some hefty-looking fans that would not have looked out of place powering an aeroplane. On the left-hand side were two enormous pens, with metal sides, containing the stuff of some people's nightmares. In this room Steve conducted research on the free-running rats and mice.

The first pen contained Common Rats. Its floor was covered with hay, and it was fitted out with various food dispensers, pallets under which the animals could hide, and logs along which they could run and scuttle. Every now and then one would run across the floor, and then another, and then another.

"There are about sixty rats in there," Steve said. "Would you like to have a walk round inside? It's fine as long as you don't touch anything."

And that's just what we did. We all climbed over a ladder into the enclosure. The four of us walked around with rats at our feet, rats here and rats there. They were big rats, with their trademark heavy bodies, long, snake-like tails and a somewhat mean-eyed look. I was excited to see my children walking around as if it were inside a play area. They did not have the slightest fear. They had volunteered to come and had no qualms whatsoever. If nothing else this year, I knew we had imbued our children with an ease around rodents, which might just be useful in later life. Even when a rat approached Emily and motioned to chew her shoes (rats will chew the shoes of sleeping humans), she was completely unfazed; in fact, she giggled.

The next pen contained House Mice. Hundreds of them. Indeed, the hay on the floor really did heave with their bodies. In common with rodents generally, mice are a delight individually, but here in their multitudes I could imagine why they could be the stuff of nightmares. Their pen was more of an adventure playground than the Common Rats' one: there was a bicycle to crawl over, an inviting cupboard, and all sorts of small runs and entrances to keep a rodent interested.

Then, at last, we came to the Black Rats. These were in an ante-room, well away from the rest. According to Steve, these animals were a good deal shier than the rest. And he only had a few of them.

The Black Rats' isolation and paucity here at the barn reflected their impoverished status as a British mammal species. These days there are at least seven million Common Rats in our country, not including the places where people prefer not to count them, such as sewers and rubbish dumps. The Black Rat, on the other hand, survives with barely a foothold. There is a population on the Shiant Islands, in the Hebrides, and a few in Ireland. Other than that the species occurs in some dockland areas, notably Tilbury in London. There are said to be fewer than 2,000 Black Rats at any time in Britain and Ireland.

It's all so different from centuries past, when the Black Rat held sway. Originally from India, this sleek animal was here by Roman times, and soon became abundant wherever people lived. It is said to have been the main vector for the plagues that decimated Europe's human population in the fourteenth century, although there is some dispute about this. Even up until the beginning of the twentieth century, it was widespread, but more or less confined to docks by the 1950s. As for the Common Rat, this Johnny-come-lately from the steppes of Central Asia was first reported in Britain in about 1720. From this point, it settled here and, little by little, spread all over the country, often seemingly displacing the Black Rat. There seems to be little direct conflict between the two species – indeed they often coexist. It seems that the Common Rat is just better-suited to our climate. It can live outside, even in the winter, while the Black Rat is usually confined to buildings all year round. It seems that the spread was simply the result of one animal being more successful than the other.

Funny, isn't it? People squeal and protest about the Grey Squirrel taking over from the Red. But this particular colour change seems not to have bothered the public at large at all.

Of course, nobody is genuinely likely to extend much sympathy to a Black Rat. To most opinions, rats of all hues are just bad news. And no wonder. The average group of 10 rats produces 146,000 droppings a year, together with 541 urine productions. This contamination is worse, in economic terms, than the actual amount of food that they eat. And rats are carriers of some nasty infections that can be passed on to human beings. None of this engenders much generosity towards their kind.

But the truth is, Black Rats are smart animals. I would even go so far as to say they are beautiful. They have bigger ears than Common Rats and their tails are thinner and not so snake-like; their coat is coal black and they have larger, almost beguiling eyes. They move around faster and less deliberately than Common Rats, in a more mouse-like manner. We stood among them and were excited by them.

Steve and Maggie offered us some tea once we had seen all of their rodents, and talked some more about them. It seemed an appropriate toast. It couldn't have been champagne for this contrived end to our quest to see 50 mammals. Tea was about right.

But actually, the Black Rats themselves were pretty cool.

## December 31st – The Last Weasel Run

It was hard to believe that, half way through the three-hundred-and-sixty-fifth day of the year, it was still possible for us to drive around in the last of the light and have a realistic chance of adding a mammal to our total. But it happened to be true. We had not seen a Weasel and since Weasels are active day and night, throughout the year, it was quite possible that, on a serendipitous drive through rural Dorset, one might run across our path.

Don't get the impression, though, that this was something of an afterthought and that we hadn't tried looking for Weasels before. Every drive that we had made throughout the year could in theory have allowed our paths to cross with this mini-carnivore, and on a number of occasions we had been on dedicated Weasel-checks. On Boxing Day we had been to a renowned stake-out, Durlston Country Park, and failed to achieve anything but getting extremely cold, windblown and sick of looking for mammals.

The previous year I had seen a Weasel along a dirt-track a mile south of our house. This triggered quite a number of drives along the same track, which also happened to be a potential detour on the school run, as well as other local trips. But although we must have done this, all we ever saw on the Weasel Run, as we called it, was the occasional Fox.

So it was that we dedicated 45 minutes on the last day of the year to giving ourselves a chance to see the sausage-bodied vole-eater. We drove along slowly, along the quietest, most rural roads we could find. To help the kids along, we took Carolyn's recently acquired *Mamma Mia!* CD (yes, she got the CD *and* DVD), as an accompaniment to our all-but-forlorn journey.

Maybe it's just because the songs of Abba take me back to more wistful days, or whether I was emotional as the year was drawing to a close, I don't know, but the drive made me feel overwhelmingly melancholy. In truth, I have never yet acquired the mental strength to get through *The Winner Takes it All* without wanting to burst into tears, but on this drive I realised that we were driving the last rites of our mammal-watching year, and it made me very emotional. The kids would never be this young again. I would never be this young again. Only Carolyn would remain, officially, exactly the same age next year. Our project was over.

Of course, we never saw the Weasel. It, and the year was slipping through our fingers.

wood mose

# Epilogue

In the end, my family did see 50 species of mammals in the calendar year of 2008. Towards the end, a few of our sightings stretched the limit of our boundaries as to what we should count, but it would be churlish to suggest that this mattered very much. For the record, I worked out that we made expeditions to see 62 species in all, which works out at more than one every week. Also for the record, there is no doubt that my children have seen more British mammal species in the wild than any of their peers. Personally, having seen a couple more than the rest of the family (Weasel, for example, in Norfolk), my total now exceeds that of all but a handful of enthusiasts. So I need not be embarrassed any more.

So that was the end of the year, and this is the epilogue. And, since you've got this far, I suppose you're reading on for some big pronouncements and wise conclusions.

But we weren't doing this to change the world. Or ourselves. Carolyn will inform you that I have the same bad habits as I did before. The kids still, very occasionally, misbehave. Carolyn has not turned into an enthusiastic devotee of wildlife. We just spent a year looking for British mammals, that's all, and it was fun most of the time.

Does a year of mammal-watching mean that we love or care for each other more than we did before? Of course not. Does it mean we are more tolerant with each other? Perhaps, at times.

OK, I expect that our family life was enriched during the year. We spent a great deal of time together, and did a whole host of things we would not normally have done. We went to sea, went to Scotland and Wales, stayed up late many times, and got hotter, colder and wetter than we would otherwise have done. We met a host of characters that we would never have met, and of course, some of these had four legs, or two wings, or indeed six legs. In the end, when it's all mashed together, that will mean shared memories, conversations and laughs.

Would we do it again? Well, perhaps not the same thing, but something similar – you bet we would. And, since it's Epilogue time, why don't you?

I think I should leave the last word to the children.

On November 16th, Emily wrote the following essay. It was completely spontaneous, penned purely on her own initiative. It gives her perspective on some of the events of the year (the transcript is reproduced below):

> Mammals are little things except whales and dolphins. We've seen forty-seven mammals including a mink. They are very smelly. We haven't seen a dolphin. Once we went sledging with two feet of snow. It was fun. My Dad's been on Autumnwatch… with Kate and Bill Oddie. It was set on Brownsea Island. One day we went to Brownsea. When we went to the café a red squirrel ran under the table. Granny and Grandpa came too. I'm now going to mention Jacob. You might think it is funny but he was a waiter at the Grant Arms Hotel on that trip. Steph came too and of course Mum and Dad and my little brother Sam.
>
> By Emily Couzens, Age 6.

In the depths of December we were at supper and the conversation turned, as so often in families, to our kids' hopes and dreams. We asked Sam what he wanted to be.

"I want to be like Daddy," he said. Of course, I felt warm and contented inside. Yet I hope that every four-year-old son thinks the same.

"How exactly do you want to be like Daddy?" asked Carolyn.

Sam thought very hard, frowning as he did so. Then a light came on, and he stated, with great emphasis: "I want to write about Wood Mice."

# Acknowledgements

In a project such as this it is impossible to manage without the help of a great many people. Some are mentioned in the pages of this book, while others played unheralded, but often equally valuable roles. Thanks are due to them all. By their sheer number I fear that I might have missed some out, for which I apologise now, and hope that no offence is caused.

My greatest thanks are to my wonderful, loving and understanding family: Carolyn, Emily and Samuel. So many thanks, and I love you very much.

Thanks too to Carolyn's parents, Roger and Celia, and to my mother Charmian Couzens, for your encouragement of (and participation in) the project. And a big thank you to our extended family and friends for all your encouragement and tolerance through the year.

Big thanks to Gareth Jones at André Deutsch, plus also Rod Green and Penny Craig. I am grateful to all of you for bringing this book into existence.

Thanks to Mike Dilger for your excellent foreword, and for encouragement through the year.

All sorts of people helped us out in dozens of ways, and my grateful thanks to them all. Special thanks to John Dixon, Sally Humphreys, Fergus Collins, Nick Tomlinson and June Roy for your help and encouragement throughout the year. Also to Sue Herdman and John Stachiewicz at the National Trust for very important encouragement early on.

For various help during the year, I would like to thank the following people: John and Mary-Lou Aitchison, Nancy Aitken, Chris Ashurst, Robert Atkinson, John Altringham, Ross Baker, Sandra Baker, Sarah Bamber, Pete Banfield, Bernard Baverstock, Tom Brereton, David Bullock, Philippa Burrell, Jacqueline Caine, Ian and Lisa Caley, Phoebe Carter, Bob Chapman, Fergus Collins, Amanda Cook, Maria Court, Adam Curtis, Steve Davis, Jim Day, Edward Drewitt, Barry Dyke, Sue Eden, Cliff and Ann Edwards, Phyl England, Jon Flanders, Jan Freeborn, Iain Friend, Holger Goerlitz, Martin Goulding, Richard and Liz Hallam, Gareth Harris, Martin Harvey, Graham Hatherley, Steve and Margaret Havers, Steph Hawkes, Anna Hobbs, Nick and Jackie Hull,Tony Jaques, Mark Jefferys, Martin Kitching, Steve Laurence, Richard and Barbara Mearns, Dave Mallon, Joan Morrad, Colin Morris, Anna Muckle, Stephen Moss, Dave Nurney, Peter Oakenfull, Matthew Oates, Julian Owen, John Poland, Ian Rabjohns, Jonathan Reynolds, Penny Rudd, David and Ann Scouse, Sophie Stafford, David Slater, Christine Sleight, Derek Smith, Ralph and Brenda Todd, Roger Trout, Alison Tutt, Toby Virgo, Lynn Whitfield, Rebecca Wright

Aside from these individuals, I am grateful to the following groups and organisations: Bat Conservation Trust, College Lake Wildlife Centre, Cotswold Water Park, Dorset Bat Group, Great Fen Project, Kimmeridge Bay Jurassic Coast, Hebridean Whale and Dolphin Trust, Herts and Middlesex Bat Group, Mammal Society and Surrey Bat Group.

The following companies and/or societies either sponsored our mad project, or played a vital role beyond the call of duty: Alana Ecology Ltd; Ardnamurchan Charters; BBC *Wildlife* magazine; Bird Watching and Wildlife Club; Carl Zeiss Ltd; Chester Zoo; Country Innovation; Dorset Wildlife Trust; National Trust; Northern Experience Wildlife Tours; People's Trust for Endangered Species.